Travels of The King and I

Walkin' and Rollin' Around the World

Also by Sue Snyder

The Queen of Eleutheria
A Memoir
2007

Miracle People
An Inspiring Anthology
of Differently-Abled Beings
2018
(Available on Amazon)

For information contact the author at
suesnyder0625@gmail.com

ISBN 978-0-9796134-6-3

All opinions are those of the author and are not meant to recommend doing any of the crazy things she has done.

This book is dedicated to all the
"differently-abled beings" hoping to travel the
planet and all the angels who have assisted us
over our many years of traveling.

We are forever grateful.

Travels of The King and I

Introduction

"What was your favorite part of the trip? What did you like best? Why do you travel? Don't you miss home? Did you take a lot of pictures? Can I come over and hear all about it? Why did you choose that place?"

These are questions we get asked over and over, I suppose because most folks can't figure out how we travel—Richard in his Rascal—and me on my well-worn feet and legs. It's not easy but we figure we've got to travel and see the world while we can. I'll be 78 next June and Richard's body deals with 53 years of MS (multiple sclerosis). I'm pretty energetic and strong. He's the brains. We're a team. We meet life's challenges and joys together. Often, when we return from a challenging road trip or long-distance plane ride, and we get back to the place we call home, I think, "I can't do this again." Richard feels especially drained from our travels. But soon we're planning where to go next.

Last fall we stayed in the Yosemite Valley Lodge for five days. The shuttle-bus drivers all got to know us and lowered the bus when they saw us waiting. We loved it there. Soon after that, maybe next Spring, I want to take an Alaskan cruise. Cruises are much easier for The King. He gets around the ship, up and down, fore and aft, in his Rascal and always gets to know the crew. It's common, when we cruise, to hear, "Good morning Richard." And "Good afternoon Richard." And "How can I help you Richard." He's a love-magnet.

I suppose it's a matter of trust, knowing that if we get in a seemingly impossible situation, there will be Angels to help us. People are loving and caring and always wanting to assist. We know that Angels will appear when we need them. We feel safe. We feel loving and loved. What more can anyone ask?

March 11, 1995

A Few Notes on Traveling with The King

"Travel is fatal to prejudice, bigotry, and
narrow-mindedness."
Mark Twain

Summer of 2004: France and The Netherlands!!!!!

When we received the invitation to Roger's Surprise 50th Birthday Party, we said, "Sure, why not? Let's do it!" We hadn't seen him since he and his new wife moved across the sea and started a family. And I said, "As long as we're flying across the sea, let's visit France." Then we began to plan a trip to Roger's new hometown of Leiden in the Netherlands. We contacted a travel agent who specializes in helping folks like us enjoy life. Due to a life dominated by an MS-ridden body, Richard gets around in an electric cart called a Rascal. His legs aren't strong and he's kinda off-balance. But we travel on.

Sam, the travel guy, found us Rascal-friendly hotels in Nice, Bloise, Orleans, Paris, and Leiden. Anita, Roger's wife, would check us in to the Holiday Inn in Leiden where she works. Sam also reserved accessible vehicles with ramps, a couple of tour guides and a driver in Paris. All we had to do was pack our bags and get to LAX early Friday morning, June 18. As teachers we are so fortunate to have ten weeks in the summer to explore the world (and create lesson plans for the next school year). Sadly, we had lost Richard's mother in April. I knew she would be happy to know her beloved son was still capable of having adventures. The week prior to flying, I'd said good-bye to my 12th grade students. Graduation is always a sad--happy time for me and my students.

We travel light: small bags containing two or three outfits that still look okay but things we are willing to leave for hotel maids. Dump an outfit or two and purchase new tee-shirts or other souvenirs. This would be an 18-day trip: two weeks in France and four days in The Netherlands. So, we flew out of Los Angeles at 3:30 on Friday and landed at Charles de Gaul airport at 11:00 a.m. on Saturday. We transferred to a plane that flew us on to Marseille Airport. But then something weird happened!

It took a couple of hours to find out that our luggage and Richard's Rascal had been taken to Orleans. Oh, no! We met the nice Nice people (who spoke no English) and were delivering our Boxer. Boxer!? It's huge. OMG! Besides being big enough for 12 people to sit in, the ramp that I had to pull out the back was another 8 feet long. The GPS didn't know any English. We didn't know much about GPS and nothing about the French Language. "La Gouche. La Gouche." GPS would repeat this over and over. We finally understood it meant, turn left. Ha Ha. We were completely exhausted by the time we got to Novotel Hotel in Nice two hours away from the airport. We grabbed a couple of salads for dinner and collapsed into bed at 12:30. Fortunately, we'd packed toothbrushes, moisturizer, a hairbrush, and my favorite little crocheted green hat in our carryon bag. We slept until early afternoon on Sunday.

At 2:00 we received a phone call that our luggage and the Rascal would be dropped off at the Nice Airport and would be available by 4:00. We drove our giant Boxer to the airport. Richard waited in the van. The luggage was fine. The Rascal was not! It had been disassembled. Its seven pieces were securely strapped and wrapped on to an airport luggage pallet. I cried as I put it back together, piece-by-piece. Airport assistants tried to help but they'd never seen such a thing before so I did most of the work. After putting it together, we dragged the luggage out to the car where Richard awaited. Deep breath! Let's go!

Exhaused. Hungry. No language skills. Not fun but . . . we travel on. Back at Novotel Hotel, we walk to Promonade de Anglis for dinner. Interestingly, the owners of the little Italian restaurant, named Piccadilly, where we had dinner, are a young newly married couple. She was from Poland and he was from Russia and they cooked some mighty fine Italian dishes.

In Search of Broccoli or "The 66 Euro Cupcake."
Monday June 21, 2004

The next night we ate at Hotel Sofitel. Our third evening in Nice, France, we walked (I walked, Richard rolled along in his Rascal) to a nearby hotel and ordered fish of some sort. Richard's came in a nice little filet. Much to the horror of my squeamish little stomach, mine still had a face. The French-speaking Chinese maitre 'd gladly dissected the poor thing before my eyes. I'd only seen this operation performed in the wilds (due to my attraction to fishermen, I suppose) so, to see Nemo, as I named my dinner, assassinated did little to improve my appetite.

Two glasses of wine fogged my memory enough so I was able to devour the pitiful lump of white bony flesh, the spoonful of eggplant pate and a handful of overly-steamed vegetables. Being students of Religious Science and

realizing it's all good, we giggled our way through dinner. I, in my crocheted hat, Richard in his bearded countenance, hoping we looked French. Accompanying us to dinner was our newly acquired and little-understood digital camera. We took pictures of each other and a timed picture of ourselves with the click of several mysterious arrows and buttons.

Feeling noble because this dietetic meal left us a bit slur-tongued and still hungry, we boldly ordered dessert. Neither one of us could be considered big eaters and rarely order dessert but on this occasion, we decided to share what the menu presented as "warm chocolate cake with strawberry liqueur and compote." I had saved the $50 for Paris that Carlos and Stephen gave me for my 60th birthday two years ago, and now made the decision to use it as a down payment on this dinner.

Judging by the American-sized portions of desserts, we quickly assessed the situation and ordered one serving (uh parfum) of this richly described "warm chocolate cake with strawberry liqueur and compote," and two spoons. In his Chinese-tinged French, our maitre'd warned us that it would take fifteen minutes to produce this masterpiece. We assured him we would be patient. As we waited, we speculated on how grand, how extraordinary must a dessert be to cost 12 Euros, about 15 American dollars and require an extra fifteen minutes, a fourth of an hour, one percent of a day to prepare.

We decided, why worry; we had Carlos and Stephen's gift, plus ATM and VISA cards and about 70 Euros.

After some minutes of anticipation, where we occupied our time flirting with each other, our waiter delivered a large oval plate which held a small cupcake-sized brown lump poised near a small, very small pink stain. A thoughtfully bisected strawberry, slightly smaller than medium size, lay near the stain. How many twelfth grade essays on "All Quiet on the Western Front" had I read to pay for this treat, I wondered? Then, in a flash, I recalled that generous gift so lovingly bestowed on me by our friends C&S. Yet, how can I tell them how foolishly I spent their hard-earned money?

For just that flash, I felt a pang of un-Religious Sciencey guilt. One intake of "Peace, be still and know that I am Goddess" and I enjoyed the heck out of my half of that warm moist chocolately cupcake and my half of the strawberry. But, where was the compote? The pink stain, I suppose was the liqueur, but it seemed to have evaporated before we got to it. This meal was memorable because we were just two lovers enjoying dinner on the French Riviera, and while enjoying our wine and flirting, we promised to love each other no matter the size of dinner or dessert. I did vow, however, to give up eating any flesh in any form. Nemo is safe from me. Total bill for dinner was 66 Euros-about $90 in American money.

P.S. A few days later, in Bloise (pronounced Blue-ah) we discovered a Chinese restaurant that served rice and veggies. The first night we ate there we ordered just one plate of broccoli plus other veggies, rice, and soy cakes. It was so good, so just-what-we-needed, we returned the next night, repeating our feast, plus we ordered an extra plate of broccoli. Life is good!

Tuesday June 22, 2004

We were determined to spend time walkin 'n rollin' on the famous Promodade de Anglis but when we got there in our huge Boxer, there was no place to park so we drove back to our hotel and left the giant. It was just 3 kilometers to the PdA so we got there walkin' and rollin' to the shore of romantic Nice.

Why I packed the top part of my bathing suit . . . after all, we're in France, on the Riviera, where women of all ages go topless at the beach. I mean it: 2 year olds and 82 year olds. No tops! When a woman (like me) is seen at the beach with a full bathing suit on, you know she's probably from Orange, California.

We took pictures of me imitating statues, we fed the hungry pigeons, and we shopped for hats. I got a cute straw one. As we strolled through one plaza, a group of 25 young school children spoke French! I was amazed that these little kids already spoke a foreign language. Then I remembered where we were and of course they spoke French. That's their native language. That made me wish we'd taken a few lessons.

We visited Grasse, the Capitale des Parfums. Due to my hyperosmia, Richard went into the Parfum factory without me. What we learned: a network of sixty companies employs 3,500 people in the city and surrounding area. Additionally about 10,000 residents of Grasse are indirectly employed by the perfume industry. Almost half of the business tax for the city comes from the perfume sector and that exceeds both tourism and services. The main activity of perfumery in Grasse is in the production of natural raw materials and the production of concentrate, also called the juice. A concentrate is the main product that when diluted with no more than 80% alcohol, provides a perfume. Also food flavorings, which developed since the 1970s, account for over half of production output today.

This represents almost half of the production of French perfumes and aromas and around 7-8% of total global activity. During the 1960s and 1970s large international groups bought up local family factories. Soon after, their production was relocated overseas. Just 30 years ago most companies were focused on the production of raw materials. However, an overwhelming majority of the modern fragrances contain synthetic chemicals in part or in whole.

Grasse perfume companies have therefore adapted by turning to aromatic synthesis and especially to food flavorings and successfully ended a long stagnation. The Grasse perfume industry cannot compete with large chemical multinationals, but it benefits greatly from the advantage of its knowledge of raw materials. In addition, major brands such as Chanel have their own plantations of roses and jasmine in the vicinity of Grasse.

And we traveled on . . .

Wednesday June 23, 2004

From Nice we drove 390 miles to the quaint town of Clermont. On the way we visited Avignon, former home to Catholic popes. Between 1309 and 1377, during the **Avignon papacy**, seven successive popes resided in Avignon and in 1348 Pope Clement bought the town from **Joanna of Naples**. Papal control persisted until 1791 when, during the French Revolution it became part of France. The town is now the capital of the Vaucluse department and one of the few French cities to have preserved its ramparts. The town itself is beautiful with its gardens and fountains and quiet spots for daydreaming. We spent the night in the luxurious hotel Clermont Ferrand. Tomorrow we head for Blois (pronounced "blu-ah").

Friday June 25, 2004

This morning, after a great breakfast at our hotel—Mercure Blois—we met our guide, Martine, in the lobby at 9:00. I drove. Martine narrated as we toured the Loire Valley. The Chateau of Cheverny was a gift from some king to his mistress. That's an interesting story but even more interesting to tourists are the 70 trained hunting dogs that entertained royalty. Wow! What more could a king want? A wife at home raising his kids. All manner of helpers at home, a mistress with her own Chateau, and lots of time for hunting with all those dogs. What did we love most about Blois? The food in the Chinese restaurant Le Shanghai. Yes! Veggies! Lots of them. What a great way to spend my 62nd birthday. Tomorrow we're off to Paris!!!

Saturday, June 26, 2004

After a full day's drive we met the young man who was to be our driver for most of the next five days. It was 16:00 when we connected with Cedrick at Orleans Fleury les Aubrais train station. We had a chauffer!!! Our first stop was the awesome Palace of Versailles. Talk about luxury. And stairs everywhere. Richard could not go into the palace, so I went on my own. The principal feature in The Hall of Mirrors is the seventeen mirror-clad arches that reflect the seventeen arcaded windows that overlook the gardens. Each arch contains twenty-one mirrors with a total complement of 357 used in the decoration of the galerie des glaces. The arches themselves are fixed between marble pilasters whose capitals depict the symbols of France. These gilded bronze capitals include the fleur-de-lys and the Gallic rooster. Many of the other attributes of the Hall of Mirrors were lost to war for financial purposes, such as the silver table pieces and guerdons, which were melted, by order of Louis XIV in 1689, to finance the War of the League of Ausberg.

The surface surrounding the palace was deep-set cobblestones. When I noticed a teacher with several students in wheelchairs, I stepped forth to help. One large young man could not move his wheelchair at all, so I got behind him and pushed him up the hill to the front of the palace. His teacher was very grateful and the young man bowed his head in a gesture of gratitude.

And on to the Chateau Chambord. It was a little-used hunting lodge back in the day. But on the few weeks a year when the king and his entourage came for a visit, all the food, furniture, and furnishings had to be brought with them. This was no easy task, as there were often as many as 2,000 people coming for a visit. The funny thing is a mystery to me: the toilets in the three-story Chateau are in the attic. Imagine working out in your garden and having to . . . nevermind. The château features 440 rooms, 282 fireplaces, and 84 staircases. Four rectangular vaulted hallways on each floor form a cross-shape. You'd think they'd have a few fancy restrooms, but . . .

As we strolled—I mean walk 'n rolled—across the bridge to the Chateau we met up with a group of tourists on bikes. Most of them from northern California. They were touring France on two wheels. Then we came upon a family trying to take a group photo, so I offered to take their picture with their camera. Even through they spoke German, I understood their gestures and their "Dankas". I love connecting with people by taking their pictures for them. Even if we don't share a common language we can communicate.

I remember being dropped off at our hotel and Cedrick insisting he'd be back at 21:30. It was a surprise he'd planned. As Cedrick drove us into Paris, he circled the Eiffel Tower several times so that we could catch the 23:00 p.m. light show. That's when the Tower becomes all aglow. As we circled, Cedrick mentioned that he wanted to show us Zhon Dark, which we interpreted as John Dark. Then, there it was: a statue of a woman on horseback. But . . . that isn't a John. When he pointed it out to us we realized he was saying Joan of Arc. As we traveled about with our delightful driver, Richard sat in the front seat beside him. I sat in the back, scribbling notes and taking in the sights.

Sunday, June 27, 2004

Today we met another tour guide. Her name is Kathryn. Her assignment is to show us around Paris. She took us for a hike up to the Village of Sacre Coeur. The Basilica of the Sacred Heart is commonly known as Sacre-Coeur and is a Roman Catholic Church and minor basilica, dedicated to the Sacred Heart of Jesus, in Paris, France. A popular landmark and the second most visited monument in Paris, the basilica stands at the summit of the butte Montmartre the highest point in the city.

Sacré-Cœur Basilica is above all a religious (Catholic) building, shown by its perpetual adoration of the Holy Eucharist since 1885. It is also seen as a double monument, political and cultural, both a national penance for the defeat of France in the 1870 Franco Prussian War and for the socialist commune. It is the most rebellious neighborhood, and an embodiment of conservative moral order, publicly dedicated to the Sacred Heart of Jesus, which was an increasingly popular devotion since the visions of Saint Margaret Mary Arloque. The basilica was designed by Paul Abadie. Construction began in 1875 and was completed in 1914. The basilica was consecrated after the end of World War I in 1919.

And the Louvre, most famous of museums. Wow! Since Kathyrn was guiding us and Richard travels in the Rascal, we got to go to the front of the loooooong line and got in free. The Louvre, or the Louvre Museum, is the world's largest art museum and a historic monument in Paris, France. A central landmark of the city, it is located on the Right Bank of the Seine in the city's 1st arrondissement. It first opened on August 10, 1793 with 537 paintings and 184 works of art. Now there are about 38,000 objects from prehistory to the 21st century, which are exhibited over an area of 72,735 square metres (782,910 square feet). Louvre is the world's most visited museum, receiving 10 million visitors annually. (When I chaperoned 50 high school students to Europe in 1983, (eight countries in 31 days—I know, huh? What was I thinking?) there was no air-conditioning in the museum and it was hot. Now it is much more comfortable. And there were fewer high-schoolers in the museum today. Then we asked ourselves, "Why have we not visited the Huntington Library in Pasadena, California together?" We put the HL on the bucket list.

The pyramid, a beautiful glass structure that stands out in front of the museum, and its underground lobby, was inaugurated on 15 October 1988 and the Louvre Pyramid was completed in 1989. The second phase of the Grand Louvre plan, the Pyramid inversee (Inverted Pyramid), was completed in 1993. As of 2002, attendance had doubled since its completion.

The heartbreaking painting of Pieta of Villeneuve les Avignon by Enguerrand Quarta was completed in 1400. To stand and look at Mary holding her dead son brought tears to my eyes. Imagine a mother looking down at her child. I wondered if the artist ever imagined how touching is his work, still. The Mona Lisa by Leonardo de Vinci—famous polymath—was worked on from 1503-1506. This painting is one of the most viewed in the world. It's an amazing feeling to stand in front of that mesmerizing smile and contemplate what de Vinci felt with each brush stroke.

Another day in Paris. Thank you Mom and Dad Snyder for making our travels possible. We hope you're looking down at us and thinking, "An inheritance well spent." And I promise you that I will continue taking good care of your precious son.

Monday and Tuesday June 28 and 29, 2004

Imagine waking up in Paris with your favorite person in the universe on the sixth floor of Novotel Paris Les Halles. I know, huh? A dream come true. We had two days on our own exploring Notre Dame and the Eiffel Tower and the Arc de Triomphe. A funny thing happened at the Tower. The two guys in the ticket booth were not quite sure what to do with Richard. After all, the Eiffel Tower is a series of steps. No way could he and his Rascal maneuver the staircase. "Aha!" (That's "I've got an idea" in any language.) They looked at Richard, said something in a foreign language (could have been French) and shuffled us over to the freight elevator—the one that takes food up to the restaurant—and directed us to enter. So we did. We landed nearly at the top. What a gift. What a view. What a thrill. We felt so blessed to have caring people around the world come forth with great ideas. We love to travel. They love to help. It all works out fine.

Wednesday, June 30, 2004

Yet another dream comes true. Giverny: home of the beloved artist Claude Monet. Cedrick picked us up at 9:00 for the trip out to Giverny. It's about 75 miles from Paris to Giverny. About and hour and a half drive, unless Cedrick is driving. In that case, it's only one hour. Before visiting Monet's home, we stopped at a romantic little restaurant for an early lunch. Cedrick declined to join us. He sat in the corner eating and making plans with his girlfriend—by cell phone.

Frenchman Claude Monet was born on November 14, 1840 and lived for 86 years. Early on he decided that painting inside a studio could only be boring. He wanted to express nature and so began creating his paintings outside, which came to be known as plein aire. Monet gave the world one of his first paintings "Impression: Sunrise" in 1872. Monet was known as one of the "impressionists". As the story goes, a well-known art critic and journalist by the name of Louis Leroy thought Monet's style of painting was not real enough. Leroy used the term "impressionistic art" as a derogatory term but the impressionist painters decided that was a beautiful way of describing their art and appropriated the term "Impressionists" for themselves.

Imagine the feeling of being in Monet's famous paintings: In Giverny we strolled through the gardens of pink and red and purple flowers. Bushes and trees. The famous lily pond. The bridge. That boat which appears in many of his paintings. I got to tour his home. (Too many steps for The King and his Rascal.) I was surprised by all the Japanese artwork in the living room. The kitchen I loved. Painted bright yellow and blue. The walls were covered in bright blue tile.

Monet's ambition of documenting the French countryside led him to adopt a method of painting the same scene many times in order to capture the changing of light and the passing of the seasons. From 1883, Monet lived in Giverny, where he purchased a house and property and began a vast landscaping project, which included lily ponds that would become the subjects of his best-known works. In 1899, he began painting the water lilies, first in vertical views with a Japanese bridge as a central feature and later in the series of large-scale paintings that was to occupy him continuously for the next 20 years of his life.

And tomorrow . . . we take the train to Holland. We've got to get there in time for Roger's surprise birthday party.

Thursday July 1, 2004

This morning at 9:00 we met Cedrick in the lobby of our hotel and he drove us to the Train Station. After good-bye hugs we boarded the train to Holland for a 300-mile journey at high-digit speeds. We arrived in Amsterdam and met our new accessible vehicle: a Kangoo, a small truck with two seats in the front and a ramp we'd pull out the back for the Rascal. Excellent! No more driving that bulky Boxer.

After being on the train for a bit over three hours—we then drove our Kangoo to the Holiday Inn in Leiden. It was a fifty-mile drive that took us a bit over an hour. Imagine our surprise to find our hotel lobby was a huge, multi-story terrarium with a fish and turtle pond, trees and plants. A beautiful place for breakfasts and just relaxing. We spent the rest of today catching up on sleep and relaxing. Tomorrow, the reason for this excursion to Leiden will become apparent. We'll be the surprise guests at the surprise party for long-time friend Roger.

Friday, July 2, 2004

We spent most of today at Leiden's Horticulture Center at the University of Leiden. This is the oldest botanical garden in Netherlands. Plants came from all over the world during the last four centuries. We were guided through the gardens by one of the students and, as they say in Holland, "De reuzenwaterleli Victoria amazonica is de parel op de kroon van het kassencomplex." And we agreed, the flowers are beautiful.

So we ordered salad and sandwiches for lunch in the little cafe, found a cozy table with a window overlooking the gardens and then realized . . . Anita, Roger's wife, is going to pick us up at the hotel in 45 minutes. Yikes! We un-ordered lunch and hurried out to the Kangoo and sped back to the Holiday Inn. Anita picked us up right on time, drove us over to their Leiden home. She hid us on the patio in the backyard. About 20 adults and five children began to assemble. Everyone was excited. Our job: sit still and keep quiet.

Roger had been sent off on a bogus errand. When he returned and walked in the front door there were shouts of "Surprise!" "Surprise!" "Surprise!" Much laughter. Hugging. Shaking hands. Roger was really surprised. Anita and her friends had laid out a beautiful buffet of yummy food and a birthday cake with 50 candles. The table was decorated with lots of candles and beautiful pink, yellow, purple, and white flowers. After he stopped laughing and was just getting comfortable, Anita announced that there was another surprise waiting out on the patio. Imagine his shock when he discovered two friends had flown from California to be with him on his birthday. We didn't laugh. We hugged and cried happy tears. He was REALLY surprised!

What a great party. We got to meet Anita and Roger's neighbors and friends. We got to meet their precious children: Nancy and Christiaan—and their three little friends. I'd forgotten how much energy they have. We witnessed summersaults, tumbling, and piggy-back riding acts. Even with his arm in a sling, Christiaan hung in the midst of the action. Such a "guy". One of the men at the party remarked to me: "Your president, he's a cowboy, right?" I laughed. He was talking about "W".

Saturday July 3, 2004

In his little boxy car, Roger drove us and his two kids over to the town of Delft, home of Delft University of Technology and that beautiful Delft Blue pottery. We visited the Peace Palace in Den Hagg. We didn't get to go inside but learned that it is the seat of the Cabinet, States General, Supreme Court and Council of State of the Netherlands. We learned that the Peace Palace is the temple of peace and justice. We stopped off at Veronica beach so Roger could show us where he and Anita first met. We visited the Oude Kerk, which was founded in 1246 and the spire was added in 1325. It was the highest until the Niewe Kerk was built in 1584.

Most people don't drive cars in The Netherlands. They ride their bikes. And, for sure, very few own the big vans that we are so used to seeing in the U.S. Someone told us that families only have two children because the cars are so small and gasoline runs about $6.00 a gallon. So driving our little Kangoo was a challenge, as the streets are pretty much taken over with bicycle riders.

Sunday July 4, 2004

What touched me the most about visiting with our precious friends, was the way 9-year old Nancy followed Richard around and seemed to want to make sure he was safe. Sometimes she would hold his hand as he drove his Rascal. My thought was that maybe she's going to be a doctor. We spent today at Vlinders aan de Viet visiting the butterflies and the birds. Nancy helped Richard feed the birds and loved holding the green parrots on her arm. Aunt Pat, Roger's sister spent the day with us. She came all the way from Colorado to celebrate her "little brother's" 50 birthday and spend time with her niece and nephew. Another beautiful day in a beautiful part of the world, with beautiful people. How blessed we are.

Monday July 5, 2004

Time to go home. We got up early. Packed our bags, left the Holiday Inn at 7:00 a.m. and met Anna Dekker at Schiphol Airport at 8:45 to surrender the Kangoo. We are scheduled to fly out of Amsterdam at 11:35 a.m. and arrive at LAX (after a change of planes in Cincinnati) at 6:15 p.m. This was such an incredible journey. Beautiful world. Beautiful people.

Tuesday July 6

We're home! It's quiet! No action! Yay!!!!!!

November of 2007   Greece with Jerri

Every now and then we receive an email from Rev. Blaire (Unity Church in San Diego) and his sweet wife Meredith inviting the congregation (plus family and friends) on an excursion of some type. This year the notice came in January. "Who wants to cruise the Greek Islands and spent time on Corinth? Also, we'll be visiting Athens, Delphi, Kalambaka, Thessaloniki, and we'll spend a day in Ephesus, Turkey." Rev. Blaire named the trip "In the Footsteps of Paul."

Curious about St. Paul's letters, and the sites in Greece, we decided to take the trip . . . until we learned Richard on his Rascal would be pretty tough. So we decided not to go . . . until I told Richard's sister Jerri about the trip. Her response? "Heck, I'll go with you. Can my bro stay home alone?"

It's only been two months since the "dog-thing" which left me with both a fractured back and left wrist. Because I am persistent about doing my exercises and in-pool therapy, I decide to wear my back brace and wrist strap and take the trip to Greece. I am cautiously optimistic. After conferring with several of our friends who promised to be sure Richard was well fed and looked after, I decided to take a break and go-for-it.

And now Jerri and I are sitting at Gate 101 at LAX awaiting our 2:30 p.m. Lufthansa Airlines. We are excited! We sit here drinking green tea and eating homemade egg salad sandwiches. We're awaiting the other eight who are traveling from LAX. Don't see anyone who looks like fellow Greece travelers. We'll be in Frankfurt, Germany around noon tomorrow, just passing through, then travel on to Athens.

We're aboard now. Speeding towards our destination. At 640 mph, after five hours the plane is going over Greenland. In another four we'll touchdown in Germany. We have met several of our travel mates: Bill and Mary Jane, Diane and Paul, Ellen and Andy. Sitting on the plane I study Athens Acropolis. Also a bit of Greek Mythology, which, ironically, I taught to ninth graders at Santa Ana High several years ago. Watched the movie "License to Wed" which seemed kinda frustrating until I figured out the real purpose of marriage school. Robin Williams always funny. Now for the plan: we should arrive in Athens by 4:30 p.m.

Tuesday, November 6, 2007

Here we are in Athens! In the Tatania Hotel. We had a lovely buffet dinner last night and met many of the 67 American travelers from California. We're from San Diego, Orange, Corona, and Sierra Madre. The city lights were brilliant last night as we bussed from the airport to the hotel. I got my camera out too late for a good picture. Don't understand any of the signs. Our host on the bus spoke Greek, English, Spanish, French, and Japanese. She told us of the cave of stalactites. In Greece, they're called stalag-titties, so they use the American word.

Hotel Tatania has a rooftop garden, complete with an Olive Garden Restaurant and a view of the Parthenon, which we will visit—with my camera—in the morning. We'll be off to Corinth then back to Athens. Most shops close at 2:00 daily and open again at 8:00. One of the many things I love about traveling is meeting other travelers and, of course, the people who live in these countries. This evening we met five Arizona women at dinner. We had a great time talking, listening, and laughing. We'll be having a "getting to know you" get together tomorrow evening. I am so tired I must get to bed. I slept for about 90 minutes this afternoon but am still really beat. And Jerri is nodding her head, yes: it's time to get to sleep. Time to turn the lights off. Good night. So when Jerri says, "Good night, Sis." I'm already asleep.

Wednesday, November 7, 2007

One year ago today, I hiked down into and back up the South Rim of the Grand Canyon—a nine-mile walk in the early morning hours. Today we hiked up and back down from the Acropolis here in Athens. The place was busy with cranes, scaffolding, and marble polishers; workmen of all sorts, busy replacing the stones of these crumbling structures. On top of the entry gate is a sign: "The Parthenon, the porch of Caryatids and the Propylaia", which is the "monumental" entrance next to the Temple of Athena Nike, the Acropolis Museum.

Down the hill a bit is the Shrine of Asclepius, who was the son of Apollo, either by Coronis, daughter of Phlegyas or by Arsinoe, daughter of Leucippus of Messenia. He was the brother of Eriopis. Asclepius was married to Epione, with whom he had five daughters: Hygieia, Panacea, Aceso, Iaso, and Aegle, and three sons: Machaon, Podaleirios and Telesphoros. He also sired a son, Aratus, with Aristodama. Asclepius was so busy producing children; you wouldn't think he had the time to think up such complicated names.

Next we visited the theatre of Dionysus, the Theater of Herodes Atticus, and the Chapel Spiliotisso. My favorite was the Caryatids: draped, sculpted female figures, supportive Goddesses so to speak, used as decorative support in place of columns or pillars, called in Greek: Karyatides. The most famous Caryatids of Greece stand guard over the Erechtheion of the Acropolis in Athens. To show our support, Jerri and I posed in front of the other Goddesses.

Me and Jerri in front of Caryatids.

The weather is beautiful—a sunny 60-ish. I can see storm clouds over the mountains. The bus dropped off most of us at the Platika where we browsed and shopped and ate. Just like tourists are supposed to do. My plan: eat only one spanukapita a day. I love this cheesy spinach pastry. And, believe me, they make 'em huge here in Greece. My plan? Buy one in the morning and snack on it all day long.

Thursday, November 8, 2007

Now we're on a bus, the Blue Bus, heading for Corinth and the Corinth Canal. We're passing Asharodito Goddess of Love. Motoring through the industrial area, sprinkled with sheep yards. Gina, our guide, is very knowledgeable—also tired as we near end of tourist season. Rev. Blair led us in a sing-a-long, and "I am vitally alive." Rev. Donna used the daily guide to remind us about healthy habits, which made me wonder why Greek salads have no green leaves in them. Hmmm . . .

Now we're crossing the Canal of Corinth. Scorpios Island is west of Greece. The Corinth Canal connects the Gulf of Corinth with the Saronic Gulf in the Aegean Sea. It cuts through the narrow Isthmus of Corinth and separates the Peloponnese from the Greek mainland, arguably making the peninsula an island. The canal was dug through the Isthmus at sea and has no lock. It is 6.4 kilometers (4 mi) in length and only 21.4 meters (70 ft) wide at its base, making it impassable for most modern ships. Nowadays it has little economic importance and is mainly a tourist attraction.

The Onassis family is buried here in Corinth. Athena, granddaughter heir to Ari Onassis, seldom visits Greece, married an Argentinean. It seems she/they own a big portion of the shipping industry. Jackie Kennedy kindly agreed to receive only $15 million upon the death of her husband Ari. Sounds like a good deal to me. The water here is quite polluted; no one goes into the ocean. The air is very smoggy. We're driving by vineyards of grapes and olive trees. According to the experts, Santorini and Macedonia have the best light for growing food. The farmers here produce pistachio, fruit, and melons. The figs, they say, take only 20 days to ripen. Earlier today I tried eating one of the Greek-grown persimmons but it was sooooooo acidic, I couldn't do it.

We're listening to our tour guide tell the story of Demeter and Persephone. As Goddess of fertility and the fruitfulness of the Earth and the flourishing of the cereal crops on which mortals depended for their food, Demeter was a Goddess of immense power and importance. The root of her name—meter--is the Greek word for mother. Hades wanted to marry Demeter's daughter Persephone but was denied that wish. So, he took her down to hell. After months of trying to find her beloved daughter, Demeter discovered where Hades had taken poor Persephone. She was able to rescue her daughter but, because Hades had fed pomegranate seeds to Persephone before she ascended out of hell, she would have to spend half the year with him. That explains why we have a few months when crops don't produce. It's all Hades fault. But the good news? The crops flourished again and people were able to raise food. Cereal crops, once again, became abundant. So, thank Demeter when you eat your morning bowl of cheerios. Or toast.

We are told that of Greece's some 3500 islands only 200 are inhabited. In all of Greece there are 33 billion olive trees; two million on Lesbos Island. Interestingly, olive trees only produce every two years. When ready, the olives are shaken off the trees. I keep humming "The sun'll come out tomorrow" although we're getting strong, bright rays through the dark clouds. Rain? Maybe. We're prepared with jackets and umbrellas. We are now arriving at Quienta Beach, the resort for European tourists. It's three miles of beautiful sandy beach. Right now, everyone on the bus seems extra quiet, perhaps due to last night's riotous dinner party at Yallop of Pegos in the Plalsa of Athens. Uumpa for ouzo.

At 11:00 this morning we walked up a rocky pathway towards "Acropolis of Aphrodite" where—many years ago—1,000 priestesses lived. They were titled the "Cult of Prostitution." They would walk down to the village in search of customers. Interestingly, the bottoms of their shoes were implanted with the words "FOLLOW ME." I would think they and their customers would be exhausted by the time they got back to the fortress at the top of the hill. All that remains of this grand fortress are some crumbling walls, some orangish stones, and a bit of scaffolding.

Repair work goes on and on in this ancient land, as does my munching on my daily spinach pie. As we travel along in our big bus, Gina tells the story of Apollo falling in love with Daphne, a forest nymph. It seems she turned into a Laurel tree, but Gina declares that most think she turned into an oleander bush. Another adventure this afternoon: stopping at a pottery workshop, which is owned, operated, and was created by a wealthy family here in Corinth. Beautiful gifts of statues, jewelry, and pictures. I looked, appreciated, and left. Now the sun is shining and I am so grateful people are returning to the bus.

This afternoon as we all gathered together at the Agora in Corinth, Bob, the Unity Church organist, read from St. Paul's letter to the Corinthians. It was one of the highlights of the trip:

Chapter I Corinthians 13

1. If I speak with the tongue of men and of angels, but do not have love, I have become a noisy gong or a clanging cymbal.
2. And if I have the gift of prophesy and know all mysteries and all knowledge, and if I have all faith, so as to move mountains, but do not have love, I am nothing.
3. And if I give all my possessions to feed the poor, but do not have love, I am nothing.
4. Love is patient, love is kind, and is not jealous; love does not brag and is not arrogant.
5. Love does not act unbecomingly; it does not seek its own, is not provoked, does not take into account wrong suffered.
6. Love does not rejoice in unrighteousness, but rejoices with the truth
7. Love bears all things, believes all things, hopes all things, endures all things.

8. Love never fails; but if these are gifts of prophecy, they will be done away, if there age tongues, they will cease, if there is knowledge, it will be done away.
9. For we know in part, and we prophesy in part,
10. But when the perfect comes; the partial will be done away.
11. When I was a child, I used to speak as a child, think as a child, reason as a child; when I became a man, I did away with childish things.
12. For now we see in a mirror dimly, but then face to face; now I know in part, but then I shall know fully just as I also have been fully known.
13. But now abide faith, hope, love, these three, but the greatest of these is love.

After an amazing day in Corinth, with another Greek salad for lunch, and witnessing the bridge over the Canal of Corinth go down down down so far that a tugboat pulled a ship through. Oh! I wish I'd had my camera ready. But alas! It was time for a siesta on the bus. Our fellow travelers must have been worn out also. All were quiet as we rode back to our hotel. Once back in our room Jerri and I both took naps. I soaked in the bathtub for 20 minutes. Ah, that was excellent. Jerri took a shower; we donned clean clothes and went up to the rooftop Olive Garden restaurant. Out on the deck the Acropolis, the hills of Athens are brightly lit and often photographed. We took pictures of us and the sights. I shall need new batteries soon.

We went downstairs in the hotel for dinner. Halleluiah! A bottomless bowl of spinach. I ate a whole plateful, then had several samples of dessert: pana cotta with burnt sugar, baklava, and crème puffs with pudding and chocolate frosting. Real chocolate: the dark kind.

After dinner we all attended a "getting to know you" meeting where we stated our intentions for the trip. Great sharing from each person. Some wanted to see more of the world in order to gain an understanding of the culture. Some wanted to get away from work obligations. Two people were interested in researching their Greek heritage. I wanted to be a better listener and give the people I interact with a chance to think out loud and feel free to share.

When we got back to our room I heard my back complaining: "What were you thinking? Not wearing my back brace today?" I may have pushed too much. Life is good! It's almost 10:30. We need to be up at 5:45 a.m. We'll be off to the Port of Pirus for a 3-day cruise. Yippee!! And so to sleep. Efarista (Thanks) and Palakana (You're Welcome).

Saturday November 9, 2007

This morning we had our suitcases outside our hotel room at 6:45 a.m. We needed to be ready to leave at 8:15 with passport and cruise ticket handy because we'd be leaving the mainland and headed for the Islands of Greece. What a day this has been! At 5:45 we hopped out of bed—in Athens—dressed, had breakfast and loaded the busses for the cruise by 8:15 a.m. Fruit, scrambled eggs, toast with marmalade in Hotel Titania. Last night's waiter was back in early a.m. Our guide, Gina, spoke very little on the way. Her back was hurting; her feet were hurting. She's had an extremely busy season.

It was only a 30-minute ride to Pierlas, where we boarded in a most amazing process. Our passports were collected. We were given boarding passes, which allow us on and off ship. Our luggage was taken to our rooms. Jerri and I will share Cabin #7228. 'Twas a simple little room with two little beds and a little bathroom. No deck. But what the heck! It's a 3-day trip around the islands of this beautiful country.

We sailed towards Rhodes—or Rodeths--as the Greek speak. We hiked up into the hills to the Church of the Virgin. It's a newish stone church alongside a very old missionary-style uninhabitable building. Irene was our tour guide. When we left the bus she reminded us to be on time and if five minutes late we would sing a song. If we were 10-minutes late we'd sing and dance for fellow travelers. If 15-minutes late, we would sing to ourselves. Three people were late. All sang; we helped. I shared one of my most favorite songs, written by Debra Alden of Orange County fame. *

Grateful for the morning
Grateful for the sunlight on my face
Grateful for the feeling,
Grateful for the knowing,

Grateful for the love that's in this place
Grateful for believing
That God is all there is
God is all there is.
God is all there is.

*Used with permission of composer.

And I am filled with gratitude that I get to travel the world, to spend time with people and learn their cultures and to spend time with my beautiful and precious sister-in-law. But I miss my darling husband.

Our group sometimes is a bit scattered at mealtime. There are 67 of us with San Diego Unity. At dinner this evening we did enjoy the company of Ellen and Andy Munoz and Becky and Jim White. Andy was so interested in high school reunions. He kept asking me to tell more. We all got on the topic of times we'd ridden, or missed busses in various parts of the world from Alaska to Mexico. Jerri and I talked about our herb gardens.

One of the totally amazing sights on the Island of Rhodes is a statue of the Greek sun god Helios, erected in the city of Rhodes on the Greek Island by Chares of Lindos in 280 BC. It is one of the Seven Wonders of the Ancient World and was constructed to celebrate Rhodes' victory over the ruler of Cyprus, Antigonus I Monophthlmus, whose son Demetrius I of Macedon unsuccessfully besieged Rhodes in 305 BC. According to most contemporary descriptions, the Colossus stood about 108 feet high—the approximate height of the modern Statue of Liberty. Although it collapsed during the earthquake of 226 BC, its parts are preserved and may some day be reconstructed.

The island is neatly divided into two parts: the old walled city and the new town, which has been built around it. What I loved most about the island were the many beautiful mosaics in the churches and museums. I'm always amazed at the craftsmanship, the persistence, and the patience that went into creating these gorgeous pieces of art. In the Palace of the Grand Master we walked on mosaic floors, up marble staircases, observed statues carved of stone, and took pictures of Medusa. You probably remember from listening to your 9th grade English teacher explain her as a monster, a gorgon described as a winged human female who had snakes all over her head instead of hair. She was the daughter of Phorcysand Ceto (author Hyginus thought she was really the daughter of Gorgon and Ceto). As the story goes, Medusa was beheaded by the hero Perseus who then used her head to help turn onlookers to stone. He used her head as a weapon until . . . he gave it to the goddess Athena to put on her shield. So, Medusa actually became an evil-averting device called Gorgoneion. I know, my teachers didn't tell me about her either. So, Perseus was the son of the god Zeus, but that's a really long story.

Sunday, November 11, 2007 - Patmos Island

Yesterday was somewhat overcast, rained a bit on Rhodes then rained hard during naptime. I was awakened at 5:30 by heavy rain and wind against the window of cabin #7228. A half-hour later we were up, dressed quickly and were greeted by a delicious breakfast of Greek yogurt with granola, walnuts, and honey—served with a cup of delicious hot tea. Today we're touring Patmos Island. At 7:00 we're off on bus #9 to see the Cave of the Apocalypse where St. John wrote (actually he dictated) Revelations, which is part of the Christian Bible. Seems he was brought here in chains then let go to pray, write, preach, and convert the natives of Patmos. Imagine trying to convince worshippers of many gods to believe in only one and try to explain this Jesus guy, the great example—not the great exception. I wish with all my heart that Richard could experience this place. The steps, the hills, the cobblestone streets: he probably couldn't handle it. I miss him. The bus ride back to the ship provided spectacular views of the island from atop the hill. Pictures were taken everywhere. I try to photograph the signs to remind me of where I took pictures.

Back on board, we've pulled away from the dock. Several passengers missed the boat and had to be collected and delivered by tender. We didn't have much time on the Island of Mykonos for shopping but I did purchase a Greek tee shirt and a wooden picture of Madonna and Child. We are now on our way to Ephesus, Turkey. Hope we have more shopping time there. Marina, a shop owner told us that her apartment is upstairs above her store. From her living room window she can see when the cruise ships pull into port. That's when she goes downstairs and unlocks the door to welcome tourists. It was so nice talking with her and learning about the island. When not actually in her little shop selling things, she is in her apartment creating pictures and jewelry to sell.

Later, back on the ship, I'm sitting on the sundeck in the beautiful warm sun. It's almost 50 degrees. We're properly bundled. I overheard a woman remark that St. John was not chained in a cave without food or water. Someone in the Catholic Church reported warm clothing as chains. Hmmm. We may never know. Our third quick stop was on the Island of Mykonos.

In Greek mythology, Mykonos was named after its first ruler, Mykonos, the son or grandson of the god Apollo. The island is the location of the great battle between Zeus and Giants, where Hercules killed the giants that lured them from the protection of Mount Olympus. It is said that the big rocks on the island are the petrified corpses of the giants. The name of the battle? Gigantomachy, of course.

Mount Olympus was home to the Greek gods, who lived atop Mytikas peak (meaning nose). Of its 52 peaks and gorges, Mytikas is the loftiest at 9, 570 feet and is one of the highest peaks in Europe. In 1938 Mt. Olympus was declared a National Park, the first in Greece.

We are now cruising to Ephesus, Turkey. Hills on the island appear smaller. The sun is shimmering brightly on the sea. There is a slight breeze but will probably be downright windy as we pick up speed. Our guide in Ephesus will be Mickael. Ephesus is one o the Seven Wonders of the World.

So we had a grand tour of Ephesus and I've decided it is my favorite place. I felt as though I was in a movie set. The village streets, temples, libraries, theater went on for a mile. Much of it was just recently uncovered. We took more pictures of Ephesus than anywhere else. We also purchased postcards and a book on the history of Ephesus. The city is famous for its Temple of Artemis, which was built about 550 BC. It has been declared one of the Seven Wonders of the Ancient World. We strolled through the streets and saw many ruined buildings including the Library of Celsus and a huge outdoor theater that could hold 25,000 spectators. At one point, Ephesus was an important port but over its first 1,000 years the silt built up. It was further ruined by an earthquake in about 614 AD.

The Library of Celsus was built in 135 AD. The pair of columns on the second level frame the windows as the columns on the first level frame the doors. The statues that are there today are copies of the originals and stand for wisdom: Sophia, knowledge: Episteme, intelligence: Ennoia, and virtue: Arete. The library was built to honor the Roman Senator Tiberius Julius Celsus Polemaeanus.

We walked by the Marble Street, the Palace of the Council, and Nike the Goddess of Victory. We stood before the Memorial to Memmuis, which was built to honor the grandson of the dictator Sulla. Many of the walls of the Agora (the marketplace) are still standing. Two things that I witnessed today were very touching. We all so enjoyed watching Dave, the handsome and personable Unity Church maintenance guy, and his passion for photography. Sometimes he'd kneel down for a better angle on something. Or he would zone in on plaques and signs and tablets to catch the wording. Second was the plethora of kitty cats that lazed about the ruins. I suppose on a cold day like today, the archeological stones gathered up warmth and made for a cozy place to take a nap. I'm sure they had plenty of field mice for dinner. It's about time to leave intriguing Ephesus.

Back on the ship we readied for disembarkation. Back to Athens. We settled our accounts, counted out $25 to tip our cabin crew, packed our bags, ate dinner, and hit the sack. At 5:00 a.m. we pulled into Port of Piereas. We were instructed to take care of immigration formalities, take back our passports, meet up with our group on Metropolitan Deck 8 and bring our white receipt. We left our packed bags outside our door for midnight pickup by ship's porters. We went into the reception area on Deck 5, ate a quick breakfast at 5:45 and were told to vacate our cabin by 7:00. Whew! We did it.

Monday, November 12, 2007

At 4:00 a.m. I could feel our ship, the Cristol, pulling into port. I peeked out the window to the bright lights of Pierius which is the city attached to Athens. Together, they house 4,500,000 people. I thought I heard rain, wind, stormy skies, but it was the sound of a dumpster being dragged on the deck, and the ship wicking sideways towards the dock. The sky was clear—a couple of twinkling stars told me so. I snuggled back into bed until 5:00, at which time I began my stretches, checked out the bathroom and brushed my teeth. The stretches were necessary—how does anyone get through the day without stretching?

I just realized it's Monday. My dear friend Tahira will be leading my Laughter Yoga group this morning at 9:00 at the Cordelia Knott Wellness Center in Orange, California. Ho ho ha ha ha my dear Laughter friends.

By 6:15 a.m. Jerri and I were in the dining room having breakfast. We dined with Joanne and Doreen from Irvine Senior Center. Joanne is the activities director—thus the cruise and trip to Athens. She takes folks on "overnighters" and wanted to visit Greece. It took a pleasant 45 minutes to get all 67 of our passports collected by Bob. It was 8:15 before we boarded our busses. As our baggage was placed outside our door at 11:00 last night, it was shuffled off the ship early this morning. We're on our way to Delphi when I spot a sign that says "Teo Pass" which we think means toll road. We'll soon be stopping at the Monastery of "Holy Luke" who was a hermit and a healer. He died before the building was finished and the village named it after him.

We pass the little village of Arahova (meaning a place with walnut trees). Fellow traveler Karla's father was born here and she was so excited about her first look at Arahova. She taught us the words fea fea fea, meaning go go go. We went by Mt. Parnassus, which is snowy most of the year. We cruised by Valley of Phocis, which claims to have one million olive trees, all privately owned. And, at last, we arrived at the Hotel King Iniohos on Ossiou Louka Street in Delphi where we will stay on this rainy night. We stowed our belongings, had a quick snack, and headed back out for the afternoon tour.

Delphi used to be named Pytho. History tells us that Delphi was dedicated to the god Apollo. It is famous as the ancient Greeks were sure Delphi was the center of the world. It is recognized by UNESCO as a World Heritage site because it had such a huge influence on ancient Greeks. We observed several female oracles that sat on tripods above some type of stream, which may have been a trance-inducer or drug of some type. Oracles prophesized future happenings.

It looked like rain as we headed up the marble-slabbed steps to the temple dedicated to the sun god, Apollo. Ruins, walkways ascended for about half a mile. I declined to climb to the very top as it was beginning to sprinkle. The view from Delphi is astounding: green hills, trees, and valleys. We walked back with Neil, as his wife Betty went on ahead. Both walked with canes. I worried about him slipping. We chatted down the hillside, getting wetter by the moment. I was grateful to be wearing Richard's dad's jacket with the water-resistant hood.

At dinnertime, I sat with Amanda and Rev. Pam. From her comments last night, I knew she felt people weren't aware that she, too, is an ordained minister, so tonight I asked her what inspired her. She'd been a second grade teacher in public school. She told us she studied for the ministry and felt that she couldn't not be one.

Rev. Blair put together a 30-minute program with singing—him on ukulele. Rev. Donna, a guy from Arizona, Rev. Marilyn, and Rev. Pam spoke briefly. As Rev. Marilyn spoke, David played meditative music on the flute he'd purchased in Kusadasi Turkey.

After our rainy travels today, we checked into our hotel. It's quaint. Neither modern nor flashy. We're enjoying it. I phoned Richard to see how he's doing without me. He misses me. He gave us the San Diego weather report and the Chargers score for yesterday. It was 5:30 p.m. here and 7:30 a.m. in California. He'll be making a second trip to Newport Subacute Convalescent Hospital to play bingo with my Laughter Yoga group. All those old folks, with various challenges, love it when Richard shows up for the afternoon. He has a beautiful connection with them. Almost before I call and hang up, I was asleep.

Tomorrow, we head to Kalambaka to see a couple of monasteries and the countryside. We'll spend the night there at the Hotel Orfeas on Pindou Street then head off to Thessaloniki for two nights and then head back to the good ol' USA, via Munich, Germany. I'm so looking forward to being with Richard, and not constantly unpacking and re-packing, but having my things in drawers and closets familiar to them and me. Just three more nights.

Dinner tonight is mushy okra in tomato sauce, cheese pie, funny little salads of vinegar, cabbage and carrots, both finely grated and served with olive oil. And dessert? Yummy apple pie. And so to bed. It's 10:12.

Tuesday, November 14

We woke up in Delphi at 6:00 a.m., showered and prepared for another beautiful day in Greece. The maple tree foliage is golden. The mountains are of solid rock. The skies overcast. We're on the bus. Gina has given us a list of books about islands. At 9:30 I feel a nap coming on. It's so beautiful driving through this countryside but . . .

After lunch in Kalambaka, we were bussed up the hill to the monasteries on the meteoras—ancient monoliths where monks live—only six of the twenty-four inhabited, one with six nuns ages 22-28. It's very meditative, quiet, a very peaceful life. They feel closer to God, being up so high. The funny thing about visiting the women's monastery is that all females must wear skirts. If you're not wearing one, they hand you one and watch you put it on. I was wearing a pair of Levi's, a turtleneck sweater, and dad's heavy jacket.

Sister Mary Catherine handed me a skirt—actually a large piece of bland-colored fabric with elastic—and I stepped into it. I pulled it up over my outfit and looked like I weighted 200 pounds. Jerri and I got the giggles in a place where we are supposed to be respectful and quiet. Ah. It brought back memories of my misbehaving in 8th grade at Our Lady of Victory Catholic School in Los Angeles. I tried so hard to hold back silly laughter so the nuns would think I was listening.

After touring inside St. Stepanos Monastery, on the tippy-top of a meteora, we walked around the beautiful rose garden on the side of a hill. There were also about 50 grape vines. Again, a very peaceful place to be (if those two would just stop giggling).

Soon we'll be traveling to Thessaloniki, named for the wife of Alexander The Great. We'll be back near the ocean for a two-night stay. The word Eleutheria comes to mind. It refers to freedom of choice in any situation, to a happy and healthy life, a spiritually awakened being: Eleutheria.

Wednesday, November 14, 2007

Today we traveled from Kalambaka to Veria to Thessaloniki. We drove through more beautiful countryside and waved goodbye to the meteoras. About 6:30 p.m. we arrived at Hotel Hotel City. (Yes, that's the name of the hotel: Hotel City.) For an hour we walked and shopped. I purchased a coin purse for me and a black Greek Fisherman's hat for Richard. Our group enjoyed a dinner of a delicious veggie soup with bread dipped in olive oil. Salad, a plate of rice, some potatoes, and a large slice of feta almost completed the meal. Dessert was interesting. We were presented with a large cake. It had maple syrup on the bottom and a blob of whipped cream on top. Yum! We loved it!

We rose at 6:00 this morning. I stretched in bed while Jerri showered. At 6:28 I got up and dressed. Downstairs for tea at 7:00. The bus picked us up at 8:15 and we were off to visit the famous Mount Olympus, home of the gods and goddesses of Greek Mythology. It is the highest mountain in Greece (9,570 feet) and is located on the border between Thessaly and Macedonia, between the regional units of Pierie and Larissa, 50 miles southwest of Thessaloniki. It has 52 peaks; one is known as Mytikas. That's the official home of the Greek gods, so they say.

Here's what we know about Greek gods and goddesses.

The king of the gods, Zeus, ruled the sky: weather, thunder, lightning, as well as law, order, and justice. In Rome, he was known as Jupiter.

Poseidon is god of the seas, rivers, floods, droughts, and earthquakes. In Rome he is known as Neptune.

Hestia is the virgin goddess of the hearth, home, and chastity. In Rome, her name is Vesta.

Hermes is the god of boundaries, travel, communication, trade, language, thieves, and writing. As messenger of the gods, he leads the souls of the dead into the afterlife. His Roman counterpart is Mercury.

Hera is queen of the gods, and goddess of marriage, women, childbirth, heirs, kings, and empires. Roman counterpart? Juno.

Hephaestus is the god of fire, metalwork, and crafts. In Rome, he is known as Vulcan.

Hades is considered the king of the underworld and the dead, as well as the god of wealth. In Rome he is called Pluto.

Dionysus is the god of wine, fruitfulness, parties, festivals, madness, chaos, drunkenness, vegetation, ecstasy, and the theater. His common Greek name is Bacchus; it was adopted by the Romans.

Demeter is the goddess of grain, agriculture, harvest, growth, and nourishment. Her Roman counterpart is Ceres.

Athena is goddess of reason, wisdom, intelligence, skill, peace, warfare, battle strategy, and handicrafts. Her symbol is the olive tree. In Rome we'd call her Minerva.

Artemis is the virgin goddess of the hunt, wilderness, animals, and young girls. She is twin sister to Apollo and known as Diana in Rome.

Ares is god of war, bloodshed, and violence. Homer portrays him as moody and unreliable. His Roman counterpart is Mars.

Apollo is god of music, arts, knowledge, healing, plague, prophecy, poetry, manly beauty, and archery. In Rome, we'd call him Sol.

Aphrodite is goddess of beauty, love, desire, and pleasure. Quite mischievous, she was, bearing children to several of the gods. Her Roman name is Venus.

Mount Olympus was declared a National Park in 1938.

At this point, the gang on the bus began singing the "Peace Song," then "Rise and Shine." Then the "Peace Song" again. We also had a chance to ask Gina, our guide a few questions, like:

"What do the cows eat here?" She looked rather confused at first and responded, "What do they eat in the U.S.? Here, they eat just the grass." So we asked, "No oats? No grains?" Her reply? "Just grass."

"Can one ski on Mount Olympus?" Gina was really tired at this point and that dumb question just got a look, which indicated we all needed to go home and rest, especially her. As a travel tour guide, at the end of a very long and very busy season, Gina was feeling like an exhausted kindergarten teacher. We let her rest. No more questions . . . until we stopped in the Slovic town of Geneva. Many of us needed to use the "water closet" and it was time for me to get another, maybe my last, spinach and feta cheese pie. Boo hoo.

Back on the bus, Gina stood to tell us a bit of history. We listened intently. We all loved her, really. She was so full of knowledge and love of her country and liked Americans, mostly. She told us that Yugoslavians have claimed their state is Macedonia, that their language is Macedonian and that they are related to Alexander the Great. This angers the Greeks, as since 1980 northern Greece has been known as Macedonia.

We'd been informed that there was a fire here three months ago which burned millions of acres. A Greek guy had told us that the government declined to renew the contract with the Russians for assistance during natural disasters. Alexander said the government is not concerned with the people. Mariana, the shop owner on Mykenos, said that since the changeover to Euros, her business has gone down a lot because, now, the American dollar is so devalued—one euro cost almost a dollar and a half. The Greeks are not happy with American government either.

The earth here, from Grevena to Kozarii, is very fertile, rich, and dark. By noon it was raining lightly and we were pulling over in Verena for a photo-op and to visit the remains of an archeological sight. It was built in 358 B.C. We walked through the old agora (marketplace) and discovered the little river by St. Paul's Church. It was small and beautiful. I lit a candle for a struggling granddaughter and said a prayer for her. Stained glass windows of several saints shone in the chapel. We got a glimpse of the jail cell where St. Paul was imprisoned for his crime of healing a young slave girl. As the story goes, an earthquake soon shook the land and cracked open the jail. St. Paul escaped and it was deemed a miracle.

Soon, we were called to assemble on the steep steps by the river for a photo-op. Messy hair, well-worn clothing, challenged muscles and weary brains made for a beautiful picture of newly formed friendships and expanded minds. What could be better than that?

Well, exploring the flower market in Thessaloniki later that afternoon was pretty good. Last-minute jewelry purchases were pretty good. Spending time with my sister-in-law was awesome. Thank you Jerri for being such a blessing in my life and being a great traveling companion.

Professor Andronikos was an archeologist who was accepted by the Greeks and paid to search for treasures. Gina had him as her archeology teacher in 1984. When the government decided to cut off his pay, he continued to search and the townspeople collected 40 dracaenas to pay him. Fifteen days later he discovered the tombs of King Phillip. Then, the government gave him all the money he needed to continue his search, which included the discovery of Little Prince Alex IV, the son of King Phillip, and Roxanne, his wife. I cannot imagine the thrill he felt at the discovery. I would have been a good archeologist, as I have persistence, patience, and curiosity.

As we approached the mound of grass the size of a football field, we noticed an opening in the earth—a doorway into the tumbus (tomb in English). Holding our tickets in our hands, we gathered in the mist—all 33 of us. Led by our competent tour guide, Gina, we walked forth to witness this incredible sight. Three large tombs, the size of a small house, had contained the tombs of King Phillip, his son, and his grandson. King Phillip was buried with his hounds, his four horses, all his worldly possessions and a young wife-to-be who willingly walked into the funeral pyre to show her devotion to her "husband". Would anyone I know be as dedicated? I would want my husband, or wife, to live fully, perhaps marry again. Hopefully, the devoted wives were drugged and felt no pain. Perhaps deep in meditation, their deaths were painless.

When I finally left the site, my cohorts in traveling adventure were well into lunch and wine. I decided to sit in quiet on the bus. Iris sat in the back with her bouquet of flowers. I may suggest we decorate the bus with them. She's carrying the flowers from hotel to hotel, courtesy of a thoughtful homebound husband.

After our travels, Jerri and I decided to go shopping for clean tee shirts. It seems everything I own is smelly. So I bought three tee shirts and a wool multi-colored vest. The shop was Sparkle Girl. I got to wear a clean shirt to dinner tonight. That felt good! And I get to wear another clean tee shirt tomorrow. After shopping we got lost. We stopped in a sub shop for directions. On his cell phone, yelling in anger, the shop owner kept giving us dirty looks. When he got off the phone, he yelled at us. "What?" I said, "Hi. We're lost. Where is the City Hotel?" I guess he didn't know any English. Then a big handsome customer came in the door.

"Hello," I said, "Do you speak English?" He said he did and gave us perfect directions. Somehow, in our chatting and shopping, Jerri and I walked about a half-mile past the turning place for our hotel. We made it back. I showered and put on a clean shirt. So nice! My new off-white tee with lace at the bottom. Elizabeth even remarked, "Oooh, cleavage." Not an easy task but I try.

After dinner we enjoyed 45 minutes of friendship. We shared appreciation for the trip, Bill our bus driver, Gina our guide, each other, Rev. Blair and Meredith, Grace. We prayed for everything. We sang little ditties. Rev. Pam's blessings, ended with "He's Got the Whole World." To bed at 11:00ish after sorting and packing in anticipation of tomorrow's early departure.

Thursday, November 15, 2007

We are on the road again. Bye-bye City Hotel. We're on our way to Amphipolis to view the Lion statue and then ancient Phillipi near Kavala where St. Paul landed on his journey. Gina thanked us for sweet words at last night's dinner. History tells us that the Turks turned cathedrals into mosques. Emperor Galarius won over the Persians. There was a fire in 1917 in the Turkish baths.

It's 9:35 a.m. and we're now on Highway 60 headed towards Filipi. There is, on the map, a town near the sea called Eleftheroupoli. We travel along quaint villages, some in ill repair, cemeteries, junkyards. Factories are being built, construction going on. A few vineyards. As always, when traveling, I find it interesting what people bring along or buy for snacks. Sugar reigns. But, there are a few apples.

Tomorrow we'll be up at 4:30 and have our bags out in the hotel hallway by 5:00 a.m. Breakfast is at 5:00 a.m. We'll be on the bus and leave for the airport by 6:00. Then we fly to Munich, Germany, and then on to LAX. We'll arrive by 3:00 and catch the bus to Disneyland where Richard will pick us up.

Ode to the Land that is Greece: Eleutheria (written November 15, 2007)

It is unlike any other country.
Frescoes, tumulas, agoras, acropolii
White-washed homes of Mikonos
Red-tiled roofs of Kalambaka
Mondsk deer, roaming cats and dogs
Shop-keepers, bus drivers, tour guides

All filled with true Spirit of Life

Cheerful schoolyard noises
Vineyards, grapes, wine, and laughter
Bringing freedom: eleutheria
The holy places, heavenly meteora
Families praying, candles aglow.

The Agean Sea and Mediterranian
Andronike's search for King Phillipi
Sunshine, rain, wind, movement
Beaches, mountains, heather and olives
History BC and A. Now. The future.
The Greece of my dreams is Real.

And in closing this story, I must thank my beloved Richard for making my travels possible, for keeping the home fires alit, and welcoming me back with love. So, my dearest: I am eternally grateful. You are endlessly fascinating. With all my heart, thee I love.

Cruising the Baltic - 2008

Saturday night. May of 2008. We get a phone call from my sister Jeannie. "Hi Sis. We'd love you to join us on that Baltic Cruise in July." I reply, "Well, the King and I have talked it over. That's a lot of money and we've never cruised and we're gonna pass." Teasingly, my sister says, "We just had dinner with Rev. Blair and his wife Meredith. There's only one accessible cabin available on the ship." I hesitate for a moment and tell her. "No. Not this time." But the next morning when I opened my eyes, Richard was looking at me with a big smile on his face. So I said, "Let's go on that cruise." He's pretty easy-going. "Sure. Let's do it."

I immediately call the Unity Church in San Diego and connect with Meredith. I let her know we'll take that last accessible cabin. "Sign us up." She signs us up and we prepare to cruise.

Wednesday, July 9, 2008

. . . and off we go! LAX to Houston. Houston to London where we will catch the transport bus to Harwich, our port of departure. Then we step onto The Jewel of the Sea. We are now sitting in the correct seats. We were in EF when we should have been in AB. Oops! I must learn the alphabet or get better glasses. Flight #1558 Continental Airlines. We are excited and alive with wonderment.

Thursday, July 10, 2008

Almost 7:00 a.m. in London 2 hours, 26 minutes away. We've been awake most of the night. It's 11:00 p.m. at home. Our seats don't recline. The plane is full. Yet we are cheerful. Plenty of time for napping once we're on board The Jewel of The Sea. At 1:45 p.m. we're on the bus from the airport in London to our ship. Ow! My feet! Ow, my back. Ow, my wrist. My arms. Very thirsty. Weather beautiful. Clouds, not too cool. 60? 65? Almost there. Got papers in order. Passports. Copies of passports.

Friday, July 11, 2008

We stood in many lines before boarding ship. Finally, we were guided to a "disabled folks" line where our Visa Card was scanned, photos were taken and ship ID created, then quickly given our cabin key-card thingy. We found our lovely suite with the big balcony. (I'm standing on it now—7:08 a.m. Estonia time.) Cabin 7610. Our first night's dinner was superb. At our table of eight were The King and I, Anne and Nancy, Rev. Blair and Meredith, my sister Jeannie and her husband Curt. Rev. Blair slept off and on through dinner as Meredith spoke. From dinner we went to an introduction show and watched an amazing juggler, I fell asleep. Richard shook my shoulder and motioned for me to leave the auditorium with him. We left for our room where we both fell into bed and slept fully clothed. I got up several hours later, brushed my teeth, took off my clothes and got back into bed.

Saturday, July 12, 2008

This morning I was awake at 5:00 but lounged until 6:00. I dressed and was out the door by 7:00. We had breakfast and then I walked the Deck 12 track for 90 minutes. Several interesting people were doing the same thing: Yadowh and his wife, Ann, originally from India—now residing in London. After the walk I returned to the Windjammer for eggs and an English muffin. I enjoyed getting to know Delores who is from Ireland, here with eight other women from her hiking group. She's been a widow for over ten years. We spoke of children, food, and weight problems in Ireland and in America. That's what I love about traveling: meeting people from everywhere.

I wondered where Richard had gone. He loves the independence provided by his scooter, the Rascal, and sometimes just roams around talking to just about everyone and anyone. At 10:15 I joined the folks from Unity group for introductions. What an interesting bunch of people we are. Several retired teachers (including us.) A couple of grandparents. Lovely people, all. Then I returned to our room and left Richard a note telling him the group was to meet for lunch at the Windjammer Restaurant.

Lunch with this group was a lot of fun. Curt told stories about his sister Joan's family, her gay ex-husband, her four children. One of our group, whose luggage was on a supreme vacation, inquired about borrowing clothes. Rev. Blair talked about his parents and their gourmet meals.

This ship is huge! Thirteen decks high. Our balcony's lovely. It looks like it could rain out there. As I walked this morning, the sun was shining brightly. It was even warmer earlier. Inside the dining area, the a/c is turned way up. The sea appears to be rolling by. We do not, as yet, catch sight of land. We will be on the sea two complete days before docking in Tallinn, Estonia, which used to be part of the Soviet Union.

Later: We are showered, coiffed, formally dressed, and on our way to the Captain's Champagne Reception. Richard in white shirt, tie, gray wool slacks, and dark blue sports coat. I am wearing a long black skirt and a backless black top. I have on my black sandals and oops! I forgot to bring black pantyhose. I have on silver and glass (fake diamonds) dangling earrings. We look amazing. So glad I've kept up the exercise. See you later.

There are 850 crewmembers aboard this ship. At our champagne dinner the captain explained tonnage, etc. Our crew director is Bobby. He's the guy in the kilt who explained tonight's Broadway show. As all this was going on, Alec, Rev. Marilyn's 12-year old grandson and I had a great conversation. He is very bright with a great sense of humor. His dad is a teacher and his mom is a physical therapist. He has a 10-year old sister and wants to be a lawyer because he "likes to argue." We laughed. I asked if he had a girlfriend. He said there is a girl he likes. Also he said girls are very forward, asking boys, "Would you like to go out with me sometime?" He told me a few of his many excuses, in a very funny way. It's easy to see he has conversations with his parents and has good social skills.

After this evening's Broadway review—which was excellent—Jeannie, Curt, Richard and I walked through the gift shop. Jeannie and I stopped to look around and the guys disappeared. Ten minutes later we parted. I called 3562. Curt was in the room. Alas, Richard is out wandering around again. Probably in the Casino. In about an hour we are to pass under the world's second largest bridge.

It is now 10:30 p.m. We are sitting by our window in 7610 when we notice our ship seems to be picking up speed. Buoys with flashing lights spotted out on the sea. Land is still a distance away. The sun has set, yet it is still light enough to read outside. Tomorrow we sail all day—arriving in Estonia early Sunday morning.

Saturday July 12, 2008

As we passed under the bridge last night at 12:30, I took pictures from our balcony. I'm not sure the pictures will be so great. We went to sleep about 1:30 and got up at 6:15 this morning. I walked from 6:40 until 8:00, showered; then Jeannie phoned. I tossed on clean clothes—no make-up, no combing of the hair. Had breakfast with Jeannie and Curt, Nancy and Ann. Richard arrived later. The menu was not great. It seemed limited. I am now at a lecture on Abraham by Rev. Larry. He tells us to "focus on the good. Abraham teaches: know what is important to me. That way I can be helpful to others. There are no accidents. No luck. No chances." Okay, I think. I have come to give unconditional love. I have chosen to experience this life, have more fun, and be gentle with myself and others. Flow with life—let go of the oars.

Dis-ease and lack indicate resistance, restructuring the conduit, like the Dead Sea; evidence of interpreting things as problems. Look for vibrational resistance. New thought. When you feel on empty, look for what fulfills you. Don't say, "I failed." It's a three-step process: ask, receive, come up to vibrational speed and accept the universe's gifts. Rev. Larry emphasized the Art of Allowing as in allowing your life to be great. He suggested finding peace where you are on your journey and letting the universe know where you are. Pay attention. After analyzing what I'd heard, I decided that there isn't anything new in the universe but awareness of awareness.

Sunday, July 13 2008

This morning we're off to visit Tallinn, Estonia, once subjects of the Soviet Union. As the story is told, in 1988, 300,000 Estonians (1/3 of the population) gathered at the Song Festival Grounds outside Tallinn to sing patriotic songs. Estonians say, "We had no weapons; being together and singing together was our power." In 1991, on the eve of an expected violent crackdown of this Singing Revolution, the makeshift Estonian Parliament declared independence. At that time, Moscow was in disarray, which made the USSR a nonentity. Estonia was free. According to our tour guide, Tia, when the communists were in control, Estonians were only allowed to sing the songs sent from Moscow, not their own songs and music. Last year at the anniversary of freedom celebration, there were 120,000 at the festival. Tina Turner, Metalica, and Michael Jackson appeared on stage. Tia declared that summer in Estonia is on July 19th.

We are now back on The Jewel of the Sea—after walking to the wrong port in the rain—big drops with wind. Just in time, as the ship was ready to pull out. We had been instructed to be back by 5:00. Oops! I walked four miles on the upper deck early this morning for exercise. Then another three miles on our tour of Tallinn. We'd had lunch at a little table on the sidewalk. Venue was small but very busy. We couldn't decide where their kitchen was. The waitress would walk around the corner and quickly return with our food. The food was okay but nothing like what we were eating aboard The Jewel.

Since we were a bit late getting back on ship we missed the 6:00 seating for the formal dinner—again. Note: When we first boarded, we signed up for the early seating for dinner, as did all 14 of the Unity group. We were assigned tables and waiters for the duration of the trip. But there are so many dining options on cruise ships often we went to one of the several buffets rather than join the more "formally presented" 6:00 seating. We never went hungry.

We DID make it to our seats in time for dinner. We arrived about 6:45. Everyone was back at their original tables. After dinner last night, Curt went to the magic show, Richard to the casino, and Jeanne and I went to listen to music. When "Rock Around the Clock" began, we decided to laugh and dance like we did in our early teens. Meredith and Rev. Blair joined us but soon the Rev. left for bed. We three women did what women do when left alone. We went shopping. I got to bed at 11:30.

Monday, July 14, 2008

This morning Richard and I got up at 5:30, showered and headed out for an early breakfast. Our bus was to leave at 8:00 a.m. We borrowed a wheelchair for this part of the journey because the Rascal was too big and bulky. Many angels helped us. We toured, by bus, all over St. Petersburg—another panoramic sight-seeing trip. What I enjoyed the most was taking pictures of people working—which will go into one of my upcoming books: Workers of the World. I was especially taken with the beautiful young woman who was watering the flowers at the palace.

Our attempt to get back to the ship on time was foiled by a stalled train. One-half hour later than expected we arrived at the dock. Richard in wheelchair—a tough call. I pushed him over to the ship where two strong young men tugged and pushed the chair up a very steep ramp. We raced down the hallway on deck 3 just to learn there is no elevator Aft on deck 3. So, we raced back. Twice maid carts blocked the hallway, so Richard would get out of the chair and stand by as I folded and unfolded the wheelchair. We proceeded. After much ado, we found elevators. Rolled in. Pushed "7". A young man jumped into the elevator and pushed "5" then a young woman got in and pushed "4". Finally—more ado, we arrived at 7610. Without delay, I used the potty, grabbed my jacket, a bag of trail mix, and two umbrellas. Somewhere in the race for 7610, we passed Rev. Blair and Meredith, Jeannie and Curt. "Don't let the bus go without me." I was leaving The King aboard while I joined the others for a tour.

Sure enough, after re-checking out with customs, Jeannie and Curt flagged me down. I am so tired, sleepy, and hungry. Well, I thought, that's how traveling is sometimes. Keep going.

We had another beautiful tour of St. Petersburg, partly by bus, then riverboat. Next we toured the palace of Yosefpov family. Wow! Fun and laughter. We enjoyed the palace and the stories told by Marina. We were back on the ship before 6:00. Tired. Sweaty and VERY hungry.

This evening we enjoyed an "opulent" dinner. Such choices! I had Latvian soup made with potatoes and mushrooms, served with a great sesame roll. Then salmon with roasted potatoes and something that looked like cabbage. It was good but I could only eat about a third of it. We shared several desserts. All were interesting but there was nothing I was crazy about.

It's 10:20 p.m. It's still light outside with very dark sky. We're experiencing a lightening storm.

Tomorrow we'll be up early again, have breakfast and be off for a Grand Tour—nine hours—of St. Petersburg, including the Hermitage Museum. Wow!

Tuesday, July 15, 2008

St. Petersburg was founded in 1703 by Tsar Peter the Great. For a few years it was considered the capital of Russia. (In 1918 the government moved to Moscow 388 miles to the southeast.) St. Petersburg is inscribed on the UNESCO World Heritage list as an area with 36 historical architectural complexes and about 4000 individual monuments of architecture, history, and culture. This amazing city has 221 museums, 2000 libraries, 80 theaters, 100 concert organizations, 45 galleries and exhibition halls, 62 movie theaters and 80 other cultural establishments. We did not have time to see everything, but we saw many beautiful sights. Around 100 festivals and art/culture competitions are held each year, 50 of them international. The most popular venue, of course, is the Hermitage Museum, one of the largest art museums in the world. It has been said that if you stood for just one minute in front of each object, it would take ten years to see everything.

Although tiring, this was a wonderful, beautiful, and amazing day. We toured from 8:30 this morning until 4:00 this afternoon and we are tired. We spent 2-1/2 hours in the Hermitage and I have to say my favorite piece of art is Flora by Rembrandt Harmenszoon van Rijn. Flora—or Saskia as Flora—a 1634 painting by Rembrandt, which shows his wife Saskia van Uylenburgh as the goddess Flora. She represents youth, spring, and fertility.

One of the really neat things about this day is that when we got off the ship, Richard in a regular wheelchair, a young man stepped forth and offered to hang out with us and push Richard around. He said he was getting a free cruise as a guest of one of the crewmembers and was happy to lend a helping hand. Again, I think he was an angel that flew down to help us for the day. We had not seen him before today. We never saw him again.

Lunch today was at the Radisson Hotel. We each had a small salad with caviar and lox. Potato soup. Rice and veggies with carrot puree. Very good. Dessert was a pear tart with lots of whipped cream and a gooseberry on top. Also, we each received a cup of tea. Our ship is scheduled to have us all on board by 5:15 and leave port at 5:30. Onward . . .

Wednesday, July 16, 2008

We slept in until 6:30 this morning! The latest ever! We showered and had a leisurely breakfast at 8:00 o'clock. We shared breakfast with Tom and Ann from Tucson, Arizona. We spoke with Sergi, our Ukrainian waiter. He spoke of Russia and freedom. He spoke of the young and the old. I felt such love and compassion for these people who had suffered under Communist rule for so many years. Now they have more freedom but do not trust that it will last. Marina, yesterday's tour guide, for example, was very knowledgeable about the history of her country. There was never, however, a spark of joy. No spontaneous joy. Did she fear us? Her job? Her life? If one has never experienced joy why would one keep living? What would be the purpose? Indeed! (Just now, for the joy, I bought an Irish coffee with brown sugar and whipped cream and accepted a scone. I am sitting at the window as the ship clips along at about 15 knots. The sea is rough tonight. As the Dali Lama says, "The purpose of life is happiness. The way to happiness is through service." (It is now 11:05 p.m. and the sun has just set.) Tonight a night at sea. Tomorrow Helsinki.

So I recognize Marina was serving us—perhaps the joy will be with her soon. Dennis Prager, on the other hand tells us in his best-selling book, "Gratitude is the Way to Happiness." Isn't happiness but a temporal measure of life? When I am feeling sad, lonely, or can't sleep, I list my gratitude. It does bring joy for all that is my life, for all that has been granted me. The grace. The grace. This is one of those times when I'm asking myself, "Did this little farm girl ever dream of, desire, or envy the cruising life? No. Never. But now that I know, I want many more. I dream, now, of a Mexican Riviera Cruise with family. All our kids and grandkids. Ah. Someday.

So, back to Russia and freedom. I cannot imagine how difficult it would be to raise children when the feeling of repression reigned for so long. Those old women on the streets, by the churches, with cups in hand, hoping a generous tourist may offer a rupple, Euro, or even an American dollar. How sad must their hearts be. And here I sit, listening to a 4-piece band. Some of the lucky tourists are dancing. Some are shopping. Some are off to the dining room again, enjoying a late evening snack.

I love what Eckhart Tolle teaches us: "Release egoic thinking, allow awareness of awareness, live in the moment, forgive, love what is, accept challenges, recognize the steps from "pain body" towards joy and viola! Joy! Grace! Love! It's all there." Bob and Barbara Gabrowski say they went to Russia years ago to bring some New Thought philosophy to people willing to see life differently. What gifts they brought. Today, Carolina, our Finish tour guide, told us quite the opposite of these Eastern Bloc populations, that the Danish, year after year, are voted the happiest folks on earth. When studied, revelations arose: low expectations combined with free education to those who pass the test for college entrance, extremely low medical costs, and grants for attending school, including hot meals. I wonder if there are requirements to stay in the country after receiving this free education—to give back.

Thursday July 17, 2008

So, today after breakfast we descended to the second deck. Several elevators came and went as people crowded in front of us—or refused to create space. After breakfast I ran back to our cabin, brushed my teeth and hiked down to the 3rd floor. At first I could not find Jeannie and Curt at 3562. The hallways were crowded with maids' carts. Frustrating. Finally, I found them, to let them know Richard was somewhere and I felt concern as to his whereabouts. So I looked for him in several spots on several floors before finding him. Finally, our group of eight assembled at the Deck 2 checkout station only to discover my "Sea Pass" key received a big fat rejection. I was told to get another new key. They claimed Monday's lost key reincarnated itself. I ran upstairs. Another key popped out of the "magic key machine." I ran back down to Deck 2. In the meantime I told our group to shuttle to Helsinki without us. We'd catch up. Finally, I did check out. Richard's half-eaten ice-cream cone would not be allowed. Oops!

The first stop of the day was to be Market Square in Helsinki. When we finally got to the shuttle Richard boarded the bus and I stood by the Rascal to see that it got on board in good health. I tried to show the driver that the speed dial needed to be turned down or it would careen out of control but he refused to acknowledge me and just stomped away. The driver's anger set off my tears. Two nice men on the bus get off and help me load the Rascal under the bus. I thank them and then remember the driver has a difficult life. Maybe there isn't much in his life to be joyful about.

We traveled on to Helsinki but never found our group. What we found was a beautiful park with fountains, statues, and flowers. We found the Market Square and Richard purchased amber earrings for me, and a one-million year old amber-enclosed tiny, tiny spider for him. Then! Strawberries, carrots, and really green lettuce, which we nibbled on, walking to the Cathedral on the hill, which turned out to be accessible only by stairs.

The carrot was the freshest. The lettuce the greenest, berries the sweetest! On a park bench, we deepened our love with juicy red sweetness! We enjoyed those red berries and wrapped up several romaine leaves to bring to dinner. (The only lettuce on the ship was iceberg and being a romaine fan, I was so happy to find some at the Market Square—known as the Farmers Market in the U.S.) A kind stranger directed us east so we could catch the shuttle back. This trip was without Rascal-boarding issues. Upon our return, we freshened up a bit and headed for the Windjammer serve-yourself café. Several precious new friends, including Rev. Marilyn and her grandson Alec, joined us. Scanning the salad bar was a no-brainer, as I collected delicious salad fixings, minus the greens, which I added back at our table. Best meal I've had.

What a wonder! Tomorrow we'll head for our great-grandparents homeland: Sweden.

As the story goes, Mrs. Mary and Mr. Sven Lofstead, our great grandparents, arrived from Sweden in 1881 and came directly to Ogallah, Kansas with their four children. As Sven said, "We arrived with $5 in our pockets and our four children. (They must have had big pockets.) Six weeks later we had five children." Eventually, they had ten children. He became a farmer and she earned money by washing clothes for her neighbors. So, Jeannie and I were excited about exploring this country, even if only for a few hours.

Our total knowledge of the Swedish language is using the word "Ja." So we use it a lot and pretend we're smart. I had so much fun just wandering around Stockholm that I almost missed the Vasa Ship Museum with its rendition of 17th century ships and various exhibits related to the archaeological findings of the ships. Although a few parts of the main ship are missing, it is a wonder to see and imagine the sinking and revival of this huge work of art. There were many exhibits and models portraying the construction, the sinking, and the recovery of the ship. The Vasa had been underwater for three centuries before being rescued. Such a quick Sweden.

Back to Jewel of the Sea for a good night's rest. To Denmark tomorrow.

Saturday, July 19, 2008

We were up at 6:00 this morning. Showered and off to breakfast with Neal and his wife Betty, Ann, Nancy, and Rev. Blair. Today, in Copenhagen, we took a bus tour and visited that famous statue called The Little Mermaid. It is a bronze sculpture created by Edvard Eriksen in 1913 and depicts a mermaid becoming a human. The sculpture sits on a rock by the waterside at the Langelinie promenade. She is as famous as our Statue of Liberty. Many of us got off the bus to take her picture.

Countries outside the United States of American are old. If we see a building at home that is 100 years old we seem astonished. In Europe and the Scandinavian countries it is not uncommon to visit buildings that are centuries old. A couple of interesting facts about this part of the world. Gasoline is about $7.50 a gallon and people really like, actually like, eating herring. It's true. Herring is a popular dish here.

Sunday, July 20, 2008

Happy 44th birthday to our dear son John today. We wish you could be with us and see this amazing part of the world.

Today, while Richard took the bus tour to the famous Vigeland Sculpture Gardens of Oslo, I took a hike. With a group of happy hikers, I walked through 5-1/2 mile of forested hills. Our hands were cold. Our feet got warm. When we arrived at the Famous Olympic Ski jump ramp, one of our group asked, "Is that your husband?" I turned around to see my beloved Richard riding his rascal into the gift shop and museum. The tour carrying Richard, my sister, Curt, and a bunch of others had just arrived.

Since I was wet and cold, my sweet sister loaned me her gloves. Our hiking group of 12 brave (maybe foolish?) souls left Jewel of the Sea in the harbor at 9:30 this morning. We walked through town with a knowledgeable tour guide and learned all about Oslo. Then we walked another mile to the train station, which stopped at Hard Rock Café for a potty break. We caught a train that took us up the mountain. We then walked 5 miles to various landmarks: an Old Catholic Church, several ski lodges, some old thatched roof homes. After the famous ski jump, where it drizzled non-stop, we marched down the hill to another train station. After a 40-minute ride, we disembarked and walked back to the ship.

I stopped at the Latte Bar for tea and a nice chat with Margie. After a much-needed hot shower and shampoo, it was off to the Windjammer for a great buffet dinner with Curt and Richard. Tired but happy, we next moved to the theater where we enjoyed the entertainment. A troop of tango dancers stepped and swayed to the music. Jacquie Scott sang us to sleep with some classics and a few of her own making. And so to bed.

Monday, July 21, 2008

We sailed all day today, our last day, on heavy seas. It was rather rough crossing the Northern Sea. I walked for 2 hours on Deck 5 from 6:15 - 8:15 a.m. Along the way I met my sister and Ann. Later we all got a chance to catch up on sleep and do a bit of reading—and writing.

Tuesday, July 22, 2008

We docked in Harwich Harbor at 4:30 a.m. I took spectacular pictures of the sunrise and lights in the harbor. We were off the ship by 8:30, on the bus, and headed back to London. We'll be there in two hours.

Wednesday July 23, 2008

We're in London! We left Copthorn Tara hotel at 9:00 this morning and didn't return until 8:00 this evening. We toured Windsor Castle and saw the Queen's Doll House complete with miniature Rolls Royces, clothes, and the beautiful English Country Garden. Did we shop? Oh, yes! I bought a beautiful yellow blouse—made in India—and a purse—at the Castle. In Bath I bought trail mix, dates, chocolate-covered walnuts. At Stonehenge, we ate egg-salad sandwiches.

Stonehenge is about two miles west of Amesbury. It consists of a ring of stones standing on edge. Each stone is about 13 feet high and seven feet wide. Estimated weight is about 25 tons. It is believed that it was constructed from 3000 BC to 2000 BC. Perhaps as a burial ground. Human bones have been found on the site. Stonehenge is owned by the Crown and is managed by English Heritage. The land around it is owned by the National Trust and was added to UNESCO's list of World Heritage Sites in 1986.

In Bath we were surprised when we rented headphones for an explanation of England's famous Roman baths and the voice was that of Bill Bryson, one of our favorite authors. He and his wife and four children live in England and in the United States. He's a history buff so this was a perfect fit. We enjoyed learning that the Romans built the baths in 60 AD in this valley of the River Avon. The hot springs are said to be natural healers. The cobble stone streets were a bit of a challenge for Richard but he managed to maneuver about the city.

Bath is located about 90 miles west of London. The Abbey here was built in the 7th century and was a religious center for many years. It is said that

Jane Austen lived in Bath in the early 19th century. After the Blitz during WWII parts of the city had to be rebuilt.

On the way back to London, I mentioned to our tour guide, Tom, that I'd always wanted to visit Tinturn Abbey in Wales. After reading William Wordsworth's poem, "Lines Composed Above Tinturn Abbey" I felt drawn to this ancient site. He immediately picked up his little cell phone and called a friend. Tom let us know that his friend would drive us, and Richard's Rascal, to Tinturn for a mere 400 pounds. That's about 800 in American dollars. For a second or two I thought that was too much. Richard immediately, said, "Yes. We'll do it." When we figured flying back here in a year or two, renting cars and a room, meals, etc. 400 pounds sounded like a bargain.

Thursday, July 24, 2008

Our driver for the day is another Richard. He's 45, married for ten months, and lives just outside London. He picked us up at Copthorn Tara at 7:20 this morning in a Voyager van, on our way to Wales, and the Wye Valley to visit Tintern Abbey. Wordsworth wrote this in 1798. He says, as he overlooks the Valley, "all which we behold is full of blessings."

Wordsworth goes on to say about his youth, "changed, no doubt, from what I was when first I came among these hills; when like a roe I bounded o'er the mountains by the sides of the deep rivers, and the lonely streams, wherever nature led: more like a man flying from something he dreads, then (the coarser pleasures of my boyish days, and their glad animal movements all gone by) To me was all in all."

After two hours on the road we are nearing Wales. The countryside along the road is stunning. We talked of Stonehenge. Richard, our driver, reminded us of a mock-up made a joke about "Hay henge" because of the many bales of hay in the fields. We saw a pile of wood. The King declared, "There's Woodhenge."

We are 25 miles from the Abbey. About to go over the Severn River, which divides England and Wales. We'll use the "old" bridge to cross the river.

We are in Wales!!! Three miles to Tinturn. Passed a racetrack.

Beauty and Peace surrounded us. Quiet. For two hours we breathed-in Tinturn Abbey. We talked quietly, read the history, took pictures, drank it all in. We spoke with a young family from "mid-land" which means the middle of England. They've rented a cottage in the Village. They live near York. The mother had been here years ago and always wanted to return.

We met Tina, a bus driver, who takes seniors on outings. We had lunch with her at the Mill-a-tiny Restaurant in the Village at Tinturn. We spent no less than 30 minutes talking with Ann, who has lived at the Quay (pronounced The Key) for 30 years. Her home is directly on the Tinturn Trail. She was mowing the lawn—at the Wye River's edge. She took me inside and showed me the stone staircase that led to the second story. Another (wooden) staircase went up to her bedroom. She told us that her bedroom window looks out directly at the Abbey.

Ann's home is 350 years old—a treasure! She left the engineering business to go into psychology. She told us her partner died 18 years ago. She called herself a "Thinking Man's Crumpet," meaning she is smart. She seemed lonely and in need of connecting with someone. Today it was with us.

This was one of the best days of my life! Seeing Tinturn Abbey was a life-long dream—high on the bucket list—and I am delighted with what I felt and with what I saw.

Tomorrow we leave our hotel at 5:05 a.m. on a bus to the Gatewick Airport with our group. Meredith and Rev. Blair will head to Edinburg. The rest of us—28 travelers—back to California. I wish there was a magic way to be home instantly.

Friday, July 25, 2008

We are on our way home. Gatewick Airport. It's 8:20 a.m. We depart at 11:30 am. Three hours to write, read, shop, drink one last cup of tea. We are filled with gratitude for the pleasures life has brought us. To see the world, to watch the children, to know that we are all in this together. For health and wealth. Fun in the sun. No pain in the rain. No bog in the fog. To spoon underneath the moon.

Funny how, as the day progresses, so many unexpected events can occur. But! Let's focus on the good. It's almost 4:00 in New Jersey. I attempt to reach Sallie or Beth. We will need a ride from LAX.

Now, as we take off from New Jersey we figure it's 2:10 California time. A six-hour ride will get us home by 5 o'clock. And now recalculate for the good news: Richard finally got his package of dried mangos open. Yum. I'm waiting for tea to go with my "Cranberry Flapjack cookie thingy."

From now on, when I'm feeling stressed, I'll meditate on the Peace of Tinturn.

Saturday, July 26, 2008

We're home! We love home! Yay! We love it here. But . . .when's our next trip? Stay tuned.

Do you love me, yes?
Do you love me, no?
Ask me in the morning not now.

May 2009 Cruising the St. Lawrence in Canada and East Coast

Wednesday, May 20, 2009

Wowee! The alarm sang out at 3:00 a.m. Actually, I was up and out of bed 90 seconds early and silenced the clock radio in the bathroom. That blast woke up Kristina, who spent the night in our guestroom/office. After showering, I made egg-salad sandwiches, packed scones, unloaded dishwasher, washed up the remaining dishes.

Cathy O'D arrived at 3:35 a.m. to leave her SUV in our driveway behind the gate. She's on her way to NYC with the Orange Community Master Chorale. They will sing in Carnegie Hall Saturday evening—without me. Boo hoo ha ha ha.

At 4:30 a.m. I phoned our dear neighbor and chauffeur Fred to check his alertness. He drove over at 4:45—Kristina and I had already packed the van-all bags aboard. At 6:38 our plane is pulling back—out of the terminal. We're in a line of planes readying for take-off at 7:00 a.m. First stop: Dallas, where we'll meet up with the rest of our group. Fourteen people in all.

Safely in the air and on our way to Montreal, Canada. Kristina is drifting off to sleep. Richard is thumbing through a magazine. We are very excited. I pray—ask compassion of Quan Yin—for our sweet neighbor Carol who was on her way to dialysis this morning. So far, it's "touch and go". We're sitting on the runway, awaiting take-off. I'm awaiting my sandwich. The scones I'll save to eat in Dallas. My stomach is making noises. It's 6:50 a.m.

We landed in Dallas at 11:30. Richard's Rascal arrived at 1:00 with its batteries disconnected. We were introduced to Vaughn and Joan, Carol and Don. We were well acquainted with my sister Jeannie and her husband Curt, and friends Yolanda, her husband Gene, and Ann. We'll meet up with the final pair Randy and Terri and their son, Tom, in Montreal.

While waiting for our next flight, MacDonald's burgers, fries, barbequed beef was lunch for most of our crew. Me: I have a tofu sandwich in my bag. It is now 2:20 and our plane is to depart off in 5 minutes. What a jolly group!

We land in Montreal, Canada and are bussed over to our hotel. Dinner was at 9:30 in the pub: Goat cheese, tomatoes, French bread with yummy salad. Afterwards several of our group went for a walk along the St. Lawrence River. The Snyders decided to go to bed and snuggle at 11:50, dropping right to sleep.

Thursday, May 21, 2009

Up before 7:00. Showered, dressed, breakfast was my day-old scone. Kristina and I walked about a mile along the St. Lawrence River. She took pictures of the Big Clock. We are in the lobby of the Spring Hill Marriott awaiting our tour bus. A three-hour tour of Montreal with history. Fifteen of us. The small bus picked us up at the hotel and drove us, for 30 minutes, to the big bus. We're ready for the tour at 10:15 a.m. We learned a bit of French on the way. Arret means stop. Centre info touriste means center for tourist information. La gouch is left and la droit is right. Norman, our guide, is fluently bi-lingual: French and English. We toured Montreal's Chinatown. Oohed and awed at the fountain, hiked up the hill towards the Bascilica Notre Dame. I took a lot of pictures of "Workers of the World." That's a book I have in mind to create.

The plan is to return to Notre Dame this evening for the "Light and Sound" show. Built in 1763, today it is a two-story domed public market with restaurants, outdoor cafes, boutiques, and a rental hall with banquet rooms. Municipal office space is also available. We visited Bonsecours Market, designated a National Historic Site of Canada in 1984 on rue Saint-Paul in Old Montreal.

An interesting challenge occurred. Just blocks from the hotel, at the corner of Saint Pierre and Margurite-D'Youville, Richard's Rascal gave up. Richard is on his cell phone trying to contact the Canada office for new batteries. I've pushed for several blocks. The batteries are drained. With less than two days before we board the ship for an 8-day cruise, a scooter with no power is a deal breaker. Loaned to a friend for the last year, he "borrowed" it back for this trip. But it wasn't' well-maintained and now, in Montreal, we have a problem: the batteries are kaput. (What's French for "no mas?") He makes contact and is talking to someone named Sonny—somewhere in Canada. It sounds as though batteries may be delivered to our hotel. Good! I only have to push four more blocks. And only half of that is uphill. Puff, puff.

Across the street we found a small pavilion with bathrooms, an ice-water drinking fountain, and viola! Beneath the water basin was an electrical outlet. We plugged in for 40 minutes to garner enough charge to get us back to Spring Hill Marriott—via a few shops and restaurants. After the charge we found Von's Café. Before Richard could order a sandwich, I had the attendant filling a box with salads: couscous, corn with tomatoes, and spinach. Next, we learned the sandwiches were all sold out anyway. So Richard decided that our 4:20 lunch/dinner would be plenty for both of us. So we ate it all.

With just one-half an uphill block to go, the Rascal quit again. So I pushed Richard up to our hotel. Since the lobby smells like fresh paint, I decided to sit outside around the corner on a bench, and pen a few lines. I left Richard in the newly painted odiferous lobby. Weather is in the low 80's. A bit of breeze coming from the west. Sunshine.

I'm thinking there are too many people on the planet. I understand the population explosion began when humankind developed farming. That allowed for less "gathering and hunting", the need for more farmhands, and permanent shelter. Just a thought. The good news is the package-delivery service promises to be here tomorrow morning. New Rascal batteries are to be brought to our hotel.

Kristina and I passed a tee-shirt shop on our afternoon walk. One shirt in the window read:

"How to Impress a Woman"

1. Hold her hand
2. Hug her
3. Kiss her
4. Cherish her
5. Compliment her
6. Buy gifts for her
7. Tell her you love her
8. Smile at her
9. Wink at her
10. Tell her she's beautiful

"How to Impress a Man"

1. Show up naked
2. Bring beer

We got laughs from several people about the tee shirt. Last night, since Richard was stuck at the hotel, Curt brought him a Subway sandwich. I had dinner (spinach salad) with Ann, Kristina, Yolanda, Gene, Randy, and Terry. They all ordered crepe desserts with ice cream, and chocolate sauce. After dinner, Kristina and I walked around St. Paul Ave. and observed the restaurants, the music, and the fountains. By 9:00 o'clock I was done. We decided to call it a night.

Friday, May 22, 2009

We had "hotel-style" breakfast on the mezzanine floor. Powdered eggs, potato triangles, and English muffins. We ate with Vaughn and Joan and Curt. Then I left with Kristina and Ann to search for a real French breakfast. After leaving the first bakery, I explained to Kristina that the French have coffee and bread in the morning. At the next bakery Ann and I shared a chocolate croissant and an almond paste pasterie. I also had chai tea. Kristina bought an almond paste thingy. She claimed she is a chocolate addict but never eats it for breakfast. I put a piece of our chocolate croissant on her plate and told her not to eat it but she did and said it was delicious.

Our plans change and change and change. Since Richard needed to charge his newly-installed batteries for three hours, and Kristina needed to be back at the hotel by 3:00 for a tour, we agreed that we (K & I) would take the underground subway to the botanical gardens and Richard would join us by taxi at about 12:45. Good thing we brought our cell phones. I phoned him and learned that the shuttle folks changed their minds—he would have no shuttle service today.

The gardens were stunning! Jardin Botanique de Montreal, is a huge and gorgeous 190-acre plot of gardens and greenhouses. The Chinese Garden, The Japanese Garden, and the First Nations Garden were our favorites. Well, maybe it was the Alpine Garden we loved the most. The trees: maple, birch, and pine. The wildlife: Canada Geese, herons, squirrels, ducks, and turtles! Oh, but the flowering gardens were stunning. Flowers of every color imaginable were photographed for my upcoming picture album of this wonderful trip. Everywhere we looked, I kept saying, "Wow! Wow! Wow!" But . . . we needed to stay on schedule, so after a good spinach salad at the jardens we started back. Got on the underground about 2:00 and arrived at our stop "Place de Ames" at 2:30. Kristina was to meet Anne at 3:15. I came back to the room where my happy husband had eaten the second half of last night's sandwich.

Saturday, May 23, 2009

We're on board the Holland America—Maasdam Iberville Terminal in Montreal, Quebec. We'll be pulling away from shore at 5:00 p.m. All fourteen of us and one Rascal with power to spare. Yippee!!!

Sunday May 24, 2009

Richard wasn't feeling great yesterday and is still a bit punky. He hung out in the room when I went to meet with Kristina and Ann for a two-hour tour of Quebec. We visited the Frontenac Chateau, which was a beautiful long walk uphill. FC claims to be the most-photographed hotel in the world. The Canadian Pacific Railway opened it in 1893 as part of its chain of luxury hotels. The FC sits atop Cap Diamant, a cliff that cascades into the raging St. Lawrence River. Then Richard phoned! He's feeling better and riding up the funicular, which gives free rides to the handicapped. (Please don't tell him he's handicapped. I swear he doesn't know.)

Once we were in the hotel we took the elevator to the 8th floor and had a peek out the window. And there, in the bay, was our ship. The view was spectacular. Explorers that we are, we found another elevator that took us to the 17th floor! We peeked out the windows in the stairwell. Wowee! We took a few pictures. What a gift, on this beautiful day! We then descended to floor RC, the reception area. Everyone was so nice. We ran into Yolanda and Gene, Joan, and Ann. Carol was in a wheelchair, being pushed by her husband Don. We later learned that by tripping, two bones in her foot broke. Yikes! We also learned that my baby sister Jeannie was feeling sick. Curt took her back to the ship. Boo hoo.

Later today we visited the famous Notre Dame of Quebec. This Cathedral has been on this site since 1647, although its life was never easy. Built on the site of a chapel constructed by Samuel de Champlain in the year 1633, it was burned in 1759 during the Siege of Quebec. In 1922 it was torched a second time by the Canadian Ku Klux Klan. Again, it was rebuilt. In 1989 Notre Dame of Quebec was declared a National Historic site of Canada.

Our group met at 4:30 for cocktails and snacks, which included three kinds of meat. This vegetarian just smiled.

Monday May 25, 2009

Happy Memorial Day back in the U.S.A. Last night Richard played video poker in the Casino aboard ship. He won the $1875 jackpot and gave me $500. Well, that paid for his trip. I'll save my gift for something really special.

We didn't get up until 8:20 this morning. Sailing eastward, we were instructed to set our clocks ahead one hour. I had set my alarm for 7:00 but shut it off. This morning I walked around the promenade only once. It was very cold out there. Richard and I finished breakfast in the Lido (where I am now having lunch at 3:00) then I lingered over tea. Kristina appeared in the restaurant so I lingered some more—until 4:30. Then Ann and I walked the promenade four times. At this point I returned to our room for some quiet time. I'm currently reading John Jake's "The Gods of Newport" about rich people living in the late 1800's. The ocean is just drifting by—wakes and waves—cloudy skies. I feel a nap coming on.

Here we are: temperature-controlled environment, excess food, hot showers, entertainment, lectures, shopping, and piped-in music, cruising up the St. Lawrence River towards Novia Scotia and the Atlantic Ocean. Dessert for lunch today was maple-raisin-walnut bread with warm cream pudding. That was at 3:15. Dinner is in two hours. I better get out there and walk for at least 45 minutes. As I'm walking I hear a poem flying by. A poem dedicated to Yolanda.

There's no travel agent like Yolanda
She'll take you to Canada and beyonda
Doubt you'll have a great time with Yolanda
Whether traveling by cruise ship or Honda.

There's no gal whom Gene is more fond a
Than this young beauty named Yolanda.
Especially dressed up like Queen Rhonda.
Looking even better than Mary or Wanda.

She gathered our money by the ton—duh
Did you think you'd get all this for Nada?
To see the world you cannot squanda
Besides, then we'd be here without Yolanda.

You've probably heard of Swami Beyondananda
He's the guru of us all in the ponda
Fish-fowl-human, all who are fonda
Our precious, dear, inimitable Yolanda.

So, I wrote the Yolanda poem and then ran into Joan and Ann. Vaughn has been ill for two days and they're searching for crackers, hoping he'll recover soon. I told them of the poem and because this is a working vacation for Yolanda we'll have a gratitude ceremony for her on Friday evening.

After dinner this evening we visited Randy and Terri's suite. OMG! Such luxury! Then we saw Ann's pictures on the television and returned to our own little cabin for a good night's rest. Another great day at sea. Oh, Richard won another jackpot. There were two jackpots for the video poker players on the entire cruise and my guy won them both. This one was $1200 which means our cruise is free—unless he goes back to the Casino.

Tuesday May 26, 2009

Up at 6:00. Showered. Yummy breakfast with Richard. Omelet with veggies. Fruit. Tea. Our tour—The Ultimate Anne of Green Gables Scenic Tour began at 8:45. Four delightful hours of riding the bus and walking through the house and barn. The Haunted Woods, Lovers Lane, looking at the Shining Waters Lake—all of Anne of Green Gables Fame. A young girl dressed like Anne—complete with long red braids, met us at the gift shop, offering a raspberry cordial. I bought a doll and books for our granddaughter Rylee's birthday. In September she'll be 8, the perfect age for reading Anne of Green Gables. I bought books 1, 2, and 3, and I intend to read 2 and 3 as I was enchanted by the first book. The little farmhouse was charming and sweet. Our imaginations are such a gift. We all pretended this Anne is for real.

Then an interesting thing happened. I'd walked down the hillside's wooden steps to take a little walk in the Haunted Woods and upon preparing to ascend the steps fifteen minutes later, I asked myself this question. (Remember, I'm only 67 years young.) So I said to myself, "Has she still got it?" Feeling strong and self-assured, I attempted to run up the hillside's wooden steps but . . . I tripped, fell, and smashed my digital camera. Guess what I'll be doing with part of the money Richard won and gave to me? Read on.

Back on ship at 4:30. I need a nap. At 5:15 I woke up and realized we were out of port. I left our room on Deck 8 and checked out the Rotterdam Dining room. No sign of anyone from our group. I knocked on Kristina's door; she was readying for dinner. Richard was reading a book. Jeanne and Curt were ready. We finally all gathered and met on Deck 7 for 5:30 dinner. Tonight's treat: stir fried veggies and rice. As our waiters served us in style, I wondered if they had ever seen such an abundance of food. I wondered if they wished they could send some home. Were their families well-nourished? What were their thoughts about all these chubby Americans?

The economic downturn does not appear to be affecting the folks aboard ship. The shopping continues. I think the seasick pills are what are making me so lethargic. I feel so sleepy most of the time, especially at dinner when I chew up two little pink pills. So—to bed at 10:00.

Wednesday May 27, 2009

Sydney was founded in 1785 and served as the Capitol of Cape Breton until 1820. The British incorporated it as a city in 1904. In August of 1995, it was dissolved as a city and became part of the regional municipality. At one time it was the biggest steel producer in the world but after WWII weapons were no longer a priority. The population declined until someone decided this would be a great tourist attraction and they were right.

Today our group was scattered in all directions. We're in Sydney, Nova Scotia at Cape Breton Island. We looked at the crafts that are created on St. Breton Island. The winters are cold. There is lots of time for storytelling and creativity from jewelry-making, knitting, weaving, glass items--mostly jewelry, and making maple syrup.

After a delightful tour of historic Olde Sydney, we were directed to the only and the best camera shop on the Island. I bought a new camera. (Thank you Sweetheart. You're the best.) This one has a more powerful zoom, and quicker response. We charged the camera and took pictures of a Scottish Bagpiper and the Ceilidh Fiddle.

I'm sitting in a rattan-like plastic chair on the 2nd story of the cruise ship terminal. It's about 45 degrees outside and windy. The giant fiddle on the dock is named the Largest Ceilidh Fiddle in the world. Its purpose is to greet incoming cruise ships. It's 60 feet tall, designed and constructed by Cyril Hearn. The fiddle is made of solid steel and has been dubbed "Fidheal Mhor A' " meaning the "Big Fiddle of the Ceilidh" which is a Gaelic word for "visit".

The search for maple butter continues. Richard likes this stuff.

Thursday May 28, 2009

Early up. Breakfast with Kristina. We rushed to make the 8:20 tour to Peggy's Cove. Now. How did Peggy's Cove get its name? Some say there was a lady named Peggy and the cove was named after her. The real (they say) story is that Peggy was the only survivor of a wrecked ship. The town's most handsome bachelor found her on the beach and they eventually married. The cove was named after her. (They say.) After taking many pictures, reminding Curt to "hold the comments" Jeanne and Ann and I returned to Pier 21. Richard and I had lunch with Curt. We took a one-hour walk along the boardwalk checking out the island. Richard and I toured Pier 21 for souvenirs, and then enjoyed the upstairs museum about the immigrants. Of the one million young men who served in WWII, in 1945, 10% married women in Europe. These "war brides", 48,000 of them, came to Canada, bringing with them, 22,000 children. That's 70,000 new citizens.

My mom's name was Nova. She was born on November 4, 1913. She died April 23, 2003. She never made it to Nova Scotia. But some of her ashes did. I wandered up a hilly path to a small museum where an artist had her studio and her apartment. I explained to her about my mom and asked her if it was legal to bury someone's ashes. She pointed to a flowery pink bush outside her studio/apartment/ museum and said, "Why don't you bury them under that little bush." So I did.

Again, we enjoyed dinner in the Rotterdam Diner. Not much luck for us vegetarians. How I long for a big green salad, some veggies, and rice. Again, this evening, we adjusted our clocks one hour, this time getting back the hour we lost on Monday. Yay. More sleep. This evening at dinner we gifted Yolanda with two tablecloths. I read the poem I'd written for her. We all thanked her. It was "formal night". We'd been out all day—sweaty and unkempt—but did our best. Kinda. Thank God for shawls.

Friday, May 29, 2009

Bar Harbor, Maine. We're sitting at the window in the lounge area watching the tenders transport cruise guests from ship to shore. The King (sometimes called Richard) and I are waiting for Jeannie and Curt for our trip ashore. We'll walk and shop and snap photos. At 12:30 Richard and I will hop on a bus for "The Best of Both Worlds"—to return at 4:30. We're hoping the ship will wait for us. Tomorrow we land in Boston and will spend three days there—seeing the sights. We'll be home late Tuesday, in four days.

The Best of Both Worlds was so foggy we had to pretend we could see the mansions, mountains, and the ocean. Bar Harbor is beautiful. I know because I bought several postcards. It was drizzly and rainy the whole day. 'Twas tricky getting from ship to shore, getting Richard down the ladder—and the Rascal aboard.

Dinner tonight was our last dinner aboard ship. The cooks, the waiters, all kitchen help and servers put on a show, beginning with the "napkin ballet". They were all smiles. It was time for us to show our appreciation. After dinner, most of us went back to our rooms to pack. Richard went to say goodbye to his gambling buddies.

Saturday, May 30, 2009

Up at 6:15. Ready for the day. By 6:45 we were docked in Boston Harbor. We had breakfast outside on the Lido Deck. At 8:30 we were ready to disembark. My brain remarked:

Hark! A lark! Marc! Marc! (Our nephew) Shark! Shark! Shark! Let's Disembark!

We phoned the Ultimate Livery Shuttle Service. Pam—middle aged and very out-of-shape came to pick us up. No way could she lift the Rascal or a heavy suitcase. Curt did all the packing. Thank heaven for Curt. So—we're off to Zero Nine Hotel in downtown Boston—across from the Boston Commons. Our sweet friend Kristina, sister Jeannie, her husband Curt, Richard and I will spend a few days exploring Boston.

We hauled our bags into the hotel and turned everything over to Sam the bellhop. Our rooms were not ready so we followed the red line on the sidewalks and streets. It was 73 degrees with no rain in sight. Perfection. We saw the sights: Paul Revere's home where he fathered 16 children. We visited the famous North Church ("One if by land, two if by sea.") Had lunch at a replica of Cheers Pub outside Quincy Market. Oh, yum. Shandies with Fish and Chips. Then we walked and walked. Got back to the hotel at 5:30. Everyone seemed to need a nap. In the evening we dined at Kinsale—another noisy pub. Got to bed at 10:00.

Sunday May 31, 2009

Leap Frog Activities? Five's a crowd? Follow me. No, follow me. No. Follow me. Where's the bathroom? Boston Commons? Oceanarian Aquarium? Make Way for Ducklings? It was a riot walking around the city with five delightful beings, who all wanted to do something different. We laughed a lot.

We had a wonderful breakfast in our hotel dining room: fresh fruit, juice, tea, pastry, toast, and English muffins. We all talked a lot about what to do. Yikes! It's tricky to get five people organized and agreeable. This afternoon I could not stop laughing. Kristina needed the bathroom a lot and there didn't seem to be many toilets in this city. I jokingly said the next time a friend wants to travel with me, I'm asking for a sonogram of her bladder. We always have to consider how Richard can get the Rascal into a building, onto a boat, upstairs in museums, or into restaurants, pubs, shops, delis, stores, and old churches.

Here's an example of our organization: Richard led us from Boston Bay back to our hotel, Nine Zero. The rest of us questioned his guidance until we realized he needed curb cuts. We were almost back to our hotel—a side trip to Barnes and Noble, when we did stop at that famous bookstore, originally to listen to a woman singing Willie Nelson tunes. K, J, and I sat on a wall to listen. J. soon joined C., who was looking at the outside book display.

Naturally, they had to enter B&N to pay for their chosen books. So, K. decides to go inside to use (you guessed it) the restroom. Onward we marched towards the Boston Commons where yet another stop—at—you guessed it. The hotel! We needed to drop off books at the hotel. Richard waited on the sidewalk. As long as we were at the hotel, I zoomed upstairs to use our restroom. I zipped back to the lobby and sat in a chair next to Kristina for a few seconds. I mentioned that I wished I'd changed shoes—into sandals. Kristina reminded me that Jeannie would be a few minutes, as she needed to wash the bird poo off the top of her shoes. We laughed—got back on the elevator towards room 407. We changed shoes. Kristina used the—again.

We changed shoes. Jeanne and Curt met us on the elevator going down. At last! We proceeded to the park. We laughed a lot at the rate of our progress and our different opinions. We took lots of pictures—Jeanne and Curt and Kristina rode the swan boat on Swan Pond. Richard watched. I circled the pond, taking more pictures. I met a nice woman in the park, pushing a stroller. She told me she lives in Detroit and is spending a week in Boston taking care of little Leslie while dad is away working and mommy finishes up her 4th year of residency/internship. This nice lady led me to the famous "Make Way for Ducklings" and told me the story.

It seems Mr. and Mrs. Mallard had eight ducklings named Jack, Kack, Lack, Mack, Nack, Ouack, Pack, and Quack. When they wanted to cross the busy road near the park, a kind policeman named Michael asked that several police cars come stop the traffic for the family. The book "Make Way for Ducklings" was written by Robert McCloskey and published in 1941. Over two million copies of the book have been published. I took lots of pictures of the mommy and her babies made of brass. Then I rushed to catch up with my own group.

We strolled through the public gardens. More photographing. After that, Kristina wanted to visit Beacon Street Neighborhood. Richard and I went our own way. Jeanne and Curt went to the hotel to rest. We (The King and I) visited the frog park pond, bought yummy peaches, Greek yogurt, and trail mix at Lambert's groceries. We had dinner in our room and watched the movie "New in Town." We also packed for tomorrow's return trip to sunny Southern California.

Tuesday June 2, 2009

Up early. Packed. Breakfast. Curt wanted to work out. Richard wanted to be on his own. Jeanne, Kristina, and I visited a beautiful old home in the Beacon neighborhood. The home was exquisite but the tour guide kept us in four rooms—15 loooooong minutes per room, before we escaped.

More pictures of Workers of the World—an upcoming book. Some day.

Ultimate Livery Shuttle Service driver Leo arrived at our hotel at 1:00. The hotel clerk had gone after our stored luggage. Akeem, our valet, helped with luggage and loading the van. Curt and Leo lifted the Rascal up and into the van. By 1:30 we were at the Logan Airport. It took until 2:30 to get tickets, check in the Rascal, take three pounds of luggage out of Richard's 52-pound suitcase, take the elevator downstairs, walk back to under the tarmac, take another elevator up to the second floor. We bought snacks and boarded Delta flight 1749 to Salt Lake City, Utah. We'll be home in five hours. Yay!

I can't wait to sleep outside and see our tomato patch and take a bath. The first attempt at landing in Utah was a new experience. We didn't. We were approaching the landing strip—after seeing two flashes of lightening when the pilot decided landing was too risky: the wind had suddenly shifted 180 degrees. So up we went, causing some anxiety in some passengers. We smiled, held hands, and I said, "If this is it, I'm glad we met."

We did a 180 and settled into a perfect landing. We all applauded the pilot. Our connecting flight was late coming in from Colorado. We waited patiently at Gate D-9. Then the Delta clerk sent us on a wild goose chase. "Hurry! Get to Gate C-10. If you run, you can just make it." We rushed all the way from Gate D-9 to C-10—a good ¼ mile or more. Yes, more. When we got to C-10, we were told, "Sorry. It just pulled back. Hurry back to D-9." Ha ha.

Later: Home at last, safe and sound, and a bit tired. But, VERY happy.

September 2009 - FYRT

"The winds of God's grace are always blowing.

It is for us to raise our sails."

From the Bhagavad-Gita

As you may know, my dear sister Jeannie, and I are about to begin our FYRT. That's for Frozen Yogurt Road Trip. Our plan is to leave California bright and early on Saturday, September 19th and return about October 3rd or 4th.

We'll be hitting all the high spots between California and Old Faithful Lodge in Yellowstone National Park, via Sedona, Santa Fe, Hugoton, Kansas (now there's a town you won't find on most maps), Kearney and Omaha, Nebraska. The trip is three-fold: first and foremost we will be joining up with our three girl cousins: Julie, Barbie, and Sharla. They have convinced us that everyone MUST experience Nebraska's Junque Jaunt at least once in a lifetime. Also, cousins are really fun and we want to spend time with them.

In case you have not heard of a Junque Jaunt, now you know. It's a coordinated link-up of 250 miles of garage/yard sales and flea markets. Now don't ask me why anyone would need to spend two whole days searching for treasures among other people's junque, but apparently this is done in Nebraska every year. I guess if you don't have the beach, and the ocean is too far away, you simply must find a way to entertain yourself. Needing nobody else's junque, I volunteered to tag along and take pictures.

Secondly, Jeannie and I will be testing frozen yogurt across our great nation. We've been told that frozen yogurt is mostly a California thing but I've searched the web and found a few places that have a container or two amongst the cartons of ice cream. So, we have volunteered to be testers, checking for taste, texture, caloric content, melt factor, appearance, and all important qualities of each product. Also, we'll be interviewing employees and makers of frozen yogurt in order to get a more educated slant on our project. This isn't exactly like bar hopping but one of us does have a propensity for consuming a certain amount of coconut frozen yogurt with almonds every afternoon. Never mind which one. Lots of blue-eyed blonds are that way.

Thirdly, we think it will be fun to chuck the grocery shopping and cooking for a couple of weeks. Our dear husbands, Richard and Curt, promise they can survive without us. It is not without some apprehension that I proceed with this journey, as Richard will have a few challenges managing without me, I think, I hope. (If you want to check up on him, please do.)

So, why am I telling you all this? Several friends have asked us to blog our FYRT and after much googling and checking out blogging, we've come to the conclusion that we just want to keep in touch with a few family members and friends as we travel throughout this great land. You are on the list. If you'd just rather not know what we're doing, please send a polite note of declination and we'll happily omit your email address from the list. So, that's about it. See you in October.

Love and Blessings, Sue

FYRT Log #1

In the beginning . . .

Two sisters started life together in a little town called Willowbrook, in sunny Southern California. Sue was three years, seven months, and seven days old when her baby sister Jeannie arrived on the planet. Later the family of six (we had two big brothers) moved to a little farm in Dominguez Hills.

Life would take them to so many places; most of them wonderful. After they retired from many years of teaching, they decided it would be a good idea to do some traveling,

Saturday September 19, 2009

We drove from California to a beautiful B&B in Sedona, Arizona and spent two nights on the creek. What did we learn there? To say YES to life!!!

Yes to 4-course gourmet breakfast in our lush B&B. Yes to climbing the red rocks, taking oodles of pictures. Yes to tart and tangy frozen yogurt with hot fudge topping. Yes to sitting creekside after cooling dusty feet in the water, listening to herds of cicadas tuning up for their song of gratitude. Most of all, we learned to listen to our inner voices and to pay attention to what they say "yes" to and to always say yes to peace, love, and joy. Listen. Listen.

Tomorrow's plan: hike the West Fork Trail in Sedona early in the morning,

Sunday, September 20, 2009

Today's four-mile hike on the West Fork Trail took four hours. We forded Oak Creek dozens of times, philosophizing about life without 90 degree heat, tired feet and sweaty dusty boots; and being grateful for a strong battery in the silver Toyota when someone left the lights on. It's true: Spirit is everywhere and in all of us.

Monday September 21, 2009

Today we're on our way to Santa Fe, New Mexico. We saw beautiful scenery: mesas, mesitas, red rocks, and tiny towns for 422 miles. Lucky for us, we arrived before the streetlights went on, had Chinese take-out for dinner but no frozen yogurt in sight.

Tuesday, September 22, 2009

After a lovely breakfast at the Lamplighter Inn, we were off to the Governors Palace, St. Francis Cathedral and a whole lot of walking. Predicted high for the day: 55 and 22 low. Ho ho ha ha ha. Thanks to the girls at the First Community Bank for letting the California girls use the restroom, drink their coffee, and directing us to Rick at Marcy's Card Shop where Rick offered a free map of Santa Fe and pointed out the best places to visit.

Thanks to Kathy at the Bank who called Jeannie's bank in California to inquire about the ATM card. Wow! A power outage in San Diego. Whodathunkit? Thanks to Allison for the two-hour walking tour of Santa Fe. Thanks to Clay, our waiter at The Shed, for introducing the lightweight Californians to The Shed's special margaritas. (They taste nothing like the ones in California.) Besides confessing his weakness for older women . . . oops! Besides confessing his growing lack of interest in college, Clay spent an inordinate amount of time educating them (the older women) to correctly pronounce guacamole. Disclaimer: Because of the lack of frozen yogurt in Santa Fe, the duo was forced to endure frozen margaritas; Salud!

Cousin Barbie phoned to be sure the California Cousins Sue and Jeannie were on schedule, which of course, we were. What the heck is triple sec anyhow? Wheeeeeeeeeee. And what road trip would be complete without a stop at Denny's for hash browns and Wal-Mart for non-California clothing: socks, jackets, vests, slippers, tee shirts, and fleece jammies for the unexpectedly non-Californian weather?

Wednesday, September 23, 2009

Then there was the unexpected fifty-mile northwest detour instead of the northeast route. Ho ho ha ha ha!! Rod Stewart, Elton John, Daniel Nammod got them through a long day from Santa Fe, New Mexico to Hugoton, Kansas for a night's stay with young cousin Kate and her husband Trevor in the home-mansion they built (with a little help from their friends). Katie made the most awesome veggie salad, interesting homemade strawberry yogurt for dinner and blueberry muffins for breakfast. The mansion has 5 bedrooms, 4 bathrooms, a kitchen, family room, living room, Trevor's saloon, Trevor's gunroom, Katie's photography studio, a laundry room, and a storage room. Not bad for a couple of young newlyweds. Thank you for entertaining us and putting us up for the night. We so enjoyed getting to know more about you.

Thursday, September 24, 2009

Today was ancestors' day at Gaeland Cemetery in Orion, Kansas where Grandma Mary Cox and Grandpa William Cox are buried near his parents George Matthew Cox and Susan Mary Fanny Cox, Great Uncle Thomas and Great Aunts Annie van Martar, Mathilda and Lydia. An enlightening experience to visit them at last.

Orion, Kansas is a one-house town. The lady of the one house, Charlotte Rebarchek and her daughter-in-law Jenny came to meet us at the cemetery and took pictures of us at the gate of the cemetery. Please pray for Jenny as she is contending with a brain tumor. Thank you.

As we left Gaeland Cemetery, I spotted a name on a tombstone and my loquacious sister and I had the following conversation: You have to have a sister to understand this:

I miss Effie Mae. (name on tombstone)
Do you miss Effie Mae?
    Yes I do miss Effie Mae. Boo hoo
Do you miss Bubba?
    No I do not. Bubba was a thief and a pig. But I do miss Porky.

The salvage yard in Grainville, Kansas is run by Terry Cox, originally owned by his dad, Frank Cox. After a conversation with Terry, it was determined that the Cox family came from Missouri and that all Cox families originated in England. All are probably distant cousins.

The Kansas countryside is breathtaking, awe-inspiring, also giddiness provoking. Thousands of acres of cornfields, bio-grain fields, fluffy clouds, rainstorms and the most beautiful rainbow ever witnessed by womankind. Rather like one gigantuous IMAX Theater. Lots of violet.

Onward to cousin Julie's home in Kearney, Nebraska for more time with cousins Katie, Barbie, and Barbie's friend Bev. Tomorrow, all will rise early for Nebraska's Junque Jaunt. We hear Julie is whipping up a batch of margaritas for us. Cousin Barbie is whipping up a batch of banana-coconut frozen yogurt. Our Cousins are so COOL!

Friday, September 25, 2009

Cousin Barbie's fun breakfast of homemade coconut-banana frozen yogurt set the mood for a fun day for six junking and jaunting women in four SUV's. Leaving Kearney at 7:30 a.m. we headed for such sights as Cairo, Ravenna, Hazard, Mason City, Berwyn, and Broken Bow. By noon we'd bargained for a wild assortment of Early American furnishings, books, pictures, valuable knick-knacks, CD's, windows, magazine racks, and other treasures including several eagles for Curt's new home office. Lunch today was in Broken Bow at The Arrow Restaurant; dinner was at Huckleberry's BBQ Pit.

Again, the scenery was spectacular from a brilliant sunrise to a miraculous sunset. Imagine the pine-tree studded Nebraska Sandhills awaiting the biannual migration of the Sandhill Cranes. More raindrops, clouds dancing, showing off the livelong day. Creeks, rivers, ponds, miles of cornfields, pine trees, late-blooming wildflowers, grassy hillsides, an occasional deer sighting, everything a road trip should be.

Grandma Sue, Great Aunt Jeannie, Cousins Julie, Barbie, Sharla, and Katie sang Happy 18th Birthday to Courtney in Oceanside by cell phone around noon Nebraska time. What a delight for all. Dear Courtney came into the world the very day Dr. Seuss left the planet on September 25, 1991. To think she's now a soccer-playing college student. Oh, my!

Tonight we will sleep at the Winfield Inn and Suites in Arnold, using two of their ten rooms.

Saturday, September 26, 2009

The Inn offered a nice little breakfast on Saturday: various pie-ala modes for lunch at Uncle Burt's Country Hotel, dinner in the local Dive. So far, the FYRT has taken us 2000 miles, including several U-turns. Tonight we'll be resting at the Rodeo Hotel.

And what do Nebraskans do on Saturday evenings? Watch the Cornhuskers in the local Dive, drinking beer and shandies. Go Big Red!! In the Dive, people yell, applaud, and cheer as Kent Pelvelka tries to explain this exciting game. By halftime, Nebraska was so far ahead, the cousins decided to go back to their rooms at the Rodeo Hotel with Sharla as the designated driver.

What's happening with the official frozen yogurt test? As time and experience has revealed, California is the uncontested leader in this field. If you're searching for the best yogurt, it seems to be either Cherry on the Top on Glassell Street in Orange, across the street from Renee's Jewelers or The Yogurt Place in Escondido across the street from American Auto Clinic where Jeannie's son, Marc works. However, the traveling sisters vow to continue the search for one more week before making the final decision, although Barb's yogurt has been the best on the road.

For the next two days, it's Aunt Ruth and Uncle Floyd time in Omaha. And so they travel on . . .

Sunday, September 27, 2009

Is there anything as frustrating as being unable to connect to your Internet? It's rather like being unable to breathe, sort of. The traveling sisters have been unable to go online for two days!!! #$%$^&**%$@# (Obviously when you get this, they will have reconnected.) Not to worry, Jamie from "Omaha Nerds" is on the way.

Yahoo! Computer's back up, thanks to Mr. Jamie from Geek in Omaha. He and his family are packing up and heading out to Yellowstone early in the morning. So, we caught him just in time.

Here's a question: Are these things funny?
Roadside sign: Pork Work Ahead.
California here we go, all the way to Omaho
Ya got yer shoes, ya got yer feet, so then ya got yer shoes and yer feet.
And then ya got everything ya need.
We seed lotsa men an we did not flurt no sir.

Monday, September 28, 2009

Disclaimer: Intellectual Stimulation is a MUST when driving 918 miles in one day. We left Aunt Ruth and Uncle Floyd's in Omaha at 3:55 a.m. and arrived in Jackson Hole, Wyoming at 5:30 p.m. (having gained an hour of Mountain Time) so that's 14-1/2 hours.

To keep ourselves entertained, we composed several poems. The following flowed flourishingly and fastidiously forth . . .

Both burly bowlegged Buford boys from Burwell brazenly blasted baby beebee buckshot back on the bumpy brown bumpers of the blue Blazers bolting about the byway. Barb's blissful burgers bought in Broken Bow beat buggy blueberry bagels with blackberry butter.

Silly singing sisters in their sexy sixties seldom sit still, seriously sir. Since Saturday, seemingly sighting several succulent silver snakes slinking somewhat shakily southward, Sue's Sis suddenly spotted seven silken slimy strawberry slurpees. Sipping special sundaes and sticking special stamps and stickers on SUV's, surprisingly, showers of sacks simply slipped, somewhat slowly, on Sinclair.

The wild women of Western Wyoming, while whittling whistles, wanted water whenever wondrous wiley Willy waddled away. Whacky wildebeests watched wicked witches wear winsome, worn, and weary waders while wolfing warm watermelon wine.

Now: If your mind is not stimulated, you may wish to take your own FYRT. The poetry continued to wax with great license:

Orion's bright stars gently smile down.
No sun had yet risen in the east.
The silver Toyota left town the road
Trippers' laughter hadn't ceased.

With grumpy Bubba Lula and sweet Effie May
Keeping company, the livelong day,

Imaginary friends are really so cool.
They make no demands, are never cruel.

All towardsing at Yellowstone Park
Barry Manilow crooning his songs
Singing in the name of love in the dark
With nary a howl, chirp, or bark.

By eight, the sun finally rose.
At Arby's for coffee and tea they stopped.
Yawned a bit and stretching their toes.
Then Westward the singing duo hopped.

Farmsteads and barns are everywhere
Horses and cows without a care.
Many miles with fences of barbed wires.
Keeping all safe from big fast tires.

Wheat fields, corn, and milieu grow.
Alfalfa grasslands mightily flow.
Cell phone towers sometimes appear.
For talking with Uncle and Aunt so dear.

"Unka Poyd" at 95 is quite the groom.
Ruth is 91 yet has that youthful bloom.
October the 7th marks their 70th year.
Years of fun and years of cheer.

'Twas sad to leave them once again.
Causing in the heart a mighty pain.
Yet the road trippers continued their quest.
Seeking adventure at it's very best.
From California to Omoho.
On to Jackson the twosome go.
Tomorrow it's on to Yellowstone.
A few more days and they'll be home.

Highlights (in no particular order) of the FYRT 9/19/09 - 10/3/09

1. Biggest and best highlight: Hugging Aunt Ruth and Uncle Floyd hello.
2. Time with cousins: Julie and Ken, Roger and Sharla, Barb and Jim. Katie and Trevor, Jamie and Scott, Brock and future wife Virginia, Tommy, Tyler, Ross, Addie, Isaac, and Tripp McGuire.

3. Snow in Yellowstone National Park (America's 1st NP)
4. Jim's cookies and veggie wraps in Sedona at the Oak Creek Inn B&B
5. Hiking West Fork Trail in Sedona
6. Guided walking tour in Santa Fe, New Mexico
7. Conversations with people from all over the planet.
8. Tracking down treasures at the Junque Jaunt.
9. Driving 918 miles in one day.
10. Laughter Yoga with the Omaha elders
11. Singing with the Everly Brothers in the silver Toyota.
12. Ancestral cemetery in Orion, Kansas.
13. Photographing elk and eagles in Yellowstone.
14. Lounging, dozing, reading, writing, laughing in Old Faithful Inn
15. Sweet frozen yogurt in Jackson Hole—for Jeannie.
16. Tart frozen yogurt in Sedona—for Sue
17. Laughing and laughing and laughing at just about everything.
18. Green salad, seeing Katie and Trevor's beautiful new Hugoton home.
19. Triple Sec (whatever that is) at The Shed in Santa Fe, NM.
20. Julie's margaritas and Barbie's banana coconut frozen yogurt.
21. Watching Nebraska skunk LSU on TV in Burwell's local Dive bar.
22. A bajillion thanks to Cuz'n Barb for planning and executing the JJ.
23. Much gratitude that . . . there were no lowlights.

Friday, October 2, 2009

Note to husbands from our hotel in Salt Lake City, Utah. Dear Richard and Curt: Get ready. Your ever lovin' wives are comin' back to y'all.
An they did not flurt no sir.

ETA in Orange 7:00 p.m. tomorrow
ETA in Escondido 9:00 p.m. tomorrow
Final Episode of the FYRT:

A song by Jeannie Reed and Sue Snyder:

California here we come.
All the way from Yellowstum.
Where showers of snowflakes start in the fall.
Each morning of dawning Sisters laugh and sing it all.

Hungry men say, "Hurry home."
That's why they can hardy wait.
Open up that garden gate.

California here we come.

Saturday, October 3, 2009

All in all, the road trippers traveled 4,444 miles in Jeannie's silver Toyota. Leaving Provo, Utah this morning at 6:00 MDT (5:00 a.m. PDT time), we arrived at the Snyder residence in Orange about 4:00. Jeannie arrived in Escondido a bit after 5:00. Richard was relieved, happy, overwhelmed, excited, joyous, and grateful to have his best friend back home. Curt will be just as thrilled to see Jeanne again when he returns next week from taking his 89 year old father to his WWII Air Force reunion in the mid-west.

Thanks to all of you for encouraging us, for responding to our log-blogs, and to those of you who helped The King get through this 15-day period. Bless your hearts. Tons of love. You are the best. Special thanks to Beth and Sallie and Joann and Fred. You are very much appreciated.

They laugh about anything.
Sweet Jeannie and Tart Sue

Italy 2010

"Though we travel the world to find the beautiful, we must carry it with us or we find it not."

Henry David Thoreau

Buon giorno Friends and Family

On Wednesday, September 1st, I will fly off to Italy to meet several friends in the airport near Venice, oh my! I'll spend six days riding gondolas and singing O Solo Mio and then take the train to Milan where I'll view Leonardo De Vinci's Last Supper and take a three-hour tour of Milan. Then it's on to Varenna, a tiny fishing village on Lake Como. After five days there, we will ride the train down to Florence where Richard will be waiting in the airport on Sunday, September 12th.

Then we're off to Tuscany for eight romantic days and nine romantic nights in a farm villa with six friends. We'll visit Florence (Michael Angelo's David at the Accadamia), Pisa, Sienna, Cinque Terra, and a few other places. All of this in a rented van. Whether the gelato is better in Florence or Olde Towne Orange will be determined by this expert gelato-tasting team.

The last six days Richard and I will roam all over Rome visiting the Campidoglio, Castel Sant' Angelo, Colosseo, Palazzo Barberini, the Pantheon, Piazza Navona, the Roman Forum (Foro Romano), San Clements, the Sistine Chapel and the Vatican, the Pope, and of course, St. Peter. The Hotel Mecenate Palace has roof-top dining and a view of St. Maria Maggiore. (Somebody's gotta do it.)

We've been practicing our Italian:

"Dove la stazione?" (Where is the train station.)
"Dove un buon economico ristorante?" (Where is a good cheap restaurant?)
"Mi chiamo . . . " (My name is, I call myself . . .)
"Mi sono persa." (I'm lost . . . female)
"Mi sono perso." (I'm lost . . . male)
"Ho . . . (I have)
"l'alito cattiva" (bad breath)
"la ridarella" (the giggles)

If you wish to NOT receive our bloggy emails, please let us know, we'll take you off this list. If you DO want to be on our bloggy email list we'll leave you on.

We don't promise to send many as we'll not be carrying our laptop, just stopping in different places and seeing how it all works. If you don't hear from us until we get back, don't worry, we're just busy. We'll fly home on Monday, September 27th.

"The only prerequisite for enrollment
in Earth School is an open mind that knows
there is more to know and a willingness
to step into the unknown, over and over again. It is only through the portal of one's own curiosity, inquisitiveness, courage, commitment, and faith that one can continue to advance."

Dennis Merritt Jones

September 1. 2010

Miracles of the day

1. The plane flew.
2. The plane landed despite flat tire.

Who'd a thunk its:

1. Piano bar in Airport at Atlanta, Georgia
2. Soldiers off to Afghanistan (with Grandma Sue's hugs)
3. The pleasure of traveling is the discovery of new . . . (add your own word)

We landed. The plane came to a quick stop just as the runway became a stopway. After listening to our pilot explain our problem in Dutch and Italian, finally, in English we learned that "We have a flat tire. The tow truck is on the way." Of course, no tow truck can pull a plane with 120 passengers on it, plus all that luggage.

We waited 30 minutes for the buses. Once off the plane we noticed the much-photographed flat tire, resembling a porcupine with steel quills pointing at its twin. We climbed onto buses, happy to be alive, remembering Captain Sully's miracle on the Hudson. Patient tourists await luggage at baggage claim. After 20 minutes came the announcement in Dutch, in Italian, in English. Luggage would be delayed 30 minutes, which in Italy can be--and was--45 minutes. I speed-walk around and around.

An hour's cruise on the Al Laguna to San Marcos. I drag luggage up and down lots of concrete stairs, called bridges in Venice. Misconnections with Ann. Cell phones not reliable, it seems. Found Hotel Antico Panada, after asking six or seven shopkeepers. Ho ho ha ha ha!

Best of all was the sunset. Fuzzy pink clouds. Got to hotel with no sign of Margaret and her significant other, Gary, or Ann or the other Sue--Sue Page. Ironically, after writing Ann a note, leaving it on her bed, descending the stairs (rejecting elevator) I find Ann coming up the stairs. Tired. Done. A few more steps and I find the other Sue, Gary and Margaret, also ascending. I'd never met them before, but heard English. They let me know to meet downstairs for breakfast at 8:00. I continue down to the street.

Around the corner to Antichi Splendori for fettuccine salmon, white wine and dessert: fragola cassata. Pistachio, lemon vanilla tutti fruiti gelato. Wow!! Ann joined me for soup then went up to bed. I decided to celebrate with a walk and to begin the search for the "right" purple earrings. I find my way back with earrings still just a vision. And so to bed.

"Live life with no excuses, travel
with no regret"

Oscar Wilde

Friday September 3, 2010

After our 8:00 a.m. breakfast, we begin the day with a gondola ride through the canals of Venice, Mario singing O Solo Mio. Awesome.

The Island of Muran, a 45 minute boat ride away. The Island of Venetian Glass and glass factories and the glass museum with gardini. First century glass found in 1962.

Italian: fiolario - a glass maker, a glass blower
Bottles = fiole

Glassmakers create jewelry, chandeliers, bowls, plates, 300-Euro wine glasses. I pass.

Visit to Santa Maria Baptista, accepting forgiveness for past and future offenses.

Dinner at Ristorante & Bar Hotel Bartholomew. Five orders, mostly shared: fish with bones (eeuuee) olives stuffed with (eeuuee) liver, cuttle fish ink-blackened spaghetti, clams, salad, tiny plate of grilled veggies. No excuses. No regrets. There is always tomorrow.

"Do not follow where the path may lead.
Go instead where there is no path and leave a trail."

Ralph Waldo Emerson

Saturday, September 4, 2010

A quiet moment alone. Giadardi Parc a 20-minute walk from the hustle and bustle of Venice, on to Santa Elena neighborhood, mostly accessible, some bridges not. Little tiny cafes, a toyshop, magazines and newspapers. Boats boats boats, a carless island. Quaint. Quiet. Meditative. Blue Bar 7:00 a.m. offers 90 minute yogamia classes. Fishermen everywhere.

More pictures: workers of the world. Good day for a picnic. Time alone. No one to consider: me, thinking. My energy, walking fast, photo ops. My bench at the edge, in the sun, joggers tight and tanned. Old fishermen, former joggers, flesh sagging.

Caffe India: "Gelato, media per favore." Si, tiramisu ed creama-cocolite chip. Water. 2.50 Euros. Feet propped amid the trees. Pathway to more boats. Phone message to Ann: "never coming back." Smokers everywhere. No one complains but Americanos.

The Doge's Palace. Along with weaponry: swords, pistols, arrows, axes, instruments of torture, comes the invention of chastity belts. When a royal soldier prepares to ride off to war, he encases his wife's torso in this contraption which, if one uses the imagination, one might be led to the obvious conclusion of the discovery of the glassmakers' term . . .

Curiosities of the Doge's Palace:

1. The prison: prisoners: poverty, a crime.
2. Intricate portraits of heaven
3. Outnumbered by scenes of war
4. Instruments of torture
5. Ego outweighing all:

The ego: "I'm right, you're wrong I deserve it all; you do not count. Care for my every need. I use you as I wish. Feed me, entertain me, pet me, build me up. It's all about me. "Serve me, keep your head."

The Doge cafeteria for Insalatonce #3: insalata misa, tonno, pomodoro, mais, ed olive nere and a couger's peek at a somewhat arrogant and very cute waiter, resenting having to serve. Oh! That ego. The married couples peruse newly acquired historical literature, young lovers gaze into their blue and brown, hold hands. Never mind the past or the future. The young gay men leave, impatient. The only sound: groups of women laughing, cherishing their freedom, young families having not given theirs up yet. The honeymooners not hungry for lunch. A very friendly couple sits near. She checks her watch, looks up at him. "My husband will be home soon." I don't actually understand her rapid Italian but understand tone of voice and recognize guilt.

Arrivederci, Sue

"A journey is best measured in friends,
rather than miles"

Tim Cahill

Italy Blog #2 - Sunday September 10, 2010

I must give up Rick Steve's advice. "Get lost," he says. "Toss good sense to the winds." "Explore." "Discover new places. " "Meet other (lost) people."

OK. The last advice was great. I did, in fact, do all of the above. And lots of lost people came up to me. "Speak English?" "A little," I would say. Of the 200,000 tourists visiting exploring shopping eating praying loving on this island called Venice, I counted 100,000 who were as lost as I.

After three hours of happening upon tiny courtyards decorated with pink geraniums and miniature soccer players and cheerful churchgoers, I came to San Francisco's Catholic church. Calm and meditative, I sat and listened to my guardian angels' directions. Within ten minutes of leaving the CC I was back at San Marcos Piazza and Hotel Antico. Rev. Jim tells us "All is well. Trust." So I did.

At nine a.m. in Texas and Nebraska, and seven a.m. in California, it's 4:00 p.m. in Italy. Richard checks on me around 7:00 and gets the daily highlights. Never mind the lowlights. I miss my best friend, my mate, and my intellectually curious love. (By the way, Honey, please bring a jar of Trader Joe's Almond Butter with Flax seeds when you come next week. Thanks.)

Peggy Guggenheim's remodeled palace-museo was this morning's treat. (Roberta: it was really strange. I guess I'm a hopeless Monet fan.) Venice's wonderland of a hundred islands is laced together by 400 bridges and 2,000 alleys, so you can see how one could lose her way here. One pocketful of trail mix and another pocket holding a bottle of water kept me going until I found a tiny neighborhood market, in a tiny neighborhood, selling bananas and nectarines and plums. I survived and bought a new green and purple shawl, somewhere.

"Wandering re-establishes the original
harmony which once existed between man and the universe."

Anatole Fance

Monday September 6, 2010

Best Minestrone soup in a little restaurant across the alley from our hotel last night. Then, alone again, I was off to the Vivaldi concierto at Chiesa San Vidal about a mile and ten bridges away. Eight handsome young men, dressed in black pants and shirts, called themselves Interpieti Veneziani and play with passion. They smile, they yearn, and sparks fly between them. Two women from Oregon sat beside me. They had been in England for several months, living life in a tiny village and now shared the evening with me. This world is full of friendly people.

This morning I was out the door at 6:45 a.m. (that's 10:45 p.m. last night in California) for a test run on the Rialto vaporetto (water bus) up to the traghetto (train station). Bought a ticket for the 6:20 a.m. train to get me to Milano (by myself) by 8:55 a.m. for the 9:30 a.m. Autostrade 3-hour bus tour of Milan's Duomo, Galleria Vittorio Emanuele, Sforza Castle, La Scala Opera House and a peek at Leonardo de Vinci's Last Supper. After that, I bus/train/walk to Verenna on Lake Como for five nights in a home-apartment, meeting my four traveling buddies: Ann, Sue P., Margaret and Gary at the dock. TG for cell phones.

Lunch today: Left my buddies in a wine/ meat/cheese restaurant and headed out on my own. Found the Artigiande Pizza Café. Ordered veggie soup, green salad, tea. I was thrilled. I even wrote a poem for five little people in my life. Celebrated lunch by buying another shawl. Don't ask if it has green peacocks, pink roses, and beaded ends. Thanked my angels for leading me to this restaurant where I shared lunch with two New Yorkers and was served tea for almost two hours while I sat and wrote. How good can life get?

Poem of the day dedicated to Chloe, Claire, Emmy, Tabby, and Joselyn: (our Great Granddaughters)

Had I luggage space enough I would bring you pretty
pink jewels and little lace dresses. Toys of Venice,
clothes of Buona, Murona's glass necklaces.
Had I luggage space enough I would bring you scarves
and shawls and little dolls.
Italian shoes for your tiny feet, tapestries of Rialto Bridge
and Venetian pastries to eat.
Alas, your great grandma can carry no more.
I bring you nothing from this far distant shore.
I send you sweet kisses and warm hugs,
I think of your smiles every day.
Remembering your giggles I wonder:
will I ever win at "duck-duck-goose?"

Cin cin! Amore, Gr Gr. Sue

I'll be leaving Hotel Antico Panada at the crack of dawn tomorrow, dragging my luggage over the bridge to catch the 6:00 a.m. vaporatto #2 to the train station. Amore and ciao and arrivederci to all my dear family and friends. And so . . . we're off to dinner in a stand-up bar to have wine and hors' ouvers.

"Half of the fun of travel is the aesthetic of lostness."
Ray Bradbury

Italian Blog #tray (3)
Tuesday, September 7, 2010

Awake at 4:30 a.m. I leave our Venice Hotel Antico at 5:30 am, drag bag, carry purple backpack to Rialto Bridge (you gotta google this bridge, it's bella) voporetti (water bus) for the 6:00 a.m. ride to tronchetto stazion. With busy arms and in rapid Italian and much pointing, a nice man instructs me to go over the next bridge (20 steps up, 20 steps down) to other dock to catch the 5:55 boat. Driver beyond the bridge tells me to go back to first boat dock to catch the 6:35. "But my train leaves at 6:30!!!!"

I return to original dock and the nice old guy (my age, I suppose) points to the sign and gives me more instructions in his rapid Italian. Back over the bridge, remember Rev. Jim's "All is well. Trust." I breathe deeply. I remember my own words to the Laughter Club of Orange "ho ho ha ha ha" laugh at life's minor annoyances. So I smile as I get on water bus #2. We make four stops before coming to the tronchetto stazione, viewing churches, palaces, homes with water up to the front door. Venice is sinking, a little bit at a time. No telling what global warming will do to this beautiful island.

I hop off the boat, drag bag and purple backpack up 30 steps (very inaccessible for rascals, strollers, and old ladies) to tronchetto stazione. Aha! EuroStar is still on track 8. None of the doors are open!!! Oh, no!!! Breathe. All is well. All is well. All is well. I get to end of train – three city blocks long. (I know I exaggerate sometimes, but not in this case. I mean it.) All the doors are closed. I yell, "Wait for me."

I turn around and quickly walk back towards the stazione. I see a nun in the distance. I hold my ticket up in case she can see me and feels like praying. I point to the train. "Are you getting on?" I ask. She smiles at me and nods her habited head up and down. She points to the door. TG for index fingers. I grab the handle and jerk it open. It's dark on the train. I get on and collapse, knowing all is well.

Eventually, I stand up and begin pacing. No one is on this train but me. My ticket says 6:20 a.m. Finally the conductor gets on and flips on the lights. He approaches me, checks my ticket. I point at 6:20 a.m. He shrugs his shoulders and says a bunch of numbers in Italian. It is now 6:50! The train takes two hours and twenty minutes to get to Milan. I'll need to take the yellow #3 Metro from train station to Duoma for my 9:30 a.m. tour. "All is well. All is well."

A bunch of other crazy stuff happens (I got kicked out of first class, how was I to know?) Dove il bagno? Taking a chance on losing my bag and purple backpack, I leave my 2nd class seat in search of il bagno. I find one quickly and push the button for "open." Viola! The door slides open. A man is standing in the corner over il bagno. I turn my back on him and gaze out the window (ho ho ha ha ha). He reaches over and pushes the "close" button. I didn't see his face . . . or much of anything else. Ho ho ha ha ha. When it was my turn, I made sure I latched the door from the inside. Next time I'll knock.

The Milano train/metro/taxi stazione is as confusing as NYC and not much smaller. With the help of several friendly Italians, I found my way to Baggage Deposito where I handed over my bag and purple backpack. They stow bags by the hour. I was in the train stazione for 30 minutes, missed my 3-hour tour by an hour. All is well. I just kissed my 55 Euro tour ticket ciao! (Jo Jo where are you when I need you?) Wishing to continue the free distribution of American Joy, I smile.

Took Metro to Duomo Square and toured the cathedral with headset. It's the 4th largest in the world (after the Vatican's, London's, and Seville's). It seems the Dukes of Milano were trying to outdo their French and German counterparts. The structure of the Cathedral is 525 feet tall x 300' wide, has 2,000 statues. It was built to hold 40,000 worshippers and there is non bagno!! That's the way things were built in 1386. Actually, it was finished in 1810, with final touches in 1995. As a matter of fact as I sat meditating in this giant cathedral, two men rolled in a bunch of machinery and turned it on. It was either a stone grinder or jackhammer. They were doing something to the floor. There is an Italian phrase for projects that take a long time: "Like building a cathedral. " All is well.

Had a beautiful tonna insalada with a bottiglia of acqua naturale for lunch at the Aperal Restaurante, upstairs with a view of people shopping eating praying loving.

Besides the Duomo, I strolled through the Sforza Castle grounds, snapping pictures of ducks floating in the pond and took a few pictures for my "workers of the world" album. The prettiest sight I saw in Milano was the traffic circle fountain and all the flowers surrounding it. Children were sitting on the edge, dipping their fingers in the water.

Today has been a challenge. I missed seeing the Last Supper but have hopes. We'll be in Italy another 18 days. Well, maybe we can rent the DVD when we get back home. Surely there is one. Varenna on Lake Como will be a treat. Our own little home with kitchen. Kayaking by George's lakeside abode, hanging out in the village, hiking the hills, eating, eating, and eating.

"All journeys have secret destinations of which
the traveler is unaware."

Martin Buber

Wednesday, September 8, 2010

My first sight of Varenna last evening was from the train, through the misty air. What a beautiful sight. Mountains, the lake, villas, trees, flowers and stone steps everywhere. The owner of the 4-bedroom house we've rented ($25/each per night) drove to the train station to bring me, my bag and my purple backpack HOME. She'd provided some snacks for us and my four housemates, who had rented a car and drove from Miliano, bought wine and cheese and olives and bread for dinner. I have my own bedroom with a view of the lake from my bed. After ½ a banana, tea and croissant for breakfast, I strolled down to the edge of the lake (44 stone steps and long, long sloping path) to the Monastery. It's a misty day, some fog. Hope my pictures are good. Hope we have sunshine when we take the ferry to Bellagio.

I strolled around the village, made an appointment for my hair (I think I need something more Italian). Bought the makings for minestrone (the Italian word for veggie soup). Like a good Italian mama, I made a pot of soup for my bambinos and if they don't want it I'll have it for the next three days.

Wish all of you could experience this wonderland of Varenna. AND thank you for all your email responses. I'm enjoying hearing from you.

Arrivederci! Ciao, ci vediamo! Sue

"People don't take trips. Trips take people."
John Steinbeck

Italian Blog #quattro (4)

This afternoon we drove to Shienta from Veranno to hunt down Margaret's long-lost Italian cousins. All we had to go on was a letter written by someone years ago, in Italian, explaining how food was sent to the hungry Italian cousins by the American cousins during the war in the early '40's. The letter was from Olivia to her cousin, who was Margaret's nanno (grandmother).

Ann punched an address into her GPS and Gary drove. Margaret, the other Sue, and I sat in the back seat of the BMW rental. We drove up a little road, got out to take pictures of people's veggie gardens and the incredible view. A woman wandered out of her home, a young man came walking down the road. With Rick Steve's Italian phrase book & dictionary, Margaret waving the letter, and much broken Italian and English, these two charming people tried to help. Finally, the young man signaled us to follow him in his car. We had no idea.

We followed him up and around very narrow step roads into the Italian Alps. He took us to a home, where the owner, Lino, invited us in to meet his wife, and son, Luigi, and granddaughter, Lucia. After an hour and a half, we determined that Margaret and Lino are cousins!!! Margaret's grandmother and Leno's grandfather were siblings.

We didn't understand at the moment, but Leno kept asking us to stay until their daughter-in-law got home because she had taken English classes. He knew no English. At one point he said something in Italian that sounded like, "Sit down until tomorrow." We sat down and laughed. Much laughing and arm waving. We went outside and took pictures of the newly met cousins, Margaret and Lino, Lake Como in the background.

Finally, Valentina came home (daughter-in-law to Lino). The whole family jumped into their SUV and drove us higher up the mountain where the roads became steeper and narrower. After 15 minutes of driving, we stopped in the middle of the muddy road and followed our new family into the 3-story rock house at the end of the road. There we met Lino's mama, Olivia, who is about 84, 20 years older than Lino. She had a total of 13 children. Four of them had passed away, including her 18-year old son who drowned in the lake. Her cousin, Margaret's nonna, left Italy in her 20's because she was tired of babysitting everyone's children and minding the sheep. She went to America. One of her five children was Margaret's father. Olivia took one look at the letter Margaret had brought with her. Olivia said, in teary-eyed Italian "I wrote that letter thanking my cousin for sending food during the war."

There was a total of ten relatives who gathered at the house, and the five of us. We stayed for over an hour, took pictures, traded email addresses, drank soft drinks and ate chips, and left right as the rain started to come down, hard. It's only about ten miles between here and there, five miles of tunnels. . . . and so to bed.

"A journey is like marriage.
The certain way to be wrong is to think you control it."

John Steinbeck

Italian Blog #5Thursday, September 9, 2010

So, like I'm sitting on the sidewalk, eating Trader Joe's Omega trail mix right outside the Moda Dress Shop in Bellagio, Italy, across the piazza Chiesa (St. James) waiting for the Villa Serbelloni Park tour to begin. I see an Indian woman coming towards me. I put my hands in Namaste position, bow my head and greet her with "Namaste." Braba, from India, reverently bows her head and returns the blessing, "Namaste." Then we laugh. Then we talk. She leads a Laughter Yoga Club in India. I lead a Laughter Yoga Club in Orange, Ca. We laugh more and more. Jeffrey Briar is right: We will have "Peace through Laughter" the international language.

Highlights for Thursday

1. The ATM in Varenna gave me a bunch of Euros
2. The hotel across the street lets me sit on the patio and "borrow" WiFi
3. Vorrei un taglio. (I'd like a haircut). (Lady Anna, I had to do it.)
4. Ferryboat ride to Bellagio, town of high fashion and high shopping.
5. Met Braba from India Ho ho ha ha ha!
6. Walked, mostly uphill, in Paradise, otherwise known as Serbelloni Park
7. Richard phoned me with love and gratitude and anticipation.
8. I phoned Richard - "Bring almond butter, see you Sunday in Tuscany."
9. Took 75 pictures of Varenna and Bellagio (Bob: I got same pic as yours.)
10. Picked up four strangers from Canada and San Francisco at the little Marcato on the corner, brought them home to see our Villa Verenna.
11. 9:00 p.m. Flauto and Chitarra Concerto at the Villa Cipressi across the street. Matteo Ferrari on flute and Andrea Candeli on guitar. (Thank you Mike Short for encouraging me to up my understanding and love of musica classica.)

"The world is a book and those who do not travel only
read one page."

St. Augustine

Friday, September 10, 2010

Ferryboat ride to Belagio and on to Cadenabbia. Walked three hours in the botanical giardinos of Villa Carlotta, one of Lake Como's famed villas. Spent 45 minutes inside the villa studying the statues, paintings, frescos, and one huge tapestry of "country life." Then . . . a little voice said, "Go back to the garden."

I have learned to listen, to pay diligent attention to intuition. There, at the bottom of the hill was a woman, in her early 80's, looking for a way out. I took her arm and guided her up 50 rocky uneven steps, then down another 100 rocky uneven steps. She said things in German and I answered her, using my entire German vocabulary. "Ya. Ya." (Thanks to my sister, Jeanne.) The very unhappy bus driver for her tour guided her back to their bus, looking over his shoulder at me as though I'd kidnapped her. So I smiled, spreading more Americano Joy.

Sue Page, Margaret, Gary, Ann and me in Venice, Italy

Blog #6 Sunday, September 12

Richard is here with us now! He's adorable as ever, smart, loveable, charming. We're all sitting under the huge Chinese Fir tree at our round concrete table (eight feet in diameter) eating breakfast. Josh (graduate of Villa Park High, his parents live in Orange about three miles from us), our young chef, has served fruit, homemade fig coffee cake, spinach-basil frittata, marmalade, fig jam, Italian bread, butter, coffee, tea. Our view: miles and miles of olive trees down the hill, a tower in the distance, a few other villas. Last evening, for a "snack" Josh brought out red wine, white wine, water, bread, toast, liver pate, cheeses, sliced meats, fruit. Richard provided the almond butter.

Richard and I live in the "barn" near the main house. We have a huge bed, antique wooden furniture, a large kitchen, and tiny dining room. Our bathroom has one rock wall ten feet high, one plaster wall, skylight and small neat shower. The rest of our group: Ann, Sue P., Gary and Margaret live in the "chicken coop."

Three dogs roam the yard: Bobbie and Tara are little weenie dogs (Hi Sis) and Toto is an Egyptian pharaoh. All are friendly and cheerful. Today we are doing nothing! Well, Francisco will take Richard and me to Montevetilini to have the Rascal repaired.

Later: Francisco was too busy with his physical therapy session and a bunch of other stuff.

Tuesday, September 14, 2010

Oink! Oink! Happy 9th Birthday Rylee, our dear granddaughter. Today Grandpa Richard and I visited the Accademia Musio and learned more about this place as a school for artists centuries ago. For about 20 minutes, we sat and gazed at Michelangelo Buonarrotti's David, the biblical shepherd boy ready to take on Goliath. My heart overflows with gratitude that we share this adventure of discovery together. I had actually been in this museo 27 years ago and am ashamed to admit that I took about 15 butt shots of David, but then that was when I was so much younger. Don't any of you grandkids do the things I did.

As we had no Rascal today, we did parts of Florence by Taxi and some walking which was very difficult for Grandpa Richard. While he sat on a bench at the Duomo, I wandered off in search of gelato and returned with a dish of vanilla and a dish of vanilla/chocolate, which included chocolate covered mystery nuts. The gelato server wants to come to California with us and work in a Ben and Jerry's in California. I'm thinking of adopting her.

Our Rascal is now in the shop and will soon be repaired. In the meantime we've sent the crew out to dinner and will have leftovers from last night's 4-course feast. It's beautiful beyond words here, where we will live for the next nine days. Heaven all around. Not much going on . . . . relaxing.

Great news! We just heard that the Rascal will be ready some time tomorrow! Richard has wheels again.

Blessings Peace Love Joy Arrivederci
Ciao, Prego!!

Italian Blog #7 Tuesday, September 14th

We spent much of today awaiting a phone call to tell us the Rascal has been repaired. It was taken to a moped shop to have welding done. So . . .

From the tiny upstairs library at Villa Lucia, a book fell into my arms. "Olives, The Life and Lore of a Noble Fruit" by Mort Rosenblum, was published 1996. A journalist, author, resident-owner of the five-acre Olive Grove "Wild Olives" in Provence, France, he writes about his first meager crop of olives being pressed into oil. "When the cloudy golden liquid oozed into a clay urn, I dipped in a bread crust to check the flavor. I was ready to write psalms." (Thea: how's that for showing, not telling?)

Mort tells us "To Muslims, as to Christians and Jews, the olive means wisdom, fertility and peace. Aristotle philosophized about them, and Leonardo invented a modern way to press them. Egyptian pharaohs were sealed into pyramids with golden carvings of olives. Greeks used so much oil to lubricate their athletes that they devised a curved blade, the strigil, to scrape it off. For a time in Greece, only virgins and young men sworn to chastity were allowed to harvest the trees. When Odysseus finally came home, he collapsed into the marriage bed he had made for Penelope from a massive olive trunk."

The Prophet Muhammad likened the holy light of Allah's being to the sparkling radiance of burning oil from "The Blessed Tree, neither of the East nor the West." Islam's oldest university, in Tunisia, is named al-Zitouna: The Olive Tree. Mort quotes Willis Barnstone "If there are four elements in the world - earth, water, fire, air - then the olive has to be the fifth." Just thought you'd like to know all this. I am sitting among the olive trees, reading about the olive trees. How good can life get????

We have the most amazing staff at Villa Lucia. Francisco runs the place, speaks not a word of English. Josh, from Orange, Ca. cooks and cleans. Jeanine, of Newport Beach, when not working on her movie, helps with everything. Vanerdina cleans the rooms and does everyone's laundry. Her husband Felici tends the olives and does all types of garden and repair work. The owner is off to California to visit grandchildren and have knee surgery. We'll meet her next time we're here. All are friendly and make a huge effort to see to our comforts. Did I mention the food is amazing?

"When preparing to travel, lay out all your clothes
and all your money.
Then take half the clothes and twice the money."

Susan Heller

Friday, September 17, 2010

After four days of waiting, we finally have the Rascal back! Yippee! Now we can really travel. We visited Florence on Wednesday, borrowed a wheelchair in the Accademia where we learned more about Michelangelo then did toooo much walking for Richard. We took taxis around this beautiful medieval city. Yesterday, we went to Lucca, which is this really cool walled city. The wall is wide enough to ride bikes, jog, hike, and push wheelchairs on. So I did.

Wednesday was hard on both of us, so when I asked the young Italian girl at the Tourist Info center in Lucca if they had a wheelchair, I got a bit teary-eyed. When she brought it out I burst into tears. I'm sure she thought I was a crazy American but I was so happy I could have my favorite person in the world with me for the day. I pushed and we laughed like two little kids with a new toy.

Saturday September 18, 2010

Richard started today by tipping the Rascal and himself over into the rosebushes at the edge of the cliff at our villa. It seems he tried to drive over a huge hose and didn't make it. When he didn't come to the van, I went back to check. My heart almost stopped when I saw him lying sideways stuck in the bushes on the side of the hill. After my screaming for help, two people came running, dragged him up, then we got the Rascal up. Thank God he was not injured. He said it was a "soft landing."

After that, the day was magnificent. Cinque Terra. Everyone looks forward to hiking along this beautiful coast. Five (cinque) towns/earth (terra). As usual, Ann drove and Richard navigated with the help of a funny little thing called a GPS. When we got to Cinque Terra, Ann and the other Sue immediately took the coastal train from Monterosso to one of the other four beach cities for picture taking and a hike.

Richard and I walked 'n rolled for a few minutes when we realized it was drizzling. Up went our umbrellas. After peeking into several touristy stores and buying the hugest pair of purple earrings, like two daring kids we went up a very steep incline to the most beautiful ($700/night) Hotel Roca right on the coast. The rain came harder. We decided to have lunch. Our headwaiter, Alexandro, and our waiter, Simone, served pasta with diced swordfish, green salad, and fish with potatoes and asparagus. As their only customers, we received extra special attention, sat at the window watching the ever-increasing storm.

The steep rocky road down the hill from the hotel was slippery, wet, dangerous, and downright scary so we asked about the hotel van service. Luigi, of the very bright red hair, came immediately to help get the Rascal into his van and drove us part way back to our friends and our rental van. Then we walked through the tunnel laughing all the way, even though there were dozens and dozens of very disappointed hikers lurking under umbrellas, standing under shelters, and frankly, not doing a very good job of laughing at life's minor annoyances. Thank goodness our good friends Ann and Sue met us with the car. We left Cinque Terra several hours earlier than planned, knowing that some day we'll return. The weather predictions for the next two days: rain. Ho ho ha ha ha! Tomorrow we'll be off to Sienna, rain or shine. I remember visiting Sienna in 1983 with all those high school kids.

Blog #8

Oh! Those Pagans! In medieval times, a statue of Venus overlooked the piazza called Il Campo in Sienna. Because, the monks decided, the Black plague was brought on by such paganism, the people in 1340 ripped Venus apart and buried pieces of her along the walls of Florence, the enemy. Revenge, I guess. The highlight of Siena's Duomo is the Piccolomini Library, which displays a series of frescos by Umbrian painter Pinturicchio, telling the story of Sienna's consummate Renaissance Man who became Pope Pius II, also known as homie Aenes Piccolomini. Amazing what we learned by renting those little hand-held audio players.

Richard and I shared veggie pizza and "tonna" salad as we watched the locals and tourists mingle on the Il Campo Piazza, a wide sloping bricked-in area in the center of town. Kids race up and down the slope, families sit to rest, and tourists busily buy up souvenir booklets and shawls and gelato, and eat pizza and tonna salad at one of the many restaurants surrounding the action.

At the top of the slope, Fonte Gaia's (Fountain of Joy) water invites all to gaze at several relief panels, one that shows "God" creating Adam and pulling him to his feet. Michelangelo probably was inspired to use this idea when painting the ceiling of the Sistine Chapel in Rome. We'll check that out this week and let you know. If we look a little chubby when we return to OC, blame it on the Sinatti pasticceine in Sienna. They make the best cream puffs.

Monday, September 20, 2010

Here's a tiny but powerful demonstration of "change your thinking change your life." Ann and the gang dropped off Richard (on Rascal) and me at the train station in Montecatini Tempe yesterday morning, just a couple of windy miles from Villa Lucia, our home base. We had checked schedules for the train from Montecatini to Florence and back. Wrote down which trains would take the Rascal, waited in line, and through a kind-hearted Italian interpreter, learned that trains need 24 hours advance notice to carry wheelchair-bound travelers.

Deep breath. Again. Deep breath. So, we wandered the streets and shops (mostly closed on Sunday) a while and came upon the Funicular, built in 1898. After I repeated "sedia a rotelle" several times and pointing at the Rascal, the ticket seller nodded his head up and down, indicating that the Rascal would fit on the Funicular.

Two strong men, an Englishman and a Dutch tourist, picked up our 130-pound machina and plopped it onto the Funicular. Overcome with gratitude and joy, we rode up the steep slope to Montecatini Alto, an old old city high atop a montagna.

Zuppa at an elegant old restaurant. Windy. Clear skies. Il vista bellisimo. Walk 'n rolled up and down steep streets, taking photos of it all: the clock tower, the vista bellisimo, us. Strolling around Montecatini Terme a bit later, we discovered a magnificent Health Spa, complete with mineral water, piano player/singer, park, fountains, more photo ops. How did we get back down the hill? We followed the same road the cars were using. Aha! Life is molto bene.

Josh, our Villa Lucia cook, met us at the train station at 20:30 (that's 8:30 p.m. in OC), brought us home, gave us a container of grilled veggies, which we chopped up and added to our little pot of leftover pasta. Such a special dinner followed by the sharing of one of Sinatti's cream puffs.

Today, Monday, is Market Day in this part of town. Clothes, food, trinkets, scarves (hope you like pale pink Jeanne). At least a hundred booths enticing the locals to stock up for the week. Josh brought back fresh everything for tonight's final celebratory dinner.

We returned to "our" villa with several new tops for Sue and a fisherman's vest with lots of pockets for Richard and trinkets for some special little girls in our lives. We're sitting near the pool relaxing and writing (Thea will be proud) and not even thinking about packing up for tomorrow's drive to Rome.

Our elegant (TG for VISA) Mecenate Palace Hotel with rooftop dining awaits us. Ah, Rome. Italy's political capital, the capital of Catholicism, and center of the ancient world. Before returning to OC we'll spend five days visiting St. Peter's, one of us will climb the 328-foot Michelangelo's dome. (She did it in '83, she can do it in '10.) Then there's the Spanish Steps, Trevi Fonte, the Pantheon, Colosseum. Wow!. . . . . . . stay tuned.

Arriverderci for now. Sue

Italian Blog #9 Wednesday, September 22, 2010.

Autumn Equinox.
Full Moon

Count the Blessings: The $110/per person tour bus would not take us. Too much trouble loading/unloading the Rascal and too many inaccessible sites in Rome. However, the $25 (for me, no charge for King Richard) for 48 hours on the hop-on-hop-off bus took us everywhere we wanted to go. The driver charmed us with his acceptance and his cheerful attitude. We decided, first to get off and cruise the Tiber River, our entrance just inside the tiny city called The Vatican.

We needed to walk down 59 steps, then 150 steps on rocky pavement to the "barco" on the fiume (river). Two steps into this perilous journey, an angel appeared in the form of a handsome young Vatican "guardia." First he offered Richard his arm, then his shoulder, and then much to our surprise, he motioned for my beloved husband to accept a piggyback ride down the steep stairway. I walked behind them, with tears of gratitude, and a bit of fear, streaming. My heart and my tear ducts concur. It is never simple traveling with The King, but allowing world citizens to give their services, their love, their joy, is a gift in itself and a reminder that we can travel.

Onward to St. Peter's Basilica where many handsome young men, all employed by the Vatican, led us through back alleys, empty lots, up ramps and lifts to take us into the Basilica, built in honor of St. Peter who was put to death in 60 AD. The interior features vast mosaic decorations and is considered a precious treasure chest housing some of the most famous artworks in the world. I don't think one can view Michelangelo's Pieta and not think about a loved one who has passed on. Seeing Mary holding her dead son, Jesus, across her lap reminded me of how we nearly lost our son when he was 23. I looked at Mary and wondered, "How does a parent ever get used to having lost child?" More tears. Rick Steve writes that to call the Basilica of St. Peter vast is to call Einstein smart. We concur.

Next we visited Trevi Fountain near the Plaza Navona, where Ocean (Neptune) appears to be surfing through his wet kingdom, water gushing from 24 spouts, tumbling over 30 different kinds of plants, while Triton blows his conch shell. Actually, Triton looks like he's eating a hotdog but we decided that was an historical impossibility. Hundreds of people sat around this famous fountain, 50% of them eating gelato. By their happy faces, it appeared that the cioccolata gelato eaters were the most pleased.

We arrived at the Piazza di Spagna (also know as the Spanish Steps) to discover that the poet John Keats died in a nearby building at age 25. Ironically, he wrote "Death be Not Proud." Fellow Romantic Lord Byron lived across the square at #66 for a while. Bernini built the Sinking Boat Fountain at the foot of the steps. That's where we met Susie and her mother, Lana. Both are nurses from North Hollywood. They were wondering about the Fountain of Amore, which was featured in the new film "When in Rome." Does anyone know? We could not find it in any book. We'll put that on our "Google list." Perhaps Fountain of Amore is fictional??? (Note: We checked. No such place in Rome or anywhere.)

Thursday, September 23, 2010

Andrea Bianchi, manager of our rooftop restaurant, greets us each morning for breakfast and helps us climb the last 25 steps to the top of our hotel. The elevator stops too soon. He does everything possible to make us comfortable and speaks pretty darn good English, certainly better than our Italian. Each morning he creates a smiley-face cappuccino for The King and a pot of tea for The Queen (that's me).

Today we took the hop-on-hop-off bus to The Coliseum, which of course, was not Rascal-friendly. Nevertheless, we looked it over, pondering its usage: built in 80 AD, the Coliseum was an arena for gladiator contests and public spectacles. There were at least 2,000 people shuffling through the site, so we were just as happy to view it from the outside. We stopped next at the Plaza Navona's Campo di fiori where the marketplace was in full swing. Every type of vegetable and fruit, spice, plant and item of clothing was for sale. As we sat with a cup of caffe freddo, eating our sandwiches and watching the locals stock up food supplies, I remarked that next Tuesday I shall be at the Old Irvine Road Farmers Market to stock up our household and make soup and salads and stir-fried veggies. As wonderful as it is to have this experience, there's no place like your own refrigerator.

Next to the little restaurant where we had lunch, was a young man, possibly a victim of AIDS, who sat on the ground with a little can, hoping for a few coins. My heart ached for him, as he seemed invisible to so many. Mostly, people looked the other way as they passed him. Richard and I both had the same thought: go talk to him and hand him some money. We approached him with our best "buon giorno" and held out an E10 note. He immediately stood and smiled. He was extremely frail; many teeth were missing. I asked him, "Come si chiamo?" He said he name is "Mariano." He asked if we were from the United States and said "US is quattro in soccer." We knew he had been a soccer player by his shirt. I touched his arm and said "Many blessing to you." He said, "Have a buon giorno." "Grazia," we said. "Prego. Prego."

The Pantheon, as are so many other places in Europe, is undergoing a facelift, surrounded by scaffolding. That gave me a chance to take pictures for a book I'm creating called "Workers of the World." Men were busily sending re-bar up in buckets and dragging bags of cement about the place. Although the outside of the structure is a bit messy, the inside is a precious jewel. The church's dome is 142′ high and equally wide and was Europe's biggest until the Renaissance. The center of the dome is a huge open skylight, which must be fun on a rainy day.

As we left the Pantheon and headed for another look at Trevi Fountain, we came upon a young man that Richard had seen yesterday. He pushes himself about on a skateboard because he cannot walk. His hands and feet are stubs of bone and flesh, his body twisted, nothing to distinguish fingers or toes, but his face lit up when we handed him a few Euros. His eyes sparkled with gratitude. I couldn't help myself when he held out his hand to me. I kissed it. I thought if that was my child I would want him to feel important, to feel visible. I'd want people to talk with him. Okay. No more tears.

So, I'm sitting at Trevi Fountain, Richard behind me. We've just polished off another gelato. Orange, peach, and mango for Richard. Chocolate, mint, and chocolate for me. An Indian woman sits beside me. I say, "Welcome. I saved this seat for you. Namaste." She returns the greeting. I ask, "Do you know Dr. Kataria? He lives in Mumbai. "Yes," she says, "I know him very well." We both started clapping our hands in the Laughter Yoga mantra, "Ho ho ha ha ha." She and three friends are visiting Rome and she declares that she's not throwing a coin into the fountain because once in Rome is enough for her. We laugh. She teaches Yoga in India and, according to one of her friends, she has had at least 2,000 students.

I just know that sharing a country and a language is not necessary for sharing our common humanity. Joy, love, gratitude is in abundance. Because Richard is so sweet and gentle and kind, people from all over the world have helped him in so many ways. None of them know us. Most of them don't speak the same language we do. The drivers on the hop-on-and-off buses have been so prompt at lowering the buses and pulling out the ramps and smiling, never complaining. Men help pick up the Rascal (130 pounds) and load it on funiculars and vans and buses and over curbs. Women come up to Richard and offer assistance. Waitresses move tables and chairs to make room. And life is great.

Tomorrow: back to the Vatican to view the Sistine Chapel and the Vatican Museum.

Blessings of peace, love, and joy to all, Sue

Blog #10 Friday, September 24, 2010

Today we took the hop-on-hop-off to the Vatican Museum and the Sistine Chapel. The line to get in was at least four thousand people deep at 10:00 a.m. Richard and I went to the front of the line where an attendant stepped out to greet us. I batted my eyes at him and pointed to Richard and his Rascal. I said, "We don't know what to do." He led us inside. He directed us to go to a special window, show ID, and receive two free passes. We then stopped at the booth to rent audio equipment so we could listen to lectures on the artwork. The nice young woman said "No charge." This special treatment happens to us over and over again. In Europe, most of the time, the "differently-abled" get free passes to everything and 99% of the time, I do when I'm with King Richard.

Attendants helped us with elevators and special lifts, making sure we got to see all the important things. We loved seeing Raphael's work titled "School of Athens", in which Raphael honors the great pre-Christian thinkers like Aristotle and Plato. Included in the work, are the bearded figure of Leonardo da Vinci as Plato and Diogenes, history's first hippie, lying on the stairs in the picture. Although Raphael was known to be a bit jealous of Michelangelo he included him in the picture as a salute to his great talent.

The Sistine Chapel, the pope's personal chapel, is where new popes are elected. It is famous for Michelangelo's pictorial culmination of the Renaissance, showing the story of creation, where God is reaching out to help Adam to his feet. Michelangelo was 33 when he had completed four years of painting the chapel. No words can do justice to his talent, his understanding of theology, and his brilliant portrayals of bible story.

One of the attendants in the Sistine Chapel, who took us up the elevator, said that most days there are between 20,000 and 24,000 people visiting the museum and chapel. He said after work he just wants to sit on the beach. We understood perfectly. We'd only been visiting and we were so tired at the end of the day, we took the bus back to our neighborhood, picked up a salad and a pizza, sat on our bed in the hotel and vegged out.

Saturday, September 25, 2010

Happy Birthday, Courtney, our beautiful granddaughter who is 19 today. We love you Court. We left you a phone message with our personal rendition of the H.B. song.

Because Richard and I are both Path One Mystics (ask Joan Borysenko) we visit Botanical Gardens when we travel. It's fun, educational and satisfying to see what grows where and who imports what from other countries. We found the Orta Giardia di Roma in the Trastavere neighborhood of Rome, which Rick Steves describes as seedy. We figured the seedy part of Rome probably produced a few plants. To our surprise, today was the 2nd day of a 3-day Urbe et Erbe Tre Giorni in Compagnia Degle Erboristi Romani. We think that means lectures about herbs, for three days. We were welcomed to the garden, free of charge, and roamed the beautiful sloping hills of the garden. Homeopathic remedies were being displayed; free samples were given out, vegetarian fare for sale by the Fabrici Caffe.

Such a treat to find tabouli, ginger tofu pastries, and cioccolate cookies, all made without harming animals. We sauntered through the aromatic garden, rubbing leaves and smelling our fingers. We photographed rare fruit and palm trees. One of us tasted flowers and berries, and when his Rascal bogged down in the rocky pathway, two English-speaking seminary students lifted the rear end and yanked it onto the pavement. So much love everywhere. We viewed Rome from the hilltop garden and took many more photos.

Ironically, as we ride along in the bus and I am writing in my little notebook, the bus driver's assistant announces that because of a problem, the bus route will be diverted. As we round the corner into Piazza del Popolo, we see several hundred vegetarian Italians carrying signs "Save the Animals." I phone our friends and let them know there will be traffic delays and also to be discrete when ordering their steaks for dinner tonight.

Speaking of traffic, in Rome its crazy, chaotic, sometimes funny. We hear men yelling out their car windows at each other. Mostly they insult each other's mothers, and then yell, "Have a buon giorno" with lots of hand gestures.

Tomorrow, we'll visit Basilica Santa Maria Maggiori, which we can see from our hotel window. Rome's best-surviving mosaics line the nave of this church built as Rome was falling. We're going to spend tomorrow roaming our own neighborhood, taking it easy, deciding what we can bring home. This has been an awesome vacation. We are filled with gratitude for the great experiences, for all the lovely people we've met, for our good-natured traveling friends, for beautiful neighbors who watch over things when we leave town, and just grateful to be on the planet.

Ciao. Arrivederci. Blessings to all.

Love, Sue and Richard

PS: Liberty and Wendy and Beth: Monday 8:45 p.m. Delta Airlines Flight 1161. LAX.

"Wherever you go, go with all your heart!"
Confucius

World Peace Pilgrimage - June 25, 2011

June 26, 2011 - So many of you asked about the June 25th World Peace Pilgrimage so here's a recap of the event. First of all, I'd emailed Mandy at Mt. Baldy to ask about getting my beloved Richard, sans Rascal, up the Mt. to the Ceremony at Location #1 above chairlift #1.

She emailed back that walking/wheeling up the hillside of shale, rocks, and gravel would be an impossible task. We were undismayed, which is another word for having unshakeable faith, or maybe, utter stupidity. Anyhow, we also emailed Oscar, one of the event planner/producers. He said "good luck" which we took to mean, "go for it."

Knowing that transporting the Rascal up the chairlift would be a laughable task, I phoned our friend Gretchen Snyder (no relation), program director at the Orange Senior Center early Friday morning to ask, "Do you have wheelchairs you loan or rent?" She was delighted to loan us a chair for the weekend! I almost cried, I was so happy. I walked over to the Senior Center and pushed the chair back through Olde Towne Orange, receiving more than one questioning look.

Our dear friend, Dave Sullinger, was at our home at 7:15 a.m. Saturday. We cheerfully drove up to Mt. Baldy, about a 90-minute ride. After unloading us and our gear, and the OSC wheelchair we pushed Richard over to the registration table where we signed in and paid the $14/each for roundtrip rides on the chairlift. Dave scouted out the task of pushing Richard and chair up the road to chairlift #1 and reported it looked impossible.

Undismayed, I inquired at the "hut" in the parking lot about driving up the steep road to lift #1. Ginger cheerfully said, "Sure. Drive on up. Just leave space for emergency vehicles." Aha! We loaded back into the van and drove up the steep hairpin road. Unloaded again. Richard and Dave maneuvered up the rocky steps; I pushed the empty wheelchair around the hut and up a steep little road and met them at the lift.

The cute young guy at the chairlift hefted the wheelchair onto its own chair and up the mountain it went. Richard and I hopped (sort of) onto the next chair and Dave followed, laughing all the way. Little did he know what he was in for. Thank God for his physical strength, cheerful outlook, and enduring sense of humor. Dave, too, was undismayed. (Understand that Dave is an Artist who looks at chunks of wood as potential goblets, which he sells at the Sawdust Festival in Laguna Beach.) We were carefully unloaded at the top of the hill where new challenges awaited.

Just slightly dismayed, we rolled down a 20-foot strip of sidewalk, ending in a mountain of shale, rocks, and gravel. Dave and I managed to push Richard and the OSC chair a little way up the hill. At the point where we could no longer navigate with any progress, Richard walked through 30 feet of srg, and then once again sat in the chair. At this point four angels came along and asked how they could help. Nearing heart attacks due lack of oxygen, and the approach of dismay, Dave and I handed over the whole operation to the angels.

They, too, were heading up the mountain to the 3rd annual World Peace Pilgrimage Ceremony. More angels flew in to help. By the time we arrived at Location #1, six people were pushing and pulling through shalerocksandgravel. We collapsed in the shade on pinecones and boulders. Before the ceremony began, Dave was offered a large bunch of crispy red grapes by another peacenik, which I quickly seized and offered to everyone, "Would you like a Peace Grape?" So many happy smiles of gratitude. So much joy. We handed out unconditional love.

From about 11:15 to 2:00 we blissed out in the beautiful mountain air with 60 other Pilgrims, who had come to pray, chant, meditate, and sing for World Peace. A portable microphone was passed from Liesel Butcher of the Aetherius Society, to Rev. Dr. George Regas of the Interfaith Communities United for Justice, to Abbot Charlotte Stein from the Buddhist Dari Rulai Temple, to Sister Priya a Brahman Kumaris, to Rev. Clarence Luckey of the Bethel AME Church, to Elder Macfarland of the Church of Jesus Christ of Latter Day Saints, to Shams Rahaman a Muslim of the International Institute of Tolerance, to a Hindu-Swami Yogananda representative, to Jasbir Bashine a Sikh, to Debrah Van Zyl a Jew, to Rev. Dr. Tahdi Blackstone of the Noetic Sciences, to Jim Dreaver of Global Awakening Network, to Kabbalah Bach who blessed us with Sacred Music.

Me, our brave friend Dave, and The King

We prayed for Peace. We chanted for Peace. We meditated on Peace. We sang for Peace. Others spoke and offered prayers. Last to speak was Richard Snyder who simply said, "I want to thank all the angels who helped me get up the mountain today." This beautiful interfaith community offered so many words of love and peace. Three times during the ceremony, we were given 10-minute breaks. Does the term "Loaves and Fishes" mean anything to you? People pulled out snacks from backpacks, pockets, and lunch bags. Sharing of munchies ran rampant. It was also a time to interact and bond with other participants. The youngest Interfaith Pilgrim, Athan from Escondido was five months old and smiled the whole time.

If the fun of getting my beloved Richard up the hill was taskful, going down caused near-dismay for Dave and me. We started by taking turns walking in front of Richard and the wheelchair, with him facing uphill. It soon became apparent that the shale and rocks and gravel had other ideas. After going only a few feet, five muscular young handsome shirtless sweaty angels landed beside us. "Need help?" Sometimes I can't do anything but cry with gratitude. So I did. Four of the guy-angels each picked up a corner of the wheelchair and carried The King and chair down the hill, up a slight incline and deposited them near the top of the chairlift. The fifth angel cheered on the others. I hugged the head angel and whispered through my tears, "Thank you." I waved at the others. They smiled and flew on down the hill.

Going down the lift we viewed mountains and trees at their best. When nature offers such beauty and healing, I think we should send our countries'

leaders backpacking and chanting in the wilderness for a week or two. Greed just doesn't exist on Mt. Baldy. Hate does not exist there. War does not exist there. We were reminded of what the Dali Lama said. "The purpose of life is happiness. The way to happiness is through service." Please let us know if any of you want to join us for the 4th Annual Interfaith World Peace Pilgrimage next year. And if you'd like to "serve" by helping Dave and me getting Richard up the mountain next year, we'd be eternally grateful.

With huge hugs and lots of love, Sue

"Twenty years from now you will be more disappointed
by the things you didn't do than by the ones you did.
So throw off the bowlines, sail away from the safe harbor.
Catch the trade winds in your sail.
Explore. Dream. Discover."

Mark Twain

Journal #1 June 3, 2012 – Road Trip: Virginia and Brock's Wedding

Four rules for a successful road trip:

Rule #1. Check to make sure you've brought every piece of luggage, cooler of snacks, Baggalini of money, the 20 oz. mocha coffee with whipped cream, 2 slices of toasted Trader Joe's Raisin Cinnamon bread, the travel cribbage set with deck of cards, and most of all, do not forget to load your Blue Book Bag that contains all your herbs, meds, and books.

Rule #2. If you get 50 miles east of Las Vegas, and have been on the road for four hours and it's 8:30 a.m. and suddenly you wonder if your Blue Book Bag made it into your 2005 white Grand Caravan SXL, pull off the highway and make your partner check every inch of the interior of said white van.

Rule #3. If, indeed, the Blue Book Bag really, really, really is not with you, do not panic. Just take out your cell phone and phone our friend Sallie. She will drive over to your house, grab the bag, and have UPS ship it "overnight" to The Silver Moon Inn, in Estes Park, Colorado where you will soon spend three nights. Cost? About $125.00.

Rule #4. Look at your darling travel buddy and think how much you've been through in your 20 years as partners, and really, compared to fractured bones and blood transfusions, forgetting the BBB is pretty trivial, and ask yourselves, "What would Buddha do?" Then smile at each other; thank the Great Spirit for your families, your lives, your home, your means and ability to travel, and for friends like Sallie. (This message was sent from The Mesa Inn Hotel 780 miles from home in Grand Junction, Colorado.)

Journey Journal #2 - Tuesday, June 5, 2012

Rule #5: If someone asks you to join them on a journey to Rocky Mountain National Park (RMNP), say "yes" then make reservations at The Silver Moon Inn in Estes Park, where the patio in front of your room is right on the swiftly-flowing Fall River.

Yesterday, Bob at the Estes Park Visitor Center informed us that the road to Sprague Lake and Bear Lake is under construction and cars can only enter before 9:00 a.m. and after 2:00 p.m. We were at the head of the line at 8:00 this morning, watching a cute young thing finish off her breakfast muffin as she held up the "stop" sign. Like a couple of boy scouts, we'd come prepared with Trader Joe's Greek yogurt with honey, a couple of bananas, trail mix (thank you son John), and two Subway sandwiches. Oh, and Sue Grafton's "U is for Undertow" on audio books (murder mystery, kidnapping, abandoned and adopted babies, wild sex, private investigators, and ??? . . . we have not heard the end yet). Most of the "stop" and "slow" sign holders were young women, smiling and waving like cheerleaders encouraging - what else - cheer to carloads of hikers.

We hiked around Sprague Lake, admiring views of Hallett Peak, 12,713', Storm Peak 13,326', and Flattop Mountain 12,324', dotted with huge patches of snow. These majestic mountains mark the Continental Divide. The divide is the separation of watersheds. If a raindrop falls east of the divide, it will eventually flow through rivers to the Gulf of Mexico. If a raindrop falls west of the divide it will make its way to the Colorado River and join the Pacific Ocean.

We then hiked around Bear Lake where snowmelt mud puddled all along the "accessible" trail. The lake, the trees, the mountains, the sky are all indescribably, awesomely beautiful. There are no words. At Lily's Lake we snapped a few photos of a tuxedo and fancy-dress clad group witnessing a young couple, a redheaded bride in long white gown and a groom, faces aglow with smiles, recite their vows of everlasting love and shared dreams. Ah, young love.

RMNP guides will tell you if you don't like the weather, wait 5 minutes, it'll change. Today's forecast: high of 84, low of 53, thunder showers. So far, 100% correct. Estes Park is a village of dozens of inns and restaurants, outdoor gear shops, and jewelry stores. We understand the "river walk" goes on for four miles, river on one side, and restaurant patios on the other. We plan to explore it. Life is great! Thank you to all of you wonderful family members and friends who have replied to our JJ's.

Much love and many blessings to all of you,

Richard and Sue

Journey Journal #3 June 7, 2012

The 138-room, neo-Georgian Stanley House Hotel in Estes Park was built in 1909 by Freelan Oscar Stanley, co-inventor of the Stanley Steamer automobile. In an effort to improve his health and spend some of his hard-earned money, he and his wife moved to Estes Park and began the building of the now-famous Stanley House Hotel. Red roof, white exterior, tea served on the huge front porch, the Steamer Café downstairs, serving homemade gelato (we sampled the lemon).

So, yesterday, after spending a very long day driving the 48 miles from Estes Park to Grand Lake and back, talking with lots of people, from locals to motorcycle riders from all over the country, stopping at every marked sight, hiking every accessible trail, snapping pictures of every elk and Clarks Nutcracker, squirrel, chipmunk, flower, and rock, standing on the continental divide, traipsing through snow and mud, and looking like two old dusty hippies, we said, "Why not?"

So we paid our $5.00 parking fee to the guard at the Stanley House Hotel and parked our bug- and rain-splattered van. After unloading the rascal, and walk 'n rollin' across the pavement, we made our grand entrance. For several minutes we watched a video of Jay Leno starting up and driving his Stanley Steamer then decided to head upstairs to the Lobby just for a look around. The elevator was small so Richard and one of the other guests crowded in. I took the stairs. Unbeknownst to me, my beloved partner didn't hear the word "lobby" and flew up to the 4th floor seeing a lot more than I did. I waited. And waited. In the lobby. In front of the elevator. Several times it arrived. No King. The second time a pretty young woman in a long, low-cut dress, holding a glass of wine stepped out with her husband. I timidly (OK, I don't do timid), I boldly asked if she'd seen a cute bearded old guy in a wheelchair roaming around anywhere. She said, "You let someone in a wheelchair go up the elevator by himself?" I explained that we lose each other all the time, no big deal.

So we talked. Her maiden name was Heather Goldstein (but I'm not Jewish, she added) and her husband's name is Matt. They were staying at The

Stanley, and ready to attend a wedding rehearsal dinner. The wedding also to be held at the SHH. Heather and Matt live down the hill in Loveland, Co. He grew up in upstate New York; she grew up in Laguna Beach, Ca. She attended Top of the World Elementary and remembered one of the teachers named Kathy Reynolds (now Housden). She attended Laguna Beach High School, class of '84. This world is just full of interesting people.

We decided to have dinner at Claire's for a second night. This time, it was first night's server Brandi's twin sister Lottie who made our meal a delight. Dinner was great: Richard had fish tacos again, I had the Greek salad. When we returned to The Silver Moon Inn we discovered that we'd neglected to leave the tip. We've decided to mail it to our waitress. Ho ho ha ha ha.

Now we're in Denver for a night, having spent most of the day at the Denver Botanical Gardens where we explored all 45 gardens, plus all the fountains, ponds, streams, and a gigantic conservatory. Monet's pond was beautiful but held no comparison to the original in Giverney, France. We were amazed at the colors, the variety of flora and fauna. Plants from all over the world. Bamboo artwork. A "scripture garden." A conservatory filled to the brim with tropical trees and plants. And a huge treehouse with an elevator going right up the middle. Now, that's what I call accessibility!

When we arrived at the Botanical Gardens, it was 88 degrees and sunny. An hour latter there was thunder and lightening and it rained. An hour later is was hot and muggy again. During the rainstorm we found a little gazebo where we could have lunch: leftover chicken sandwich for Richard, Greek yogurt sprinkled with ground hemp seeds for me. A couple of cute gals walked in and of course one of us (hmm) invited them to join us. The mother, Laurie, was happy to share her stories of living in Denver and other parts of Colorado and told us to be sure to visit Chief Crazy Horse monument in South Dakota when we're there next week. Her daughter, Keegan, had been a competitive Irish Dancer for nine years, is about to begin her senior year at Willamette State University, talked about spending a semester in Bulgaria. She showed us the bright blue sleeve of her on-going knitting project.

Now we're resting up for tomorrow's 8-hour drive to Omaha and hugs from Aunt Ruth and all the cousins. Saturday is the big wedding. Nighty-night. S&R

"The woods are lovely, dark, and deep,
But I have promises to keep
And miles to go before I sleep,
And miles to go before I sleep."

Robert Frost

Journey Journal #4 Friday June 8, 2012

The drive between Denver and Omaha was littered with orange cones, construction trucks, and highway improvers. We are happy for the crews; they have jobs. Somehow we kept thinking of Robert Frost guiding his horse and buggy on a Snowy Evening. And how we had "miles to go before Aunt Ruth's." "J is for Judgment," another Sue Grafton audio book, supplemented the miles of cornfields, Black Angus sightings and stalled traffic.

Aunt Ruth lovingly greeted us as we arrived in Omaha at 5:30 Friday evening. Connected to her oxygen machine and her walker, she bounced all around her home preparing for our arrival, supervising her caregiver, Anna. My sister Jeanne and husband Curt had arrived from California, by plane, a few minutes earlier. Cousin Barb of Hermann, Nebraska danced in the door with more food for dinner. Our dear niece, Chrissy, now a Catholic nun working for hospice care, joined us. Her name is now Sister Catherine Marie but she's still Chrissy to us. Our cousin Marylyn, and son, Tim, from Houston, Texas had arrived on Thursday. We brought the California avocados, pilfered from our neighbor's stray branches.

Virginia and Brock's wedding took place Saturday in "The Hollow" in the woods of a beautiful country estate named after the owners, Scott-Lyn Yards. About 100 guests drove across the property: hills of newly mown grass, to find an assembly of chairs set up amidst soaring trees, a little chapel in the forest. A red sundress-clad guitarist provided music and song. Five bridesmaids, in golden silk gowns were escorted down the grassy aisle by a group of handsome young men followed by the beautiful and radiant Virginia, on her father's arm, glowing with happiness: both of them. Brothers Tripp and Isaac dressed in size 3 and size 4 tuxedos delivered, with great ceremony, two wedding rings on a pillow. The buffet dinner and the dancing and speeches took place in the loft of the big red barn.

How do you describe the "happiest day" when the family has recently been devastated by the loss of 9-year old Addie? It was obvious to all that Addie's parents—Jamie and Scott--and grandparents--Julie and Ken-- (Brock's mom and dad) struggled to keep focused on the present. There were tears for Addie, who we lost in March; there were tears for Uncle Floyd (Addie's great grandpa and Aunt Ruth's husband for 71 years) who we lost 17 months before that. Addie was to be the flower girl; Addie's mother, Jamie, was to be a bridesmaid. Addie's uncle was the groom. The human spirit never ceases to amaze us. Maybe some day we'll get used to the idea that loved ones pass on. For now, we struggle.

Here is a quote by Harriet Schiff, author of The Bereaved Parent that we think is helpful:

"The reality is that we don't forget, move on, and have closure, but rather we honor, we remember, and incorporate our deceased children and siblings into our lives in a new way. In fact, keeping memories of your loved one alive in your mind and heart is an important part of your healing journey."

As I send this Journey Journal to all of you and close down the laptop, thunder, lightening, and pouring rain are happening all over Omaha. The weather is exciting - especially for the science major. Nighty-night . . . Sue and The King

"When we get out of the glass bottle of our ego
and when we escape like squirrels
in the cage of our personality and get into the forest
again, we shall shiver with cold and fright.
But things will happen to us so that we don't know ourselves.
Cool, unlying life will rush in."

D.H. Lawrence

Dear Aunt Ruth, JJ #5

Thank you for sharing your warm-hearted and cozy home with us. We always love spending time with you and our special cousins. Thank you for the lightening/thunder storm; we rarely see those out West. Thank you for all the great food. Thank you for having such caring caregivers. All of them: Anna, Maria, and Margie were just wonderful to us. We're looking forward to Tommy and Brook's wedding next year - or the year after.

I loved leading our 4th annual Omaha Laughter Yoga session. Wow! Twenty laughers from 83 to 100 ½. I remember what a great laugh Uncle Floyd had. My memories of him are so clear and loving. And I remember so many of your friends who came to laugh with us.

We left our loved ones in Omaha this morning, a joyous yet tearful reunion, and are on our way to South Dakota.

We stopped in Wall, S.D. this afternoon and while Richard was window-shopping, I wandered into a little chapel. I had a talk with Addie and told her to communicate with her mom and let her know things will be OK. If Addie would just let her mom know she is still with us, all around us, loves us, we'd all feel better. I also asked Addie to nudge her mom to write a book about the grieving process. It would help so many people who have lost young children and Jamie is an excellent writer.

Richard and I are loving this journey, being together, seeing the sights, and meeting people from everywhere. Brookings was interesting and although the McCrary Gardens at SDSU was small, it was beautiful and being groomed for future weddings and receptions. And although SDSU Creamery's ice cream was good, it could not duplicate the excellence of Blue Bell, Texas's finest. We took a side trip up to Watertown, as Margie suggested, and visited the Terry Redlin art collection. He paints in the style of Thomas Kincaid, yet each picture has a distinct story to it. We spent several hours viewing his 250 paintings and 100 sketches. Then we traveled on. We visited the Badlands today, saw fossils and amazing rock formations, had a paleontology lesson by Ranger Emily. Antelope, Big Horn Sheep, lots of birds, but no bison-sightings today.

About an hour ago we arrived in Rapid City and dragged our gear into the famous old Alex Johnson Hotel right in the middle of the stunning old part of town. Lots of activity this evening. Every Thursday during the summer, there is live entertainment, all kinds of food, and kids playing in the fountains in the Old Towne Square. This evening a belly-dancing troupe, guitar players, and a balsamic-glazed green salad with goat cheese, beets, pumpkin seeds, tomatoes, and some funny-tasting olives entertained us. We ate every green thing on that plate. The hostess, cashier, server was a white-haired ball of energy named Pat. She was so helpful; we hugged her when we left. Then, of course Richard wanted to taste ice cream from the Dakota Soda Company. It was OK but not Blue Bell.

I wish I had taken a picture of one couple we saw. They were in their early 60's, were nearly covered with tattoos, he had a pony-tail, a droopy beard and belly, she had five lower lip rings, and long blond hair. Accompanying them were three pitbulls: a grown one and two puppies. Is that supposed to be cool or am I getting old?

We'll be here three full days, heading towards Jackson Hole, Wyoming on Monday. We plan to visit Lead, Crazy Horse in Custer Park, and Mt. Rushmore where four of our presidents are carved in stone. Oh! On several street corners in Rapid City, statues of presidents stand and wave or smile. Richard took a picture of me with my favorite president: John Adams. When people ask me who my hero is, I usually say John Adams, husband of Abigail.

Nighty-night and lotsa hugs.

Your other favorite niece and nephew,

Sue and Richard

Journey Journal #6 June 16, 2012

It's Saturday morning and we're sitting by the ground level 30-spigoted fountain (just like the ones at Irvine Spectrum and Aspen, only bigger). Children, mostly bare-chested 8-yr. old boys, run across the concrete as water squirts ten feet straight up. Shrieks of daring joy, chest-pounding machismo fill the air. A few tomboy-girls run through the water gigglingly.

We're watching a little pink polka dot sundress-clad 12-month old as she cautiously extends her hand over a stream of water. Each time, she touches her forehead and hair, making sure nothing is mussed. Watching the others, she decides that the real object is to run across the square but can't quite join the masses. Mom and Dad sit and watch. Big brother, about 3 yrs. old is drenched.

Across the Rapid City Square, the weekly Farmers Market offers lettuce (3 boxes of it) and tomatoes (2 boxes). Other booths display homemade aprons, sketches, and beaded bracelets made and sold by a near-sighted elderly woman (we could tell by the stitching). Can't wait until my morning yogurt is digested. I'm going back for the Enigma Restaurant's organic vegan Greek quinoa wrap. Many of the "farmers" are trying to sell "low-on-the-pyramid" multi-marketing products: Nu-Skin, Shaklee, and coconut water.

Yesterday's 8-hour journey through The Black Hills took us from Mt. Rushmore where Ranger Roger in the Sculptors Studio explained the process of carving those four guys up there: George, Tom, Teddy, and Abe. Gutzon Borglum designed and oversaw the project, which used lots of dynamite and tiny little tools. Then it was on to Chief Crazy Horse-in-progress. The sculpting began in 1949 and has a long way to go before completion. Most fascinating is the Needle Highway where tall sharp rocks, thousands of them, spiral up out of the earth. If dinosaurs were to appear in this prehistoric setting it would only seem natural. Thunder, lightening, rain poured over us as we came to a space nearly surrounded by needle-rocks. In and out of the space were two one-lane tunnels carved through the rock.

To conclude a magical day, we ate mahi tacos and wild-caught salmon and drank Riesling as we sat up on the 10th story of our Alex Johnson Hotel, gazing out the window with a full view of the city lights and more thunder, lightening, and pouring rain. The AJ Hotel is the tallest (by 7 stories) of any other structure in this part of the city, except the grain elevator over on Haines Blvd.

Saturday June 16, 2012

There's nothing quite as yummy as a home-grown Rapid City, South Dakota Farmers Market tomato after hiking a mile up the hill to Mt. Moriah, viewing Wild Bill Hickok, Calamity Jane, and Potato Creek John's gravesites, then meandering through a 120-year old neighborhood where folks on porches wave and say "howdy", then walk down 130 steps on a very steep green slope that leads back to the Old Gold mining Town of Deadwood, South Dakota. I'd spent an hour touring the old Adams house, learning history, upping my education while Richard went off to inspect the Video Poker machines at the Silverado Casino. The weather is perfect.

Monday June 18, 2012

Bye bye South Dakota at 7:15 this a.m. By 4:00 we'll be nearing Jackson Hole, Wyoming where, I recall tasting some mighty fine tartly tinged frozen yogurt at the end of a 918-mile day driving from Omaha to Jackson Hole. That was in late September 2009 with my baby sister, Jeannie. In the meantime, it's 85 windy degrees. Horses, cattle, pronghorn antelope look up from their yummy sage brush afternoon snacks and John Grisham drones on about a notorious Washington power broker, life in prison, life in Italy, CIA tricks and a possible upcoming assassination.

The Snyders are starting to ask, "Are we there yet." Robert Frost pops back in with "miles to go before I sleep."

A little poem to rival Frost:

We started a road trip last week
It's fun and adventure we seek
We've seen places that we'd never been
Some old friends but most of them kin.

Seen where all of them cattle is born
And quite a few acres of corn
Hiked hills, circled many a lake
And lots of their photos we take.

Soon we will be on our way home
Now all of our money's been blown
On fuel for our tummies and car
And all of them motels afar.

See you soon - but not in June.

JJ #7 Friday, June 22, 2012

At 6:35 a.m. we left Yellowstone behind - hoping to return someday, for more exploring of the be-jillions of accessible trails through the geysers, mudpots, hot springs and of course, that earthy fountain beside our home for three nights: Old Faithful Inn, Old Faithful itself. We spent all day Wednesday exploring many boardwalks around OF. On the way to Solitary geyser, the boardwalk gave way to a dirt and gravel trail, which the Rascal maneuvered bravely, only, alas, to be overcome by tree roots, logs, and rocks crossing our path. Always the trooper, Richard encouraged me to continue. He would wait, his Rascal basket loaded with water, cookies, and trail mix. We were both armed with cell phones.

Solitary Geyser is so named because every ten minutes or so, it squirts one mighty stream into the air. OF (Old Faithful) on the other hand (otoh), erupts every 90 minutes or so and continues erupting for about five minutes. So, like I'm mesmerized by Solitary when I notice a little sign pointing to Observation Point and I wonder what curious hiker would pass that up. Thirty minutes later, I phoned my beloved to say I'd be later. "Go have a good time", which he took to mean speed around in his Rascal, honking at little old ladies, flirting with young ladies, explaining the physics of geysers and the damage done by bark beetles to anyone who would listen, mostly foreigners.

I, on the other hand (otoh), sweated my way up the mountain north of OF and observed her from above. What a magnificent sight. Cheers from the 200 people sitting on wooden benches watching the eruption echoed up the slopes. After photographing a really cute chipmunk, three butterflies, and eight poor little caterpillars caught in some wicked spider's web, Richard and I talked by cell phone, then met, both with stories to tell. We ended the day with a healthy shot of Baileys and a cribbage game, which I allowed him to win. My mother would be proud, as she often told me, "Let the boy win." Ho ho ha ha ha.

We are now on Highway 85, heading for Oregon. Potatoes and cows line both sides of the road forever. Think cheeseburgers and fries. We're not sure where we'll be tonight - all part of our adventure. But we'll be at Matt and Kenda's in Silverton Saturday and Sunday nights, where the boys will reminisce about their hippie days and we're hoping (OK Matt and Kenda?) to wash a load of dusty, musty, sweaty clothes. On Monday we'll be visiting cousin Jim and his wife Diane and hopefully, their two daughters Courtney and Ashley at their home in Albany as we travel down to Crater Lake and Sue's Big Seven O. We hope you all get to come visit Yellowstone. Three days is not enough but it was a pretty good start. Three months would be better. Much love to all of you.

Blessings and love, Sue and The King

JJ #8 June 22, 2012

Early Friday morning (June 22) we left Yellowstone and headed west stopping in West Yellowstone, Montana for veggie omelets and cinnamon toast. We crossed borders in Montana, Idaho, then Oregon, and on a rainy evening found the little town of Pendleton (yes, the wool town) and booked the last room at America's Best Value Motel. We walked and rolled over to Como's Corner Bistro in the old part of town. Another salmon salad. This salmon topped a bed of stir-fried veggies and was surrounded by lots of yummy green things, topped with olive oil and balsamic. We liked it a lot.

June 23, 2012

Saturday morning, after a walk along the river, we were heading out of Pendleton, in our extremely dirty van, when we noticed a group of girls washing cars. Angels they were. We pulled into the parking lot and gave them the challenge of the day: a very dirty, bug-encrusted 2005 white van. This lively group of teens is the Five-time State Champion Pendleton High School

Dance Team. They let us take a picture of the team washing our car - all twelve of them.

June 25th

A misprint in last Journey Journal stated that Sue would be 70 years old today but it's not true. She is still 17.

Ah. Clean clothes.
Ah. Watermelon, cantaloupe, grapes, strawberries, blueberries, cherries, & yogurt for breakfast.
Ah. Potatoes broccoli and asparagus for dinner.
Ah. Walking around Oregon Botanical Gardens with Matt & Kenda.

Thank you M&K for the card that sings "Celebration." I've played it 50 times so far. And thanks for a wonderful day with you and thanks for being truly great people.

Ah. Homemade vegetarian chili, a gigantic salad, and the Oregon cousins: Diane & Jim and their daughter Ashley (daughter Courtney was at work at the U of O - boo hoo). A great day of reconnecting with Richard's cousin Jim and his beautiful family in their Albany home on 1-1/2 acres - wowee!!

Ah. Watching the rain again, on the drive from Albany, Oregon to Jo's Motel in Fort Klamath, just down the hill from Crater Lake. For $110 a night we have the "suite" which consists of a bedroom, bathroom, dining room, full kitchen, and a carport. We have a front door, a back door, and a door to the carport. We have five windows. There is no TV or Wi-Fi or telephone or a clock. How good can life get? Fort Klamath appears to be an "old hippie city" where everyone is laid back.

So, we arrived in Fort Klamath in the rain, checked in, and ate some more veggie chili, thanks to cousin Diane packing snacks for us. Tuesday it rained, it snowed, it hailed. Only the south entrance to Crater Lake National Park was open. All other roads were closed due to eight inches of snow falling on Monday. If Crater Lake is on your bucket list, plan to visit in late July or August. An average of 500 inches, yes, five hundred inches of snow falls each year. Crater is the deepest lake in America (1943 feet) and one of the nine deepest in the world. An explosive volcano formed the Crater 7,700 years ago. The lake is a clear deep crystal blue because there is no runoff, only rain and snow. No people pollution.

We drove as far as the Crater Lake Lodge, oohed and awed at the snow everywhere. We stopped off at the Visitor Center to watch a video about the formation of the lake: Apparently, the Indians in the area viewed the lake from the edge, never actually going down to the lake (there is only one way down and it's closed most of the year.) Perhaps that's one reason it remains so clean and crystal blue. Indians considered the lake sacred and gathered to meditate and perform ceremonies called "vision quests." American Explorers decided to create another wonderful National Park.

Wednesday June 27, 2012

Because Tuesday was a cold 35 degrees, we decided to stay one more night and see what could happen. Today was sunny and warm (55 up at the lake). We walked and rolled about ¼ mile along the lake, took lots of pictures, had tea and café mocha at the "Visitor Center and Gift Shop" then had a late lunch (Alaskan Salmon salad with marionberry vinaigrette dressing) at the old Lodge (built in 1909). Here's a challenge we thought up while waiting for our salad: try to say this five times: "cheesy - cheesish." We couldn't do it but had fun trying.

It's always fun talking with the young people working in the National Parks: they come from all over the world. Our waiter today, Tom, lived in France as a youngster, then Chicago, Arizona, and now spends his time working in different Parks. Our hostess came from Romania. And of course, we've met kids from all over the U.S., most of them working during summer vacation from college. Any of you grandkids interested? Google "summer jobs in National Parks" and check it out.

Tomorrow morning we'll head south, maybe even go home. Or maybe we'll stay somewhere else tomorrow night. We'll see how far Sue can drive on a Starbucks Frappaccino. We're starting to miss our little backyard and our family and our friends and the daily routine thingy. It's like the song. There's No Place Like Home.

Much love to all. Sue and Richard

Friday, June 29, 2012

P.S. Written Wednesday evening.

It's our last night here. We need dinner. I check the little refrigerator in our "suite." We have a bit of Diane's veggie chili, ½ corn cut off the cob, a salad with raw veggies in it, 4 ounces of tofu, and a few drops of olive oil. I fry up everything, including the salad. I serve it in a cereal bowl for Richard and a coffee cup for me. My beloved lifts a forkload to his mouth, chews, and swallows. "It's not bad," he says. "It tastes like a lot of things we've had before."

I can't stop laughing. It reminds me of something my almost 48-yr. old son said when he was four. He sat at the dinner table, looked at his dinner, then looked up at me. He squinted his eyes and said, "Is this one of your 'sperments?"

Friday, June 29, 2012

P.S.S. It's 5:30 a.m. I've been up for an hour. It's great to be home. We drove 780 miles yesterday, from Fort Klamath below Crater Lake to our little purple house in Orange. We kept saying yesterday, "What a wonderful trip we've had, we're so lucky, where will we go next?" (Sept. 22 we leave for a cruise through the Panama Canal.)

P.S.S.S. Thank you and many blessings to all of you for reading our little journey journal. Thank you for the communications and replies we received from so many of you. Thank you for the encouragement. We are blessed beyond measure to have such a beautiful bunch of family and friends.

Panama Canal Cruise

New Home September 2012

HTTP = Here's The Tangential Plan

Dear Family and Friends,

We're heading south tomorrow . . . all the way to the Panama Canal. We'll be aboard Celebrity's Millennium for 15 nights, visiting a bunch of historical sights along the way. We plan to eat, sleep, swim, and, if all goes according to calculations, it's about time Sue beat Richard at cribbage. Will let you know.

We'll spend four nights in Ole Town Coral Gables, Florida, head to the Dallas, Texas area for grandson, Billy and Christina's wedding and arrive back in Old Town Orange mid-October, or so. Will let you know.

Peace and Blessings, Sue and The King

Sunday, September 23, 2012

Dear Family and Friends,

We are asea, on our way to the Panama Canal, which we will reach Tuesday October 2. In the meantime . . .

Ah, for a spiritual transcendence of consciousness. That is, perhaps the number one reason we all love time off from our usual routines, vacations, cruises, meditation, down time. So, what the sages of the ages were telling us, "Resist not evil, practice nonviolence, practice inaction, Be still and know that I am God," is the lesson we are learning.

Instead of vigorous morning swims followed by line-dancing, power walks on deck 11, and much anticipated romance, Richard scoots about in his rascal collecting breakfast fruit and yogurt, and Bautista-- our stateroom attendant--who says, "It is my pleasure to treat you famously" – delivers hot tea to room 7137. Sue is resting quietly after her first of five acupuncture treatments and anticipating the first of five massages, due to that lower back thingy that drags her down from time to time.

Spirits of all are high, thanks to the power of Laughter Yoga and continuous streams of "ho ho ha ha ha" reducing pain while raising levels of peace love and joy. Soon, Sue will be walking without her two canes, swimming and line-dancing. Ziplining in Costa Rica may have to wait for the next trip. Thank you dear Peggy J. for delivering us to Pier B in San Diego and thank you dear Anna for watching over the little purple house on Walnut Avenue. Thanks to all of you for healing thoughts.

Shalom As-Salamu Alaykun
Blessings of Peace, R&S

Blog #2 Panama Cruise

Tuesday September 25, 2012

Greetings from Puerto Vallarta after a beautiful lightening storm and much delight in the cool wetness of an otherwise hot and humid location. Good news: Sue is down to part-time one-cane only, after two acupuncture treatments and one message. After tomorrow's hot-rock massage, she'll be twirling that thing in the air as she line dances. GREAT NEWS!! After nearly 20 years of losing cribbage games to King Richard, clearly using her new strategy of focusing on lessons in the book, "The Art of Racing in the Rain" by Garth Stein, Sue has, at long last, beat Richard at cribbage. Life is good.

Happy 21st Birthday to granddaughter Courtney, mother of our first great-grandson, two-month old Sylas Caden Toreli. Wish you could be here to celebrate with us. We send our love and hugs and 5 million kisses to both of you.

Yesterday's view of Cabo San Lucas from deck 10 was stunning. Imagine a resort in full swing. Meredith and Blair kayaking around the peninsula; Dee and Mary Jo searching for Mexican earrings, Dave photographing everything in sight; and us lounging about. My friend "Lil Sis" Cheryl and I spent four days together here in 2004 where I narrowly missed crashing into the rocks on a borrowed kayak, which would have been tough explaining to my principal when I'd called in sick for four days.

We have met people from all over the world on this cruise. The crew hails from India, Indonesia, The Philippines, England, Jamaica and Russia. Lots of cruisers here from Florida, England, British Columbia, Quebec, Maryland, and Georgia. Every single person on this ship offers us assistance as Richard rascals and Sue hobbles along. I told Richard this afternoon, in a moment of whimsy, "I wish everyone on the planet could experience the kindness, the food, the safety that we take for granted." Wouldn't the world be a wonder-filled place? Ah, peace at last.

Blessings of peace Shalom As-Salamu Alaykun to all of you. R & S
P.S. To son John, get thee to an acupuncturist, mom will foot the bill, however many treatments it takes.

P.S.S. What is acupuncture? Traditional Chinese medicine which balances the qi (chi) energy, allowing qi to flow freely which restores balance to pain-riddled bodies. The treatment is pain-free, even relaxing.

Blog #3 Panama Canal

Greetings from Costa Rica!! Sunday, September 30, 2012. Last Thursday: imagine sitting up on Deck 11 at 3:45 a.m. gazing at Orion, the Pleiades, Sirius, and Jupiter through binoculars when Suman from Indonesia, the night maintenance crewman comes up to check on us. Richard gives him an astronomy lesson and encourages him to use our binoculars. To say Suman was "wowed" is putting it lightly. He was most amazed to learn of the Pleiades, known to Native Americans as Pigs in Heaven and to the Pagans as The Seven Sisters.

Suman told us that he'd checked his Facebook earlier and was feeling sad. He'd left his fiancée behind in Indonesia for the chance to work on Celebrity Cruise ships for a few years. He is to be married in December when he goes home for vacation. "Now," he said, "I feel 'appy! Very 'appy!"

Represented on this ship are over 800 crewmembers from more than 68 countries, most of them bilingual, usually their native language and English. They've been trained to put their differences aside and to concentrate on their commitment to give the best service possible.

"The purpose of life is happiness; the way to happiness
is through service."

So says the Delhi Lama. Here's a thought: what if we made all politicians work together on a cruise ship for six months? Mitt and Barach could spend their time sorting through recyclables, Hilary and Condalesa would bus tables, while Paul Ryan and Joe Biden teach line dancing, etc. Good idea?

Friday September 28:

The oldest city in Spanish-America, Antigua (antique) Guatemala, at 5000 feet seemed the best place to build the Convent Conception in the early 1540's, which was destroyed in the 1783 earthquake. The town was built around the convent and is inhabited by Mayans whom we saw walking along the roads carrying huge stacks of firewood, babies, even small trees. A few people own mopeds, and fewer yet own cars. Most folks use the bus service when they need to go the distance.

Our tour guide Karla remarked, "I don't need a car, I use the bus. I have a friend with a car who takes me to the market." The children in Guatemala who do attend the public school wear uniforms; classes are from 7:30 a.m. to noon. About 60% of the population speaks Castilian Spanish; most of the other 40% speaks one, or several of 19 Mayan dialects. Literacy is not yet a high priority here.

As I write this, we are gazing out the window from the 5th Deck, in Café al Bacio, watching the occasional hatch zip by. We are docked, for the day, at Puerto Quetzal, Guatemala. One of the crew confided in us that the president of Guatemala is aboard, having lunch in the Millennium Casino. About a dozen young camera-clad reporters are also aboard, snapping pictures of everything and every one.

Five friendly people from India and I were stuck in Deck 1 elevator for a brief time yesterday. When the doors finally opened, Madam Chief Housekeeper advised us to wait while she went for help. The obviously married couple in the corner began to argue (language is no barrier when tone of voice is involved). She wanted to get over to a different elevator. He disagreed. Loudly. Holding my open hands out, middle fingers to thumbs, I began a slow mellow "Aaahhhooohhhmmm." Two others joined me in de-escalating the tension. Then a miracle happened: the elevator across from us landed on Deck 1 and the doors opened. All of us ran over to it and hopped in, laughing all the way up to the 10th Deck. Ho ho ha ha ha!!!

Sunday September 30:

For a fruit-grower aficionado like Richard, today was heaven. We're in Puntarenas, Costa Rica where mangoes, bananas, sugar cane, coffee, papaya grow along the roads. Roy, our bus driver, stopped often, hopped off the bus with his machete and whacked off various fruits from the trees, then Angel, our tour guide educated us about the abundance here in Costa Rica. Does this sound familiar: as inhabitants of this country become more educated and more into technology, they are less willing to work in the fields. Now the less-educated Nicaraguans come here to pick the main exports of Costa Rica: coffee beans.

Upon returning from a hot, humid, and sweaty walk 'n roll down the pier and through a huge native craft fair, we were greeted by some of the crew with iced washcloths. I wiped off my arms and legs while crewmember Alberto rushed over to cool off King Richard's feet and legs. Is that because he knows the name of almost every crewmember he has met? I often stand and watch the way the world wants to be of service to him. He's such a love magnet.

After four acupuncture treatments, and four massages (including a seaweed wrap), Sue is her normal energetic self. The crutches have been returned to the medical center and the canes stowed in the corner of Cabin 7137. Dr. Julian and Chloe are miracle workers. Life is great!

Peace Shalom As-Salamu Alaykun Puda Vita
with Love from The King and Sue

Blog #4 Panama Canal

Tuesday, October 2, 2012

The best way to cruise through the Panama Canal: Deck 11, front of ship, open deck, me tucked under the slanted windows where other bodies shaded me from the sun. Any 5-year old would have thought of it. As soon as I slid under the rails and sat on the deck floor, 39 other forward thinking folks followed, several of my East Indian buddies, bowing to me with "Namaste" which means, in Hindi, "The Spirit in me honors the Spirit in you." Cool, huh? To top off the wonderfulness of it all, I had a cup of tea made with Mother's MY-Tea-Leaf Green Jasmine tea. How much better can life get? Meanwhile, Richard is spending 75 minutes with Chloe, who gives a dynamite massage.

The first set of locks, Mira Flores Locks, was a miracle to witness. Most of the 2100 cruisers and lots of the 800-plus crew peered over the front and sides of the ship and out windows of the Oceanview Café. It all began about 6:00 a.m. Our friend Dave was out on deck at 4:30 to get a good spot. In order to get a cruise ship or a container ship through the canal it takes about ten hours and 52 million gallons of fresh water from Lake Guton. There are three huge locks on Lake Guton.

Between 38 and 40 ships go through each day, at the cost of $500 for a small yacht or $300,000 for a ship like ours. On a "bad" day, the canal brings in $3 million; most days it brings in $6-$7 million. Keep in mind that the minimum wage in Panama is $1.55. Folks who work for the canal earn about $8 an hour. The cost of gasoline here is about what it is in California - around $4.00 a gallon. There are 9,200 people who work for the Panama Canal Association (PCA); these are the high wage earners. Sometime in 2014, the new canal will be ready for use. Current locks are about 110 x 1000 feet. The new ones will be 200 x 2000 feet, nearly twice the size. Some of the container ships have to wait several days for a place in line. Adding a new canal will make things much more efficient.

Our Train ride from Colon (on the Atlantic side) back to Panama City on the Pacific side amazed us all. An hour-long trip across the Lake Guton, beside quaint villages, the women's prison, and the men's prison where former bad-guy president Noriega resides, none of these are air-conditioned. This is not a land where we could exist without our huge a/c units.

Our guide's name is Errol. He told us that his mother, like many of women of that era, was in love with Errol Flynn and named her son after the handsome movie star. "However," he said, "He was famous and I am not. He was rich; I am poor. He is dead; I am alive." While attending a university in the U.S. he fell in love with a beautiful American woman, married her, then was drafted into the U.S. Army, and served during the days of Viet Nam. They now live in the beautiful and thriving country of Panama with their three lovely children and five grandchildren.

Panama has no military. Errol told us that when a country has an army, it has a general and the guy with the weapons is tougher and tries to rule over the president. Interesting. He also told us the reason the Pan-American Highway (also know here as Dios Mio Highway) has never been completed is because the drug runners would have an easier time getting drugs from Columbia to the U.S. and Mexico. In case you were wondering.

Thursday, October 4, 2012

We are overwhelmed with gratitude for the privilege of living in North America. South America's climate is unbearable, poverty is everywhere, and we found that any time we stepped off a tour bus we were surrounded with vendors dangling jewelry or tablecloths or tee shirts in front of us. Tour guides told us to not make eye contact because then the vendors think you'll buy something.

We spent today in Cartagena, Columbia, where independence was won from Spain on 11-11-11-11. That is, November 11, 1911 at 11:00 a.m. Cartagena is actually a group of islands where the shipyards are loaded with thousands of containers waiting to go on ships to all parts of the world. Some are labeled COSCO.

For the next two days we'll be hanging out at the pool reading, talking with our 2100 new friends and eating more of the yummy food always available here. The skies have been generally cloudy, not good for stargazing. We're hoping for some good viewing before this is over. Sunday at 7:00 a.m. we'll land in Miami, Florida where we'll spend four days before heading to Dallas for our grandson, Billy and Christina's wedding, which will be on the 13th. We're hoping to fly on American Airlines, if our daughter, Dianna, still has a job there. With all the layoffs, things are iffy. Ho ho ha ha ha. Another adventure awaits.

Friday, October 5, 2012

Just heard the fourth of five lectures by the incredible Dr. Harley Thronson, the astrophysicist from NASA in West Virginia. We viewed the video that showed 3% of our galaxy with its nebulas and dust clouds and even how NGC 4438 collided with its neighbor NGC 4435, stripping it of much of its dust and gas. It's not always easy to tell whether a star is coming or going. And, from our Astronomy Magazine, we now know how to find Sirius, the brightest star in our sky. Orion's belt points north to Sirius. In case you were wondering . . . No kidding, go outside in the early morning and look. Stargazing has not been the best in South America, as the sky is so often clouded over.

Thanks to all of you for responding to our emails. We appreciate your thoughts and questions. We're paying 75 cents a minute to use the ship's WIFI and it takes about ten minutes to get online. Ho ho ha ha ha.
Much love and many blessings. Pura Vida, Shalom, As-Salamu Alaykun,

Richard and Sue

Blog #5 Panama and Beyond

We're in Miami Airport waiting for flight 527 to Dallas. We're leaving Florida a day earlier than expected. We visited the Science Museum and Planetarium, Fairchild Botanical Gardens, and the fabulous Fruit and Spice Park in Homestead (highly recommended by fellow Rare Fruit Growers Roger and Shirley and others). We've driven all over Miami and Coral Gables, waded in the warm waters of Key Biscayne Bay, stocked up on munchies at Whole Food Market, and lifted the Rascal in and out of the rental van countless times (with the assistance of countless strong men).

Traveling with Richard is a huge lesson in learning to ask for help. The heat and humidity in Miami would be pretty tough getting used to . . . we didn't. When I was younger and stronger I got that Rascal out of vehicles all by myself. Now I go for help.

We've met people from all over this world on this trip and only met one grouch: he thought the sandwich makers on the Millennium should work faster and give him more French fries. We wanted to ask him if he'd heard of the Seven Virtues. Surely one of them is Patience. But I think another of the virtues is MYOB. We did.

We hear autumn has come to Dallas. Low 70's for this weekend. Grandson Billy and Christina will be wed this Saturday, October 13th, in a friend's backyard, right outside Dallas, at 3:00 p.m. If we can swing it, we'll be on the 9:30 p.m. flight back to Orange County Saturday evening, arriving in OC at 10:30. Otherwise, lots of iffy flights on Sunday and Monday. Ho ho ha ha ha. We may be laughing a lot.

Friday, October 12, 2012

We are safely ensconced in the Fairfield Marriot just a few miles beyond the Dallas Airport. We've visited with daughter Dianna, son-in-law Bob, granddaughter Jennifer (who works in this hotel and got us the amazing room rate) granddaughter-to-be Christina (wedding tomorrow), great granddaughters Claire (7) and great granddaughter Joselyn (almost 3), and grandson Billy. Tonight the whole family will gather downstairs at our hotel for a pizza-salad-other munchies party to celebrate us all. We'll get to meet Christina's parents from Del Rio, Texas.

Last evening we attended Claire's softball game. What a joy to watch dozens of little girls in pink, swinging at the ball, sometimes hitting it, running after balls and bases. The teamwork and confidence in this group of future teachers and politicians and librarians and athletes is way up there among must-see sights on this tour.

And so we're off to meet another grandkid, Aubrey (Claire's mommy and Billy's former wife and still a grandkid in our hearts) for breakfast. Such an amazing life we lead. Thank you for all your emails and good thoughts. We are blessed to have such a beautiful family and bunches of friends.

Much love and many blessings
Pura Vida
Shalom
As-Salamu
Alaykun
Velle Dobre

Dear Family and friends,

Our cruise was wonderful, Florida was pretty good, and Billy and Christina's wedding in Texas was beautiful and amazing and so much fun. We're loving being back home in California for a be-jillion reasons. And now for some news. We have lots of friends who live in The Woods, Laguna Woods - Linda, Lee and Sheri, Tom and Diane, Thea, Helene, Cheryl, Kathie and Jack - and more. We are often there for parties, theatrical performances, dinners, Jack's baseball games, swimming, even Laguna Woodstock. Visiting friends Kathie and Jack in early September, I remarked that if we had a view of Aliso Creek, as they do, and the great floor plan they have, we'd consider living in The Woods.

So, like we've just cruised through the Panama Canal and visited Colon on the Millennium, when I drifted off to Cabin 7137 for some R&R. I checked email. Jack and Kathie reported that a home, just like theirs, across the creek was for sale. "It'll go fast," they tell us. "Shall we put a down payment on it for you?" Wow!

So, like Richard is on the ship somewhere, but I don't know where. So, like I email K&J and say "Sure. If you like it, we'll like it." By the time we docked in Miami, there were 10 (yes TEN) backup offers!!!!!! To make a long story short, we bought it, sight unseen, and after living in the little purple house in Orange for 27 years (17 for Richard) we're moving on. Escrow is to close sometime around November 8th. Before the move, we're replacing the brand new carpet with brand new wood flooring. Then, we'll be living at 907 Ronda Sevilla in condo "O" (as in Oprah) Laguna Woods, Ca. 92637. We plan to be completely moved in by December 1st.

Our little purple house in Orange will have the perfect new owners, as soon as they know the little purple house is for sale. More news as it happens.

Love, Sue and Richard

Iceland Cruise 2013 August 26

To: Family and friends
From: Sue Snyder, Travel Enthusiast
Subject: Terra Incognita

So, like my friend Jane Carter (yes, that Jane, the famous trumpet player, composer, and music-of-all kinds coach) phoned one day last June and invited me on a cruise ship that would take us from Amsterdam to NYC via Norway, Iceland, Greenland, Newfoundland, and Nova Scotia. Of course, I said "no" because I can't leave Richard for three weeks and so much going on and we're heading for Hawaii right after your trip ends and etc. etc etc. Lots of good excuses, right?

Naturally, Richard encouraged me to go. I still said, "I can't." Then I got to thinkin'. What if I'm on my deathbed in a few years, I'd be saying, "Holy Sh--! I should have gone on that cruise." Not words your grandkids should hear as you exit the planet.

Then a bunch of our lovely friends (thank you, you know who you are) offered to keep an eye on Richard if I went. Several of them are planning their casseroles right now. And Dan and Lisa promise to visit several times a week, to bring food, to (wow!) pick up things, and to see that my beloved Richard is well-cared for and doesn't get too lonely. Of course, as soon as I'm out of town he's heading to Reno for a couple of days. And I said, "You go, babe."

So, Jane and I fly from LAX to Amsterdam via O'Hare on Monday, August 26th. Maybe we'll send a few stories about our adventures. We shall return on Sunday, September 15th.

Much love, Sue

Possible Subtitles for Upcoming Adventure Stories:

1. Thelma Jane and Louise Sue last seen heading north.
2. Laughter experts spread peace, love, and joy throughout Arctic
3. Wannabe travel writers blog for free
4. Famous composer and buddy write #1 hit musical about Iceland
5. Emergency: Holland America Eurodam Cruise Ship runs out of Kale
6. Stand by for a R.A.M. (Really awesome memoir)

Blog #1 August 26 – 29

Cool Idea #1 – Gained from September S.O.M. Magazine, scientific research by Waldman and Newberg:

"Using meditation, affirmative thoughts, and gratitude, you can train your brain to become habitually optimistic. Activity decreases in your right frontal lobe, and the fear circuits in your brain can actually begin to shrink."

(See honey? I'm not crazy. ☺) This is really cool to know when you're on the Holland America with 2000+ passengers of varying degrees of optimistic outlooks on life.

So, that explains my years of saying, thinking, and believing "I am whole complete and perfect" and "I love my life" and "I am grateful for everything." My fear circuits lie dormant waiting for a negative thought to arise, but guess what? It ain't gonna happen.

Flying over the Atlantic Monday/Tuesday: Sunset: 8:00 p.m. Sunrise 11:00 p.m. (California time). Flying over UK, arriving Amsterdam 9:15 a.m. Tiny bit of sleep on plane. Then, waiting for Holland American Transport to Eurodam Cruise Ship, Cabin 8088, munching Trader Joe's roasted coconut chips. Lots of droopy-eyed, bed-haired travelers lounging on benches, no doubt jealous of our TJCC (coconut chips). Promise of transport at 11:00 a.m. Richard's watch says 1:30 a.m. California time. Confusion shall be abated with more nourishment, a bit of sleep, shower, and clean clothes. We repeat: "traveling is fun, traveling is fun, traveling is fun." If attitude slips, refer to "Cool Idea #1.

Tuesday afternoon:

Leaving Amsterdam on Holland America's Eurodam, many Amsterdamians waving from the shore. Many wind farms in the bay of Amsterdam. Architecture a mixture of very old and ultra modern. At last, boarding ship. At last, a nap in Cabin 8088 which is interrupted three times with delivery of baggage. Ho ho ha ha ha.

Wednesday August 28

A day at sea. An early-morning walk around Deck 3 for an hour. Eating, reading, a lecture on Norway's natural history, another lecture, this time on places to see in Norway. Dinner with Joan and Bruce, Aida and Marvin, Jane and me in main dining room. Formal night. Black jeans, shawl, earrings. Nighttime entertainment: Jane and I sat in the Queen's box watching seven-piece orchestra and singing quartet and four dancers. One hour of beautiful singing and dancing. To bed at midnight.

Thursday August 29

We docked by 7:00 a.m. Breakfast at 8:00. I took off on my own to walk through the City of Stavanger, Norway from 8:30 - 11:00. Beautiful Kirk (church) park and lake. Took lots of pictures of swans, ducks, and gulls. Walking through Olde Towne, noticing a salg with ½ pris shoes. Many wedding gowns and books in Norwegian Fretex Army, which we call the Salvation Army. The streets are made of Rascal-challenging cobblestones. The children's playground is made of brightly painted pipes, old rubber tires, and a giant beach ball-filled area. The kids just bounce across it. Also for their enjoyment there is a huge pile of sand. I headed over to la café François (across from F.A.).

At la café François I asked for a cup 'o tea. "Do you take U.S. money?" The barista said, "Oh, yes. Tea is $65." Then a handsome young customer chimed in, "No, that's $55." I said in the U.S. it's about $2 or $3 for a cup of tea. Laughter. "But you are in Norway. The most expensive place in the world." We settled on $4 but they didn't know how to make change. More smiles. I handed him a $5 bill and said, "Keep the change, please." More smiling and nods all around.

BTW, it was the best tea since our Chinese nephew, William, came over from China two years ago and gifted us with some real tea. As I enjoyed the tea, four Brits settled down at a nearby table - two retirement-age couples. Three of them pulled out their iPhone thingys and the fourth flipped through his map book. They were pretty quiet.

In Norway extra letters are added to words wherever possible: as in "bakery" becomes "bakervarer" and "chiropractic clinic" becomes "kiropraktisk klinikk" and "bedriftsleger siomannsleger" remains a mystery. I returned to ship at 11:15 to join the group bus trip to Utstein Island and the Utstein Monastery. To get there by bus, we traveled under the sea for about two miles in a tunnel that the government had originally opposed because of the staggering cost: $1 billion. That is, they opposed it until they were given a ferry ride across the bumpy water from Utstein Island to Stavanger on a very windy day. After most of them experienced severe seasickness, they agreed to build the tunnel. It was paid for with the people's tax money. Now, it is supported by fines paid by speeding tickets, which run $400. Not using a seat belt? That's $300. These fines now support the maintenance of the tunnel to the tune of about $1 million/year.

According to Heidi, our tour guide, the people here pay 40% of their salaries to the government. Norway now has enough in its "kitty" to pay for all medical expenses and all education and road maintenance and government salaries, etc. for the next three generations. There is no national debt.

Friday afternoon was amazing. Unemployment is at 3%. She also said that everyone earns approximately the same salary, there is not a lot of difference in the high-paying and low-paying jobs. Executives do their own paperwork; everyone is responsible for his/her job. Most people begin work at 8:00 a.m. and everyone has gone home at 4:00 p.m. (except bus drivers). No one is rich. A dinner out with wine will run about $280 in American dollars. Families don't go out for meals. No one here is obese, as in some other places in the world because all are very active and eat healthful food. However, fast food restaurants are about to land. We'll see how that affects the population. Heidi said children are carried on their first hike at three months and by three years they hike alongside their families.

Note: There are no lawsuits. It is not allowed. Everyone is responsible for him/herself. The major industries here are oil and fishing. When you retire at 67 your pension will be 67% of your last paycheck. It rains here 265 days a year. August temperatures run about 60 degrees high in the summer and 37 degrees high in the winter months. She says it's not cold here; you just have to put on more clothes. Because of the long summer days, blueberries and strawberries are the best in the world. About 60 languages are spoken here; many cultures exist side-by-side, most are open-minded.

Utstein Kloster is an old monastery turned tourist attraction. After our tour of the church and other buildings we were treated to an organ recital by Ole (he pronounced it O-lee). My heart melted when he played Edvard Grieg's Last Spring. It was that feeling you get when you first fall in love or when you look at someone you've been married to for 18 years and 5 months and 18 days. Thank you Ole. After shaking myself out of a deep trance, we were served tea, coffee, and waffles. Or, for us gf avoiders, tea. The weather today was what they call Scotch Mist. I said in So. Cal. we call it a storm. Life is totally and awesomely amazing. More news as it happens.

Peaceful blessings, As-Salamu Alaykun, Shalom,

Sue

Arctic Blog #2

Cool Idea #2: As I counted the happy faces in the Lido Restaurant on Deck 9 yesterday, I wondered why there were not more. So many couples eating in silence: he torn from an unarguably vital time in the baseball world and she waiting for attention and romance. So I got to thinking about the great thinkers of the world and think what they would think:

1. The Buddha reminded us to have high expectations and low attachment.
2. Deepak Chopra would say meditate.
3. Rev. Jim: Edit your thoughts.
4. R. Snyder: Don't believe everything you think.
5. Bhai Kanhaiya, the Sikh hero: The light of God shines from every soul.
6. Dali Lama: The purpose of life is happiness. Happiness is attained through service, as in the Crew on the HAE. (Holland American Eurodam)

The crew seems very happy (high expectations, low attachment) even though most of them have been away from their families for several months. The crew is mainly Indonesian and Filipino. The two guys who clean up after Jane and me, Fredrik and Budi, are quite personable. Fredrick said he saw his wife and three kids one month ago and will not see them again for the next 11 months. Budi has a lovely wife but no children. Bernie, who cleans the pool deck, has a wife and two children. He taught elementary school for a few years but his $300 a week salary would not stretch far enough. He will see his family in three months.

Friday, August 30, 2013

Left Eurodam at 9:00-ish and walked for 2-1/2 hours through a cool sprinkly Bergen. The only times I stopped was in the big Kirk (church) for a 5-minute break and for a few photo ops. As I walked along, I was drawn to the names of streets in Bergen and began to write them down. (See list below.) There are three cruise ships in port at the moment, all of them just for the day. We'll be traveling across the sea for the next two days with lots of time for early morning deck-walks, Jacuzzi time, reading time, writing important blogs.

Our excursion bus took us out to Edvard Grieg's Troldhaugen, which is the home he and his wife, Nina, built on the fjord in 1884. They gave it that name because of the trolls that lived on the hillside. Norway is full of 'em. It's a typical Olde Orange two-story craftsman style home with lots of windows to let in the light and views of the surrounding forest. Nature kept Grieg inspired. Down the hill from the house, Grieg had a "man cave" built so he could get away to a quiet spot for composing. We visited the museum full of pictures and sheets of original music. The highlight, of course, was the one-hour piano concert in the Grieg Concert Hall, overlooking the fjord.

Normally, Friday afternoon traffic is a bit heavy for a few minutes, but this Friday there was an accident on the road that went through a big tunnel. We were on the only other road and as everything backed up, we were 90 minutes late getting back to the ship. Our tour guide phoned the ship, explained the problem, and lucky for us, they kept the doors open. We cruise on.

Saturday, August 31, 2013.

The Lido restaurant was crowded this morning so I sat with Hines and his wife, Mika, living in Holland, originally from Switzerland. Both are retired German teachers. She is thin and fragile from osteoporosis and wears a neck brace. I cheered them up by pointing out the birds flying through the strong storm we were experiencing. We talked of skiing, hiking, teaching, traveling, and our kids. Later today, as I sat reading J.K Rowling's Casual Vacancy, she walked by and patted me on the head. Joy cometh on tippy-toes.

This morning's lecture was titled "Iceland, Land & People." Dr. Jon Sigurdsson presented stories and slides. In Iceland, when you come to a red light you'll notice that the red light is in the shape of a heart. The idea is for people to think loving thoughts and drive politely. Since the installation of these heart-shaped red lights, there have been fewer accidents. He explained that in Iceland, everyone goes by his or her first name. If your name is Richard and you name your baby Sue, her name will be Sue Richardson (son of Richard). It would be laughable to call a person his last name. He said that trolls live in the cracks of volcanic rock and they often come out to eat people. One very wise person grew giant marshmallows (at this time we viewed a picture of bales of hay wrapped in white plastic). Now, he added, the trolls eat fewer tourists. One of his pictures showed a village completely covered in volcanic ash from the 1997 eruption. Today at 5:00 in the Explorer's Lounge on Deck 2, we enjoyed an hour of Adagio - beautiful slow music on violin and piano.

Sunday, September 1, 2013

Up at 6:15. Walked on the inner decks and stairs. Outside doors closed due to stormy weather. Two more lectures by Jon Sigurdsson with amazing pictures of him, his wife, and young son hiking and photographing the 2010 volcanic eruption of Eyjafjallajokull on Iceland, which lasted for five weeks and sent most of its smoke to Europe, closing airports all over the world. His second lecture - with slide show of the town we'll be visiting tomorrow: Reykjavik, the capitol of Iceland.

Names of some of the streets I walked yesterday
in Bergen, Norway

1. Nikolarkirkeallmennince
2. Vagsallinenningen
3. Smastrandgaten
4. Olev Kyrresgate
5. Allehelgens
6. Ostre Skostredet
7. Bankgaten
8. Sparebankgaten
9. Bankgaten
10. Sparebankgoten
11. Domkirkeplassen
12. Brendenbecksmauet
13. Ovre Karskirkeallmenningen - near Krok og Krinkel bokcafe (bakery)
14. Lille Ovregaten
15. Vetrlidsallmenningen
16. Ovregaten
17. Lodin Lepps gate (near Gitzi Formalwear Shop)
18. Bryggestredet
19. Draggsallmenninge

Much love and many blessings from your traveling wife, sister, aunt, grandma, great-aunt, great-grandma, friend, Sue

P.S. Because it is VERY expensive to read my email, I don't always respond. But, I really appreciate your responses. I am so grateful for the life I lead, so grateful for each one of you.

Arctic Blog #3

September 3, 2013.

Happy Labor Day to all you in the far-away U.S.A.
Editor's note: Corrections on Blog #2. In Norway, pensions are 50% of usual pay, not 67% and we could not find any heart-shaped red lights in Iceland.

Dr. Deb Sandella (article in S.O.M.) reminded me this morning:

"The brain doesn't distinguish between real
and imagined experience."

So, imagine being blasted head-on with ice crystals in 40 mph winds, leaning backwards into the wind without falling, and trying to control my little purple-flowered umbrella. In and out of our Ford 4-wheeer several times to hike down volcanic ash trail to gorgeous waterfalls sprouting out of--what else- volcanic rock. My brain had a hard time realizing we were really slippin' and slidin' on an Icelandic glacier, being driven by a daring young man who looked like my dear son John. It was a wild ride that probably won't happen again for a while but a great adventure.

Iceland is a beautiful place where I really could live, maybe. Crystal-clear ice-cold water is piped into all the houses. Another pipe brings in hot thermal water from volcanoes. Icelanders get to take really long hot showers. Homes are heated by hot-water pipes running under the houses. All food is grown organically here, in greenhouses. At three months old, babies are taken on their first hike and at three years, they are walking the trails.

(Note to Grandma Sue's grandkids: "In Iceland, the kids don't complain about forced marches.")

Sheep dot the hillside, roaming free until their day of doom. Lunch for us today was veggie soup, but much to the surprise of my squeamish vegetarian stomach, chunks of lamb floated in the soup. Fortunately, the cook was able to find a bowl of vegetarian soup made with a tomato base. Just for me.

Electricity here is generated by the plethora of waterfalls. We drove by miles and miles of volcanic rock and ash. Several volcanoes are on the verge of eruption. GPS warns researchers when a volcano is getting ready to blow and that could mean a week or 20 days or a year, and sometimes 20 years. It's just hard to tell but when a volcano begins pouring out molten lava; homes in its path are vacated until it's all over. In 2010 several farms were buried 10-15 meters deep in ash - which turned out to be wonderful for plants (in much smaller doses), not so for whomever dusts the furniture.

Today's Adventure: Golden Circle and Horse Show. Bus picked us up at 8:30 for a multi-adventuresome ride (on streets this time). We visited the Thingvellir, Geysir, and Gullfoss waterfalls. Also we saw the geothermal area of Krysuvik and then hiked the beautiful lava fissures of Pingvellir National Park while photographing its thick carpet of moss, lichen, and wildflowers. We visited Law Rock where the Vikings held court and where the country's laws were recited to the masses below. Law Rock is also where women were often punished when people were cured or when they died because it was always their fault. (In either case, it was witchcraft.) Things have changed a bit since 930 A.D.

Just north of Selfoss, we hiked up a little hill to view the Kerid Crater Lake, which is beautiful, deep, and pretty small - nothing like Oregon's Crater Lake. When I tripped and fell at Kerid, I was far enough from the edge that my new bruises are just a reminder of my good luck. So, later, I'm rushing back to the bus after photographing the really stunning Gullfoss Falls on the river Hvita about 47 miles northeast of Reykjavik. Why? It's raining again. My tiny purple-flowered umbrella is deflecting some of the downpour. I'm wearing my purple Nordstrom Rack fur-lined waterproof boots and my $4.74 army raincoat (a recent purchase from Corporal Don's garage sale in Laguna Hills), and Ruthe's thermals and ski pants.

Then, I see a little lady sitting in a wheelchair. As I hold my purple-flowered umbrella over her, she tells me her husband is way down the hill taking pictures. It was sunny when he parked her with a great view of the falls. She is from Holland. Her name is Lilla. She is regaining her speech after having had a stroke. Hanging on the back of her wheelchair is an orange bag, which contains her magical lime-green heavy-duty plastic poncho. I unfurl it as she holds the purple-flowered umbrella and we both laugh as I wrap her up and tuck it around her tiny feet. Then I ran for the bus. I hope her husband recognizes her. In the end, I'm a little wetter but Lilla's a lot dryer. It's a good trade.

We were fed a great lunch of mushroom soup and wild-caught Icelandic salmon with rice and greens. We sat with Peter, a National Guard helicopter pilot and his young Chinese wife, June. He talked of his time in Afghanistan and his rescue duties during the Katrina disaster. They live in a far-off place called Maryland.

When I had my salad this evening, Barbara and her husband Al, from Manhattan in NYC, recommended dozens of things to do next week when Jane and I spend a few days there. Cruisers are so friendly. People are beginning to smile more. They must have read the great thinkers' thoughts.

OK. Last story: Today's bus driver did not speak much English and I can only say Godan Morgan and Godan nott, and Ja in Icelandic so when I asked him about the gold Olympic medal hanging from his mirror, I think he said "Inga ran the fastest 5k" somewhere that started with a P and is pronounced as vf. I think he asked me if I ever ran a 5k. "No," I replied, "but I've run 10k's." We smiled and I went off to photograph waterfalls. Upon my return Mr. Bus Driver pulled an OGM (Olympic Gold Medal, complete with ribbon) out of his pocket and hung it around my neck. If I understand Icelandic, he said, "You come back for our next race in November." Yikes!!

When our bus returned to the ship, all we heard was "Hurry, hurry." We had 30 seconds to hop on before it left beautiful Iceland - home to green farmland and volcanoes and glaciers. We are now heading for Greenland - land of ice and ice. I could have spent an entire week in Iceland - so many hiking trails. And don't you think it would be fun to hike up a volcano and look down inside?

Goden nott, Sue

P.S. sukkuladi means chocolate.

Ayn Rand in "Atlas Shrugged"

"My philosophy, in essence, is the concept of man as
a heroic being, with
his own happiness as the moral purpose of his life,
with productive achievement as his noblest activity,
and reason as his only absolute."

Arctic Blog #4 Saturday

September 7, 2013.

In this part of the world, (Prins Christian Sund) when raindrops are falling on your head and fog obscures the glaciers, they say "this is atmospheric" and when you are freezing and you think the weather is bad, they say "there is no such thing as bad weather, only bad clothes."

Temperatures remain in the mid-40's. So you take pictures through rain-shrouded windows and thank the weather gods for water. Then you begin to take pictures of people and pictures of pictures hanging on walls and your own cute fur-lined waterproof purple boots and wall hangings on the Eurodam and suddenly . . . you see movement on an ice floe. You snap the pictures through the rain-shrouded window. Zoom in on the picture and aha! Wildlife! A sea eagle enjoying something red. Ah - chef's special of the day - sushi on the floe. My favorite photographic achievement to date.

When the Vikings discovered Iceland and Greenland in the 900's, they wanted to keep Iceland (volcanoes and glaciers and lots of farmland) for themselves and hoped others would populate Greenland, land of ice and glaciers and ice floes and more ice. And that is why they mis-named them. On Thursday, we cruised 65 miles through Prins Christian Sund in Greenland. No polar bears. No seals. Lots of sea eagles.

The population in Greenland is 56,000 folks - mostly Inuit Eskimos living in tiny villages on the edges, below glaciers and snow-capped mountains. Greenland, said to be 20 times larger than Iceland is the northernmost point of North America. There are only about two months a year when a ship can navigate the Sund; most of the year it is frozen and innavigatable.

Thursday we traveled 65 miles through Prins Christian Sund on the long channel between the mainland and the island Sanmisoq. The Greenlandic name is Ikerasassuaq, meaning the long channel. Our ship stopped briefly at a tiny village and two of our tenders delivered 12 pizzas, cases of coke, and bags of cookies. It was said they greatly appreciated the snacks. I prayed their digestive systems would be OK with something other than seal meat and whale blubber.

When cruisers arrive, by tender, in Nanortalik, Greenland, everything opens: market, the open-air museum, the cultural center, and tourist information. The population here is 1500 and there appears to be a baby boom. Nursery schoolers on parade. On display on the "inside" museum are handicrafts: baskets, clothing, figures carved of seal bones, and boots made of sealskin, yarn, and beads. It appears that the villagers spend many long dark winter months inside in the winter, creating all sorts of clothing and crafts and artwork. Open-air museum means walking grassy and dirt paths to the peat house, the blubber house, the ancient bakery-brewery, the cow house, and the fishing house.

There are several "selvbyggerhuse" which are the houses people built with their own hands, out of sod and weathered boards. The ceilings in the old homes are about five feet high, which means you'd have less space to heat in the 10 months of winter. The newer pre-fab homes are shipped here in large containers. Most homes appear to be about 800 square feet and are painted every imaginable color from white and yellow to lime green and purple. The men fish from their wooden framed and sealskin-covered kayaks while the women's little boats are a bit larger, also covered in sealskin. They are called umiaks.

At 9:00 a.m., children from ages 7 - 15 (7 boys and 9 girls) performed several folk dances, inspired by Dutch and Scottish whalers centuries ago. Ten dances ended with the bunny hop to an original Greenlandic tune. The children were a beautiful mixture of Inuit and Dutch. They seemed to be the happiest people on earth. Most of them wore very modern-looking foot apparel, which they probably ordered online.

The Greenlandic choir: 5 women and 4 men sang five songs in their native Greenlandic and ended with Amazing Grace sung in Greenlandic. It was such a heart-connecting moment. It brought forth that S.O.M. realization that "we are all one." Bhia was right when he said, "The light of God shines from every soul."

The Amazing Greenlandic Choir

Our awesome lecturer, Jon Sigurdsson, was to leave us by helicopter yesterday, which was to take him to an airport and back to his home in Reykovik, Iceland but the "atmospheric" fogginess would not allow that to happen and since they don't operate on weekends, he'd have to wait three days for the next helicopter. So, he hopped back onto the Eurodam and is with us as we travel to Newfoundland, Canada.

We are now headed to Newfoundland, Canada. We'll spend just a few hours there tomorrow where I am scheduled to visit the botanical gardens at the University of Newfoundland at St. John's. Newfoundland's clocks are one-half hour off from the rest of the world. That is, when it's 10:30 in Newfoundland, it's 10:00 in Eastern Canada and 6:00 in California.

Thank you everyone for your emails. It's so much fun connecting with y'all. At $2.50 per minute for use of Internet – which connects VERY slowly, it would be about $10. to respond to each of you. Ho ho ha ha ha!

Note to my STEP sisters: I am looking forward to our meeting on the 19th at Aldersgate and will send confirmation to all members when I get to NYC. Much love to all of you.

Note to Dorcus: I'm 200 pages into "Atlas Shrugged" and looking forward to discussing it with you. I've got just 967 pages to go.

Peaceful blessings
As-Salamu Alaykun, Shalom

Arctic Blog #5. Wednesday September 11, 2013

Happy 222 monthaversery to Richard and Sue ☺ beginning March 11, 1995. Many of you were there at the beginning. Did you think then, that it would last? Here's the secret: All you need is a sense of humor, someone happy to marry, and separate vacations once in a while. ☺ ☺ ☺

On Saturday, Sept. 7th, we arrived in Newfoundland. The M.U.N. (Memorial University of Newfoundland) was wonderfully wet, windy and beautiful. The Newfoundlanders say an umbrella is unnecessary because the rain always comes at you sideways. It's true. Twenty-five of us brave souls toured through the beautiful botanical gardens at the university with an expert in horticulture and humor.

The 32-acre reserve emphasizes indigenous plants and wildlife. At one point we all rushed into the little (20′ X 30′) greenhouse to get out of the mini-hurricane. We spent 30 minutes in and out of the wetness before the vote was taken: "Let's head back to the nature center for hot tea and scones served with clotted cream and strawberry jam." I was a little disappointed at not getting to see the entire garden but loved the tea. I sat with Jason, one of our two young sound technicians. He left Nebraska to spend a couple of years cruising and working the lights and sounds at the Main Stage on board the Eurodam. He doesn't know our cousins from Omaha, Lincoln, Syracuse, Kearney, or Hermann.

(Note to sister Jeannie: I know you're thinking of all the times we helped mom turn the gleaned strawberries from the neighbor's acres into jam and how hot our little farmhouse got and how tired we were and how we both have an aversion to strawberry jam, BUT, 60 years later, I tasted it. It's not so bad.)

Upon returning to ship, I put on dry clothes and then took a hike around town. I sauntered by the Booby Trap (they sell bras), and headed up the hill to The Room, Newfoundland's museum, and convention center. Several ancient cathedrals, churches, and schools were built on the hillside and were visible from our ship. John Cabot's Tower on the hilltop was built in memory of his discovery of Newfoundland in 1497.

Marconi received the first transatlantic wireless message here on Dec. 12, 1901, near the tower. The old part of town is like an artist's pallet: colorful homes and shops and restaurants. The streets are very narrow, not even a VW could be driven between the houses. That evening, after our excursions, we were treated to a glimpse inside Nova Scotia's rich Celtic roots with a traditional bagpipe performance and talk with Highlander John & bagpiper Keith from the Halifax Citadel (their fort). As we sailed towards Nova Scotia we were entertained with a Cape Breton Fiddle Concert. Sisters Cassie (fiddle) and Maggie (keyboard and guitar) MacDonald form a dynamic award winning Celtic Sister duo. They call their type of music "kitchen concerts" because of all the cold weather here, their family creates a lot of music and the kitchen is always the warmest place in the house.

Tuesday, Sept 10

Nova Scotia was warm and sunny. Yay! No rain. No fog. Jane and I took the tour bus up to Peggy's Cove, perhaps the most picturesque place on the planet. It's an old fishing village with the often-photographed lighthouse, several gift shops, art galleries, a restaurant, and a coffee shop. Old wooden boats line the shore and piles of colorful ropes are stacked along quaint little cottages. An hour later we were back near the ship ready to get on the hop-on hop-off busses. What a great way to see the city of Halifax and to hear the history. The population here is about 50,000 but goes up when students return to one of several universities.

We listened to the story of the 1917 explosion in the "narrows" of the harbor where 1500 people died instantly and flying glass blinded many more. The explosion was caused by the collision of two ships, one carrying 5.8 megatons of explosive ammunition. The other 60 ships in the harbor were also destroyed. We were told that the only bigger explosions on the planet were the two atomic bombs that decimated Hiroshima and Nagasaki. Because of all the tragic deaths caused and all the damage to structures, the people of Boston, Massachusetts came to the rescue with trainloads of food, medical supplies, and glass. All the windows for miles around were shattered. Now, in memory of the kindness of those citizens of Boston, the people of Halifax send a decorated Christmas tree to Boston every year.

The April 15, 1912 sinking of the Titanic was near enough to Nova Scotia, that the folks of Halifax helped rescue some of those cruisers and brought back over 200 dead bodies. Many of them are in the Halifax Cemetery. The people here combed the beaches for heart-shaped stones and carved the names of each of the 200 onto the stones. When contact was made with families of the victims, the families were given the heart-shaped stones. Lots of nice people up here.

After all the people and excursions and history, I decided to take a walk along the boardwalk, which goes for a couple of miles. I got to thinking about the delicious beet and goat cheese salad we had in Estes Park last summer when I walked up to the menu board at Murray's on the Cable Wharf and guess what was at the top of the salad menu? Right! Beet and goat cheese salad! My waiter, Chris, a Halifax native and world traveler, brought me a cup of tea with the salad. It was delicious! I asked him if he was a student. He has a degree in psychology, likes to travel, his parents are getting a bit antsy about his moving in and out of their home. I told him how great teaching is. Who knows?

And so, we are now, at this very moment heading towards New York City. We'll arrive there tomorrow morning about 7:00 a.m. That's 4:00 a.m. California time. We've been told that we'll be passing the Statue of Liberty at 5:30 a.m., off our balcony. Jane and I will spend the next couple of days in NYC and return to Orange County, California Sunday evening. Yippee!!

Thank you, my dear friend Jane, for inviting me on this adventure. It was even more wonderful than I had imagined. Thank you. Thank you.

Much love to all of you, Sue

OMD Richard: Flight 507 United Airlines 4:40 p.m. coming down from San Francisco. Sunday. Santa Ana Airport. If you can't be there, send someone. (Lisa? Dan? Thea? Linda?) We'll wait.

OMD Richard: Please go to LW Library. Check out Atlas Shrugged, Ayn Rand.Thnx.

Arctic Blog #6

Friday, September 13, 2013

Woke up at 5:15 yesterday and saw lights outside our balcony. Dashed out the door and there she was! The Statue of Liberty, a gift from France to the U.S.A. on October 28, 1886. I love the Statue of Liberty and what she stands for but most of all, I love the little statue behind her, the one of Emma Lazarus, who wrote the poem.

"Give me your tired, your poor,
Your huddled masses longing to be free.
The wretched refuse of your teeming shore.
Send these, the homeless, tempest-tost to me.
I lift my lamp beside the golden door."

I imagine the many immigrants who were greeted by our Statue of Liberty and how they longed for a better life, how exhausted they were by the time they got to our "teeming shores." Hopefully they were greeted by someone who loves them, someone who could provide a home, maybe a job, some good food.

By 10:00 we were off the ship and through customs. Then we rolled our suitcases three blocks, looking for a taxi, and low and behold, David from Nigeria stopped his taxi, tossed our bags into the trunk and drove up to the Manhattan Club on the corner of 56th and 7th – across the street from Carnegie Hall. It took 45 minutes to go about a mile. That's just the way it is in NYC, the city that never sleeps.

If you think the 405 is a tough drive during rush hour, you should see this place. Lucky for us, we were allowed to check in our room 4 hours early. We purchased bus tickets and took off for an open-air ride around Lower Manhattan where the sun beamed down on us. Ah, it was wonderful. Then, without notice of any kind, one full inch of rain fell out of the sky. When we realized what was happening, we unwrapped our plastic ponchos and protected ourselves the best we could but by then I was just laughing. I laughed and laughed until I realized I was sitting in a puddle of rainwater on my bus seat. Ho ho ha ha ha. I was wet for the next five hours. The sun did come out again.

After I showered and put on dry clothing, we stood out in the street waving at 25 taxis before one stopped. Weirdly, most passing taxis had just one customer. So we spent another ½ hour in a taxi going about 1-1/2 miles.

Traffic again. We saw a wonderful play called A Trip to Bountiful, starring Cicely Tyson. She was amazing. The play was great. Tomorrow we'll visit the 9/11 Memorial and see Kinky Boots in the afternoon. And Sunday – hip hip hooray – we'll fly into Orange County Airport at 4:40 p.m.

This morning I took a 3-hour stroll through Central Park. Kids and moms and dads and nannies and dogs playing and . . . Anderson Cooper jogging through the park. I swear it was him. White hair, skinny. Yep, it was him. 'Twas a beautiful day. I met people from all over: Japan, Brazil, Ireland. I took their pictures, they took mine.

It feels so good being back on the continent and am sooooo looking forward to being back with my beloved Richard and the creek and the trees and my own stuff. Especially looking forward to good ole' California food. I did have a great salad at Whole Foods Market last night but home is the best. And looking forward to reading the last 608 pages of Atlas Shrugged.

Saturday, September 14, 2013

Happy 12th Birthday Dear Granddaughter Rylee. Your birthday surprise is on its way. Hint: It says, "Oink!" Love, Grandma Sue

This morning we are at the 9/11 Memorial in Lower Manhattan, site of the World Trade Center and the atrocities of 9/11/2001. I see tears and looks of anguish on many faces. An elderly gentleman, his face pained, stands at the "survivor" tree, the only tree in the area with enough energy to continue. I wonder if the man lost his sons who served on the FDNY or an accountant daughter who jumped to avoid the flames. When I ponder those 19 who caused this disaster, I think of Maslow's hierarchy of needs.

If you don't receive the basics of food, shelter, strong family ties, and a feeling of safety, you don't reach self-realization. You are then likely incapable of compassion and love, and are quick to blame, quick to buy into mob mentality of rioting, violence, and a belief of an angry god. (Maslow's Hierarchy is on Wikipedia). I see an older Japanese woman and wonder how our bombing of Hiroshima and Nagasaki affected her family and, therefore, her life.

Jane and I got our free 9/11 Memorial tickets online scheduled for 10:00 to 11:00 a.m. We were quickly admitted. About 200 people waited in the other line. We taxied from The Manhattan Club up on 56th Street and 7th Avenue in mid-town Manhattan south to the Memorial at 8:00 a.m. We enjoyed 45 minutes in the La Quotidian Restaurant with jasmine tea for me and rich black coffee for Jane. We shared a zucchini frittata and a small salad. For dessert: (yes, in NYC you are allowed a small dessert for breakfast) ½ chocolate croissant and more tea and coffee. We walked four blocks to the "path" to the memorial and another four blocks to the entrance where we were checked in and body-scanned. The sun shone brightly, the air a crisp 60 degrees, no rain in sight.

This afternoon we really really really enjoyed the musical play "Kinky Boots". Great dancing, music and story with so many nuggets of truth. And so ends, another fabulous vacation for this traveling gal. Tomorrow a.m. we catch the 9:45. United Airlines flight out of J.F. Kennedy, stopping off in San Francisco Airport for an hour and then on to Orange County, arriving at 4:40 p.m. to be greeted by the one and only Mr. Darling Richard. And that's the best part of the whole trip.

Thank you all for your insightful funny supportive comments. There's no place like home and that's where I'm headed and that's where I'm staying for the next ten days. More later . . .

Love, Sue

P.S. It's 8:00 p.m. We're back in California where it's nice and hot. There's no place like home.

Hawaii Fruit Grower Cruise 2013

Aloha #1

September 26 – October 5

We're in Hawaii with 100 other Fruit Growers from California, Arizona and several Hawaiian Island Tropical Fruit Growers. Richard has been involved with the California Rare Fruit Growers Club of Orange County since 2002, Sue tags along quite often. Some folks are island hopping, using planes and the hotel system. Others of us are cruising on Norwegian's Pride of America. We all met last Thursday evening at the University of Hawaii in Honolulu and spent two nights sleeping in the student dorms. Our cubicles at Manoa were so much fun. The elevator will let you off at one of the following floors: 1,3,6,9,12. So like, if you are in rooms 300 or 301 you'd take the elevator up to the third floor, walk down a set of very steep stairs, like Vicki and Rick Yessayian did to find their room.

We took the elevator up to the third floor then walked up a set of very steep stairs to room's 314A and 314B. We were advised to rent two rooms because each is set up for one student. After measuring the bed (32 inches) we decided we could smush comfortably each night so who needs two rooms? Bathrooms in the dorms are really really fun. They are co-ed, as are the showers. Only rule is: girls and boys are not to shower at the same time, so we did. At 5:30 in the morning before students got up.

Thursday morning we took a walk at 6:30 and after viewing the Japanese garden on campus, walked away "oohing and aahing" when the young woman walking in front of us turned around and said, "Would you like to hear some of the history of the Japanese garden?" The garden was built in the 60's and dedicated by the Empress of Japan when she planted the first tree and placed the first koi in the pond. The President of Taiwan donated the teahouse, dedicating it to the Japanese people of Hawaii. He comes every July to serve tea. His daughter was here yesterday." Cool, eh?

Thursday evening after we got settled we walked over to the student cafeteria and enjoyed Greek salad (for Sue) and Panda Express Teriyaki Chicken (for Richard). Upon return to the dorms, we noticed six East Indian students in the kitchen. They were stir-frying veggies, toasting pita bread, and dumping spices on everything. No fast food for them – slow food with lots of laughing and eating great stuff. Life in Honolulu is slow.

Friday morning about 50 of us sauntered over to the cafeteria for breakfast where we met lots of other fruit growers. Dr. Seth Williams from Portland sat with us, talking about his family (twin 9-yr old boys) and husband Dave. He's very enthusiastic about growing food, teaching his sons to not only grow food but to glean and deliver extra food to shelters in the area. After breakfast we all climbed into big vans to visit the Lyon Arboretum where we were greeted by Chris Dunn, then sent off on guided tours through the forest of fruit trees. Lots of mangos, sweet lilikoi, passion fruit, guava, cherimoya, jaboticaba, rambutan, longan, lychee, bilimbi, and jackfruit. Except for the mosquitoes, we were in paradise.

Next, we visited Frankie's Nursery where Jenny took us around the grounds, pointing out more sapote, cherimoya, the cinnamon tree, the nutmeg tree, and the amazing jackfruit tree. If you've seen a jackfruit you know they sometimes weigh 30 or 80 pounds, and although they look like a porcupine with a crewcut, they really do taste good. We were refreshed with ice-cold passion fruit juice and papaya juice. More fruit tasting there. Friday evening at Kapiolani Community College we were invited to dinner created by the culinary arts students. Emphasis at the college culinary arts school is on fruit - getting people to eat more healthy fruit.

My favorite drink was diced up papaya, mango, pineapple, sapote, and rambutans in vanilla water. Yum! Students dressed in full chef-wear and hats, cooked and served salads and herbs from the culinary garden. Our keynote speaker that evening was Chris Rollins, main guy at the Fruit and Spice Park in Florida. His slide show was titled "Sapotes in the Mist" and made us laugh about the "spitting garden" in the parking lot at the F&SP. Seems people often sample what's growing there and spit the seeds into a certain plot of dirt in the parking lot. Lots of unplanned things growing in that spot. He said that sometimes visitors to the park steal the fruit.

He spoke about a group of women in sari's who walked out of the park balancing bags of something between their knees. Another woman took three tries to toss a jackfruit over the fence towards her car. When mamey sopote was $8 a pound in the 60's people stole from the park to sell it. Now that the price has gone down to $1.50 a pound no more stealing. Now they just steal cars. Ethnobotany is being lost, he says, due to the growing of cattle in the fields. Lots of people have lost interest in growing fruit and are into eating cows. This is especially true of the Hog Plum - Spondiaspurpurea. He also talked on antidesma (acquired taste) and how something may taste good to me and taste bad to you; it's all in the genetics.

Saturday a.m. - back to Kapiolani CC for breakfast (tea, coffee, pastries and fruit: pineapple, melons, pumelo, rambutan, strawberries, and bananas).

Our very own Roger Meyer handed out awards to various outstanding members of Fruit Grower Clubs. Robert Paull talked about agriculture in Hawaii. Jim West flew in from Ecuador to talk about his life in the Peace Corps in Guatemala and his 27 years of living in Ecuador with his wife and two children. For 45 minutes Jim told us of rare fruits in South America - most we'd never heard of.

Roger spoke again: this time on his world travels in search of the perfect jujube. Martha Haber cut up and served lots of fruit at our table. She'd purchased it from Frankie's the day before. It's fun to try different fruits but if you are ever offered durian, smell it and think twice - or three times.

The head of the Culinary Arts Department explained what had been prepared for our lunch: pork, fish, veggies and fruit. We feasted again. At 2:30 our driver David (Day-veed) a horticulture student at the U. of H. drove us to the port and sent us off to Maui with lots of hugs and laughter. We are looking forward to a room with a big bed and our own bathroom and a balcony.

Sunday: Up at 6:00 to watch the sunrise (port side), have breakfast, and meet our new driver, David, and off ship in Maui by 8:00. David and his girlfriend, Julie Ann, live two hours from our port in Kahului, Maui. They, with six others, work on a farm in Hana. They're experimenting with perma culture and year round crops. On the way Rick Y. pointed out Mickey Mouse Ears (a kind of cactus) and Monkey Pod Trees. We passed Oprah Winfrey's acreage (no house as far as we could see).

On the way to our 10:30 gathering we stopped in the parking lot of the Maui Winery, which agreed to open an hour early just for the 50 of us. So, it's like 9:45 a.m. and we're sampling Passion Fruit and Pineapple wine. Standing beside Don Winterstein sampling Splash we agreed that, well, it's made from fruit and we're here to taste the fruits of Hawaii. Richard had been at the same winery in the 70's. I bought him a little box of Plumeria Chocolates as he was waiting in our van.

By 11:00 we were at Lilly and Chuck's ONO farms in Hana (ono means "good" or "delicious" in Hawaiian) 2.5 hours from our ship in Kahului. They have five grown children, several grandkids, and eight interns who help run the farm. The house is amazing: lots of wood and many windows to view the jungle. After lunch, Autumn, one of the daughters, gave us a tour of the gardens: lots of cacao (chocolate) and star fruit trees and a few coffee bean bushes. We tasted more than 30 rare fruits. Again, in paradise.

We visited National Botanical Gardens where we ate lunch (fish, rice, veggies for Richard; spinach salad for me), heard the story of the Temple of

Agriculture (or Love) then drove back to our ship. Because our caravan to ONO's came overland, circling Haleakala's southern edge, our return completed the loop, treating us to the infamous switchbacks known as the Hana Highway. Waterfalls and turnouts around every bend along the way. We stopped for a few minutes to pick up the best thing I have ever tasted, amen: Coconut Ice Cream. No dairy. Creamy smooth coconut ice cream with little chunks of coconut. OMG!!! Back on ship at 7:30. Showers, no dinner, nighty-night.

Monday, we all met off ship and were picked up by our drivers and delivered to Maui Gold Company, Limited. We visited Maui Gold, the 1000-acre pineapple farm, ate lots of pineapple right out of the field. Maui Gold, Ltd. is one—if not the only—remaining commercial pineapple facilities in Hawaii. When the owners realized they could sell their land to developers for way more than they'd ever make growing fruit, a group of loyalist workers banded together, raised enough money to buy 1,000 acres and continue to do what they've done for generations. The next time you see a Maui Gold pineapple, buy it!! Support the growers who refused to bow to BIG MONEY.

It's a good thing the drivers had machetes with them. Our van stopped a couple of times and the drivers whacked up a few delicious fresh pineapples for us to sample. Lunch was served in the packing plant. The pineapple is picked every other day; packing happens on the other days. Maui Gold harvests 14,000 tons of pineapple every year, much of it shipped to the US by plane. Every year the business gets tougher, and it gets harder to make a profit. Eat more pineapple.

The Hawaii Islands Tropical Fruit Growers is trying to change a few things here. For one thing, 90% of the food consumed in the islands is imported from other parts of the world. They are trying to get small farmers and backyard gardeners to be more involved in what people eat here.

Aloha, Richard and Sue

P.S. Seth says he had a dessert last night that was the best ever: a cheesecake-like dessert made from breadfruit and sweet lilikoi passion fruit.

Aloha Blog #2

October 3, 2013

There ain't nuthin' like sitten' on our balcony feeling the ocean breeze off the coast of Kauai after a long day of walking through Kauai coffee plantation (3,200 acres, 4 million coffee trees, $1.5 billion generated around the globe) followed by a longer hiking tour of the National Tropical Botanical Gardens. Actually, the State of Hawaii supports the gardens now after the federal government reneged on a $10 million grant in 2008 when our economy dived.

Waterfalls, fountains, streams, statues of Buddha, Dianna the Huntress, reclining nymphs, a pony, and a mermaidish beauty, all built by the Allerton family over a period of 26 years. Every kind of tropical fruit tree you can imagine. We ate miracle fruit, a tiny berry that makes everything taste sweet. After that we ate limes. Yes, they tasted sweet. We ate rambutans off the trees, sampled lichees and coffee berries. Paradise at its best. A fabulous catered lunch out in the middle of a grassy field: mahi mahi, chicken, steamed veggies, rice, green salad, quinoa salad, and another display of "rare" fruit: jackfruit, durian (don't try it), starfruit, rambutan (looks like a big eyeball, tastes sweet like a grape), papaya, mango, and white pineapple. BTW: what do you call Buddha sitting in the bamboo forest? Bambooda. ☺ After a very long day, we head back to the Pride of America tired, content, ready for naps.

"Oh What a Night Tribute" group entertained us last night on the Main Stage of the ship. They sang most of the Four Seasons 27 hits from the 60's and 70's. The audience went wild - singing most of the songs. (Yes, Kathie and Jack, the same group that sang for us in Laguna Woods last spring.) Frankie Vallie would be proud.

Yesterday, we stayed aboard in Kona, as cruisers were "tendered" to shore, not possible for cute bearded guys who need Rascals to get around. So, we slept in! Until 7:00 a.m.! Spent the day napping, reading, eating, and talking with the crew. Shared dinnertime with Vicki and Rick Y. (Sister Jeanne: Rick sends his love and says he has fond memories of whatever you two did at age 13. ☺ And he says "Hi" to Ann. ☺)

Tomorrow at 1:30 p.m. our ship will sail back to Honolulu. We'll disembark Saturday morning, catching the 11:00 a.m. flight back to LAX and "winging it" from there. Yay! We're almost home. This has been an amazingly educational tour of the islands; getting to know the fruit growers who are so passionate and knowledgeable about what they do. And we loved getting to

know our fellow fruit growers from the Hawaiian Islands, Arizona, Oregon, and California (about 100 of us) and loved getting to know our crew.

Aloha to all of you great family members and friends. We wish all of you could have been with us.

Much love and many blessings, Richard and Sue

PS Satish: Has our building been painted?

PSS Sheri: Thanks for the reminder; I'll bake cookies Sunday.

Italy Again May 2014

Dear Family and Friends,

We did it - my sister Jeannie and I took a two-week Globus journey through Italy. I've always said, "If your little sister asks you to take a trip to Italy with her, say 'Yes.'" So I did and we did and now we're back home where it's 3:00 a.m. in California and noon in Italy. We're hoping to get used to the time change soon. While we were across the sea, Richard flew up to Washington, met his brother, Steve from Juneau, and the two of them attended a Mother Earth weekend at the fairgrounds in Puyallup, then a few days in Vegas.

If you've seen the movie "If it's Tuesday, this must be Belgium" you have a pretty good idea how these 2-week bus trips are. We spent two nights in Rome, two nights in Florence, and two nights in Stressa on Lake Maggiore, two nights on Venice Island, one night in Assisi, two nights in Sorrento, and the last night in Rome. On the way, we stopped off for a few hours in Pisa, Lugano Switzerland, Isola Dei Pescatori, Milan, Padua, Capri, and Pompeii. Whew!

The first night we met 28 other travelers - all English speakers. They came from California, New York, New Hampshire, New Jersey, Oregon, Pennsylvania, Florida, Mexico, and Australia. What a beautiful group of people: all well-behaved and friendly and helpful. Errica, our Italian multi-lingual guide, is a fountain of knowledge on the history of Italy, and did a fantastic job of keeping us focused while we were awake.

There were times, I must admit, that after several days of traveling, lots of us fell asleep on the bus. Georgio, handsome and youthful driver, confidently drove us up hills, over bridges, around other busses, through mountain tunnels, and kept us on schedule for 13 days. Truly Georgio and Errica are amazing people.

So, here are a few highlights:

1. Rome: Michelangelo's Story of Creation scene on the ceiling of the Sistine Chapel. He was 21 when asked to paint it. At age 31, he was asked to depict Judgment Day on another portion of the ceiling. We found it interesting that the four angels sitting on the rocks held two books. If your name appeared in the small book, angels carried you

up to heaven. If your name appeared in the big book, guess what? Yes, you were carried down to eternal damnation. By age 71 Michelangelo was an architect, a painter, and a sculptor. He lived to be 89.

2. The little Gelato shop on the corner by Trevi fountain still has the best coconut and pistachio gelato anywhere.
3. Some brilliant engineers have stabilized the leaning tower of Pisa. And, we observed several other leaning towers in Italy.
4. Florence: After viewing Michelangelo's David at the Accademia Museum, our local guide, Leah, took us over to the Uffizi Museum to view the greatest collection of Italian painting anywhere in the world including Leonardo, Raphael, Michelangelo, and Botticellis. After viewing incredible paintings on the first floor, we began to climb the 80 steps toward the second floor. As we rounded the corner, we discovered there were another 80 steps to climb. So we pushed on and then . . . another 80 steps and . . . another 80. I was so grateful that my morning walk at home includes a steep hill that I make myself walk up without stopping. And . . .the smart people took the elevator. In the afternoon, tea time for us English descendants, we searched in vain for tea and scones but had to, alas, settle for pizza and beer - shandies actually. Life is just like that sometimes.
5. During our two-hour visit in Lugano Switzerland we walked through a beautiful park along Lake Maggiore, took lots of pictures of Dr. Seuss trees and the village across the lake and enjoyed toona salate.
6. The Bristol Hotel on Lake M. serves an interesting 5-course dinner. The hors de oeuvres buffet included squid with olives and cheese, cole slaw with ham, beans with cheese, asparagus with cheese, cheese, salami, eggplant, bread sticks, artichoke with cheese, and bell peppers. Soup for the second course, then pasta, then fish with potatoes and zucchini, and for dessert a choice of fruit cake, a bowl of fruit, or milliflori cake. I gave up after the soup but many of our brave companions ate everything!!!
7. We toured the baroque palace where Chinese white peacocks live in the gardens of the enchanting Isola Bella and later had dinner on Isola Pescatori.
8. Next: two hours in Milan. We view the amazing and fabulous Gothic Duomo, which is right across the street from La Scala Opera house. We race through a luxury department store and ride the escalators to the 6th floor (no stairs this time) to get a good view of the Duomo, then head for the Sforza Castle which has the beautiful San Senpieto Park and little lake. A blue heron flies past us and lands on the edge of the lake. We take lots of pictures. We pick up salads at a nearby

deli and head for the meeting place. See what I mean? This is a quick overview of Italy.

9. We arrive at my favorite place in the world, Venice, about 5:00 p.m. We drop off our bags at the San All' Angelo Hotel, then some of us head for the gondolas. We all fit into four gondolas, including an accordion player and a handsome, talented young singer who serenaded us through the canals. Errica led us to a beautiful restaurant near the Rialto bridge where we had the best dinner yet: cantaloupe (declined the ham), pasta, roasted potatoes and broccoli and fish in a yummy sauce. Jeannie and I didn't have time for the tiramisu so waiter packed it in boxes for us, as we had five minutes to get over to the Vivaldi concerto that started the minute we sat down in the church. We listened to The Four Seasons and Pacabel's Cannon performed by 4 violins, 1 cello, 1 base, 1 keyboard. 'Twas heavenly.
10. Next morning: cold showers, as the water heater had gone out. Brrrrrr. We see shoes in shop windows. Prices run up to 1600 Euros, which is about $2208 in American dollars. I decide to just take pictures of shoes.
11. Off to Burano, the lace island. Group lunch on the island with lots of wine. Homes here are multi-colored. People are friendly.
12. For several days, Errica has told us about the "meat coffee" served at the Caffe Producchi in Padua. All I can think is "ick". She says some people like it, others don't. The University of Padua is across the street from the Caffe and the students all like it, Errica says. Meat is not part of my diet so I know I won't be trying it. It is not until we get inside the Caffe that we discover Errica's accent makes the word "mint" sound like "meat." Aha! It's MINT coffee, not meat coffee. OK. We all laugh. We try it. It's just like mint 'n chip ice cream melted.
13. In Padua, we take a quick walk through San Anthony's Cathedral. We view the relics of Saint Anthony: his tongue, vocal chords, and jaw with teeth. He is famous for performing many miracles and he talked a lot.
14. Next stop: Assisi for one night. We visit St. Francis Cathedral, which has the most extreme decorations of any building I've ever seen. We like Assisi a lot. It's quieter than most towns, fewer tourists. Jeannie and I decide to hike up the steep road to the town square. It's about ¾ mile. I find two ceramic frogs for Richard's frog collection but don't have enough Euros. The sales clerk promises to hold them for me. Now we're looking for an ATM, which is called Banco in Italy. It costs about $138 for 100 Euros. We take pictures of everything on the way: balconies and flowers and steep steps leading up to private apartments. Lovely. Back down the hill, the salesclerk is sitting

outside, ready to lock up for the night. She lovingly wraps the frogs in a cute little black box. I hug her and we march on. We had a forgettable dinner in our San Francesco Hotel.

15. Thank goodness I brought trail mix and several baggies of homemade protein bars. Sometimes we didn't have time to eat much. Jeannie and I carried "feed bags" on the bus with us. On to Sorrento.

16. Ah! Grand Hotel Vesuvio in Sorrento is the most luxurious yet. It's raining but we can see the Mediterranean from the hotel's balcony. Next morning we are bussed to the boat dock and glide across the sea for 30 minutes. We are headed for the famous Island of Capri. On the island, we ride the funicular up to the expensive homes and hotels for a look. Wow! Beautiful gardens and homes built very near the steep cliffs. We have eggplant sandwiches and water - no gas, flat. If you don't tell the waiter "no gas, flat" you'll get sparkly mineral water. We top off our visit on Capri with lemoncello sorbet and hazelnut and pistachio gelato. After a brief rest back at the hotel on Sorrento, we are bussed down to the town of Sorrento, walk around, have fish 'n chips for dinner. I find, at last, a cute hat for my beloved Richard. Jeannie buys gifts for her husband and kids. She's great at that. Apologies to my kids, grandkids, great grandkids: All you get from Italy is a happy Grandma Sue.

17. Our last full day: Pompeii, the Roman city both destroyed and preserved by an eruption of Mount Vesuvius in 79 AD. The volcano last erupted in 1944 and is still smoldering ominously. A local guide takes us on a two-hour walk through grounds. Pompeii was once home to 20,000 people. It had been an important seaport but because of the eruption in 79 AD it is now a mile from the ocean. From about 600 BC to 79AD this was a thriving metropolis with 40 bakeries, 30 brothels, and 130 bars, restaurants, and hotels. Mosaic floors have been uncovered, also other artwork on walls - some quite, ahem, risqué. They did know how to decorate those brothels.

18. Last night was spent in Rome at the Holiday Inn on the edge of town to avoid early morning traffic. We have a final lavish dinner at a beautiful old restaurant built on beautiful old ruins. Another 5-courser. J. and I decline the beef and are served veggie omelets. Very good. We are grandly entertained by two opera students. They sing every Italian song you've ever heard and several more. They were accompanied by a talented pianist. It was great fun. Lots of laughter. Lots of vino. Lots of heart-felt sad goodbyes to our traveling buddies. The youngest of the group are planning a get-together in two years. Maybe another European tour, they say, or maybe a meetup in Miami. I hope they invite us.

Costa Rica - February 2016

Pura Vida

"If we did all the things we are really capable of doing,
we would literally astound ourselves."
Thomas Edison

Friday February 19th

Our nephew Marc delivered his mom--my sister Jeannie--and our niece Melissa and her life-partner Shannon to our place at 7:30 in the evening. Linda arrived a half hour later and delivered us to LAX in 45 minutes but, because of the traffic jam, it took an extra 30 minutes to get to Terminal 5 where she would drop us off.

Saturday February 20, 2016

It is now 12:12 a.m. Time to board 1388 to San Jose, Costa Rica. Lots of folks on their iPhones. Delta 1388 pulled out of California at 1:15. An hour later, we were in the air, headed for SJ, CR. Five hours and five minutes later, after a quick nap, we arrived in S.J. We sailed through customs with (oops!) bananas and carrots (okay).

In just a few ticks over five hours, we met our tour guide, Fabian, and our driver, Charlie, both agents with Swiss Travel in Costa Rica. We were driven to the hotel, dropped off our luggage at Doubletree Cariari by Hilton. We got a quick snack of coffee and cookies at 9:00 a.m. and hopped back on the bus for a tour of San Jose's Metropolitan Cathedral. Originally built in 1802, it was destroyed by an earthquake. In 1871 it was rebuilt in the Greek Orthodox, Neoclassical, and Boroque styles. Bible scenes are depicted in the stained glass windows and the main altar is decorated with statues of angels and a wooden figure of Christ. What a busy introduction to this beautiful country.

Next we walked through the Mercado Central where we got to know the real Costa Ricans and how they earned a living. The market was built in 1880 and is just a block from the Cathedral. It consists of more than 200 fruit, meat, fish, and vegetable stands. The overnighter on Delta Airlines left most of us tired and a bit confused. So that was enough for one day. It was a good time for early-to-bed. So we did.

Melissa and Shannon

Sunday, February 21, 2016

This morning's breakfast buffet was over-the-top delicious and bountiful. We all enjoyed the coffee. Later we sat near the La Paz Waterfall Gardens for a coffee break. We enjoyed munching on coffee bean candy. I felt a bit light-headed and decided to switch back to tea. We met Kimberly, our young little omelet maker, and we so enjoyed our outdoor meal. Fourteen of us were then bussed to Doka Coffee plantation, which was at 4500 altitude. We were given several samples of coffee and learned the old-fashioned way of processing the beans. Doka sells their raw coffee beans to Starbucks all over the world. Starbucks buys the beans from Doka but does their own roasting.

Next, a 1,000-step climb to waterfalls and a butterfly display. These friendly little winged creatures were quite comfortable landing on us. We also saw birds of every exotic kind. There were caged ocelots, cougars, lynx, and snakes in cages—venomous and non. We enjoyed a wonderful lunch buffet, which meant I could eat as much salad as I wanted. Following lunch, eight of us spent 45 minutes in the Jacuzzi: Yolanda, Pam, Ann, Antonio & Mary, Gary & Margaret and me. That evening I had dinner with my Jacuzzi mates, plus my sister Jeannie. Curry stir-fry and jasmine rice. And lots of jokes. We did get a glimpse of Shannon and Melissa but they were in a world of their own.

Monday February 22, 2016

In Costa Rica we enjoyed a bit of Chilaxation under the full moon as we viewed the Arenal Volcano. We stopped the bus three times to watch the sloths in the trees, also saw five adult monkeys, and two baby monkeys in the trees. Poisonous frogs. I missed them but was told they are very tiny, like 2.4 inches long. Our driver, Charlie, stopped the bus this afternoon to help a sloth get across the road. All the traffic was stopped. Our kind driver used a towel to pick up the sloth and carried it to the other side of the road. Thank you Charlie for being so observant.

Fabian, our guide, studies wildlife, plants, and loves coffee. He has a wife and two little kids. He knows the names and voices of all the Costa Rican birds. So far he has pointed out many turkey vultures, cattle egrets, and white hawks. He's teaching us history, geography, and explained the medical and educational systems here. Health care is free to everyone, but if you want quick service you buy insurance. Education is free but many students drop out during their high school years in order to go to work. It seems that many parents don't encourage their children to stay in school.

Tomorrow we'll be hiking through the rain forest for three hours, crossing the swinging bridges, and then—YIPPEE—zip lining. We are very excited.

Tuesday, February 23, 2016

I awoke at 6:00 this morning, opened my eyes and looked out the sliding glass door across from my bed. The site of the Arenal Volcano spewing smoke was so amazing I felt like I was in another world. According to historians, the Arenal was inactive from about AD 1500 until July of 1968, when huge explosions triggered lava flows that destroyed two villages, killed 80 people, and 45,000 cattle. Since that time, the volcano has been steadily producing menacing ash columns, massive explosions, and glowing red lava flows almost daily. Usually by late morning, the smoke from the volcano clouds our view of it, so I felt happy to see it early in the day.

Jeannie and I ate breakfast at the restaurant in the hotel near the pond at 7:00. And what did we see on the pond? A Bare-Throated Tiger-Heron searching for his own breakfast: frogs, probably. For breakfast? A bowl of yogurt with a mound of fruit, a scone, and a cup 'o java. Delicious. Charlie picked us up at 8:35 and drove us to Mistico Arenal hanging bridges. We strolled through the forest for three hours, often stopping to watch spider monkeys. Everyone with an iPhone or camera was treated to a telescoped picture taken by our fabulous guide Fabian. Today we watched four monkeys swinging through the trees all at once, as though they were showing-off for us. We also took pictures of a sleeping ocelot, cuddled up in a tree and pictures of the venomous English Palm Pitviper. He's a very tiny and very poisonous four inches of danger.

We drove over to Monteverde for Sky Trekking and the Sky Tram Tour. A few of us decided it would be more of an adventure to zipline across the canapy and be right in the midst of nature. Our zipline tour consisted of six zips. After the fifth one we stopped for a coffee break. Then we continued to fly through the air at 75 mph. Screaming and laughing: what is more fun than that? As we zipped along we got views of Lago Arenal and Arenal Volcano. We flew over deep canyons and other ziplines. When the fun was over we were bussed back one mile on rutted-bouncy roads.

On our way back to our hotel, Hawkeye Charlie spotted a chestnut-mandibled Toucan. We took close-up pictures of it, of course. Another amazing day in Costa Rica.

Wednesday February 24, 2016

Happy 67th Birthday to my dear husband back in California. I can't wait to find out what happens at your surprise birthday party this evening at Wahoo's Fish Taco Restaurant in Lake Forest. I planned it. I paid for it. Then I flew to Costa Rica. More on this when I find out how it goes.

Today we woke up at 5:00. The Arenal volcano was hidden in the clouds. Then a little bird hit our window. He hit the ground, stunned and appeared to be having a seizure. I was afraid he was dead. All of a sudden he stood up, shook his head, and flew up into a tree. Hooray for tough little birds.

By 6:45 a.m., the four of us: Jeannie and me, Melissa and Shannon had our bags up at the office and were eating breakfast. Jose Juan Carlos, a bus driver, picked us up at our hotel at 7:45 and drove over to the other hotel to pick up the other ten jolly travelers. We all rode over to Lake Lago for a 30-minute tour, but because Fabulous Fabian is so into nature, it turned into a 50-minute trip. We stopped to see every egret and heron and osprey and vulture along the shore. Such a thrill to be so close to these birds.

Next: we bussed to Santa Elena for shopping and lunch. Jeannie and I had lunch on the second of a three-story restaurant, "The Tree House." It was built around a 40' tall tree. While shopping, we bought Richard a book on tropical fruit. I wish he could share this trip with us—but the Rascal doesn't do forest trails and sky-high ziplines or swinging bridges. I am so grateful he encourages me to travel, whether he can join me or not. Thank you my Sweetheart.

One of the other neat things about Fabian is that he recognizes the sounds of the birds and the animals and can spot them in the trees, or sky, or on the water. After lunch, we met with our #1 driver, Charlie, in Santa Elena and he drove us to the Cloud Forest. Fabian guided us and pointed out a Quetzal through his telescope, which made me think how very lucky his children are to have a dad who is so into nature. A Quetzal, in case you're wondering, is a colorful bird, about the size of one of our Acorn Woodpeckers but with a very long tail. We spent the next two hours hiking through the Cloud Forest loving the outdoors: fresh air, exercise, wild creatures—sometimes poisonous—and absorbing the magnificent world we live in.

Next, we relaxed on the bus for 20 minutes as we headed for the Trapp Family Lodge in Monteverde. This little hotel was nothing fancy. The rooms were small but beautiful. Ours even had an alcove with a window overlooking the rainforest. As I sat there contemplating my life and thinking, "How did this little farm girl get to this amazing place?" Suddenly, two Chestnut-mandibled Toucans landed in a tree and looked at me. As I attempted to adjust my camera, they looked at me, smiled, and flew away. Another lesson: absorb the beauty and keep it in your mind. You don't need a picture. Jeannie and I walked downstairs for dinner.

Funny thing happened at dinner. I ordered veggie cassava and pumpkin soup. Everybody got served but me. Finally, as people were halfway through dessert, my bowl of soup appeared. Ha Ha. I'm looking forward to tomorrow. We'll be visiting coffee and chocolate plantations and factories.

Thursday February 25, 2016

This morning I spoke with my adorable, husband, via iPhone, at 9:30 Costa Rica time. That was 7:30 in the morning in California. He said the surprise party was crazy fun. Sixteen people showed up and he was very surprised. Each person stood up and told when they met Richard. He's so happy but unaware that I planned the whole thing. Between the wonderful staff at Wahoo's and our friends Kathie and Jack, the party was a great success. Sorry I couldn't be there, but that's how life is sometimes.

Jeannie and I went over to the breakfast room in the Trapp Family Lodge and enjoyed coffee, scrambled eggs, a rice/bean mixture, and delicious little coconut cakes. We pretty much relaxed with a short walk and some down time until we headed out to lunch at Bon Apetite Café for a serving of pasta with veggies and a salad followed by a big slice of apple pie with Vanilla ice cream. It was kinda too much. Right at 4:00 we were ready for our tour of a coffee and chocolate factory. Then this evening we'll be taking a night-watch tour in the forest. Spooky, eh?

I had no idea! We walked around the coffee bean plantation, up and down long hilly trails through the plants. We also got to see where they grew the cacao beans for making one of our favorite treats: chocolate! In the "factory" part of the farm, the beans were on top of plastic sheets that were spread over a huge area: about 100′ x 100′. The beans would dry in the sun, and then be collected for bagging or grinding. Of course we were encouraged to have another cup of coffee and got to chew on unsweetened chocolate. Hmmm. Interesting.

This evening, we met Eric, our guide for tonight's tour through the dark forest, as we search for shining eyeballs in the dark. The theory is we won't necessarily spot the big cats but if there are any we'll see their eyes. Six brave souls from our group, and a brave young couple from Holland joined forces in this auspicious endeavor. We found walking sticks, a few katydid, some grasshoppers and spiders. No sloths or monkeys or big cats, at least none who looked at us. Oh! But we did see a cluster of cutter ants. The arthropods were in abundance but no mammals appeared. And only one striped Palm Pitviper.

After that adventure, we joined the rest of our group in the Tree House. Sixteen of us tried to fit around a long table on the second floor but we finally went to the third floor, which had no branches in our area and the ceiling was made of branch-shaped boards. Leaves were painted on the ceiling. We—most of us—danced to a 3-piece band with much fun and laughter.

Tomorrow begins at 6:00 a.m. with our bags outside the Lodge. We'll have an early breakfast and be on the bus at 7:45. We're looking forward to three nights at Tamarindo Diaria Beach Resort.

Friday February 26, 2016

Today we floated on the Corobici River for two hours observing at least 15 spider monkeys, one white-faced capuchin monkey, most of them in the siesta mode. A barred owl watched as we floated by. Perched in the hollow of a tree, turning his head ever so slowly wondering how human creatures manage to stay alert all day long. We came upon a cave just above water level and spotted a school or flock or precision of long-nosed bats asleep—about 30 of them hanging upside down in formation. Also known as the "proboscis bat" they live in groups of 10 to 40. They are nocturnal and sleep in an unusual formation. They line up, one after another, on a branch or wooden beam, nose to tail, in a straight row. They feed on insects using echolocation. Each bat measures about 2.4 inches.

Our guide and paddler, Kevin, spotted a flock of storks. I asked, "The kind that bring babies?" I kindly told the storks to go away. I asked Kevin how many children he has. He said: "A 4-year old son and a 2-year old daughter. No more." Then he pointed out the "rock-a-diles" the "trunk-a-diles" and was really surprised when someone pointed out the quietly observant real crocodile hanging out on shore. As we floated by, he turned his head probably hoping one of us would fall out of the little boat. Actually, he slithered into the river and we never saw him again. We did spot many birds: a boat-billed heron (also known as the pico-cuchara), several cattle egrets (also known as garcilla bueyera), an osprey carrying talapia between his feet, a black-billed whistling duck, several spotted sandpipers, a green heron (garcilla verde), several vultures: both turkey and black. A green kingfisher flew up and down the river searching for yummy bugs.

Onward to Tamarindo Diaria Beach Resort!!

OMG! OMG! Jeannie and I shared room 204 with an awesome view of the Pacific Ocean. Shortly after our arrival, we headed for the pool for a swim, then showered and were off to a dinner of Greek salad and snacks by the sea—all 14 of us together. Can one ever observe a sunset over the ocean without oohing and ahhing? I think not.

Saturday February 27, 2016

At 6:00 we were walking on the beach. At 6:45 we had breakfast. At 10:00 we had brunch. At 2:00 we ate another Greek salad and at 7:00 we had tuna salad. We watched the sunset again this evening.

The last few days we walked the beach and the souvenir shops in the town of Tamarindo where we slept at the Diria Beach Resort. One of the guys took a great picture of an anteater strolling around the town early yesterday morning. Several raccoons and an opossum casually walked through the sandy-floored restaurant at the Latitude Blue.

We also enjoyed a fantastic fire-dance performance before dinner on the beach at the La Palapa Restaurant. Our tables were out on the sand. The waiters brought an amazing assortment of food and exotic drinks that I can neither name nor remember. I do remember that it was all delicious and that I kept an eye on the rising tide. We survived.

Sunday February 28, 2016

Today we arose early, walked on the beach, ate several times, shopped for tee shirts and books and a cute top for Linda, who will be picking us up on Tuesday afternoon at 3:30 at LAX.

Monday February 29, 2016

It's our last day in Costa Rica. We enjoyed an early-morning walk on the beach with absolutely beautiful moments of silence. It was a great time for being silent and listening to the sounds of the waves, the chirping of the birds, the voices of excited little children. It was also a good time for sitting beside the pool reading—and eating.

At our "Last Supper" together, our tour guide Fabian asked each of us fourteen traveling friends to briefly describe what we loved best about our ten days of discovering the cloud forests, the Mistico Arenal hanging bridges, zip-lining over the canapy, soaking in Arenal volcanic hot springs, floating on the Corobici River, boating across Lago Arenal, hiking in the La Paz Waterfall Gardens, the people, the history, spotting wild monkeys and sloths and margay; the Resplendent Quetzal and Scarlet Macaw and the Chestnut-mandibled Toucan, the barred owl, the kingfisher, the bare-throated Tiger-Heron; the Eyelash Palm Pitviper and side-striped Palm Pitviper, and the Nero Glasswing and Monarch butterflies; the sampling coffee and sugar cane and cocoa plantations, watching the Oscars on big screen TV in Latitude Blue Restaurant on the beach. The food! The beautiful and kind Costa Ricans! And it was unanimous: We loved it all.

Tuesday, March 1, 2016

Pliny the Elder was famous for reminding us: "Home is where the heart is."

Pliny the Elder was famous for writing the encyclopedic Naturalis Historia, which became an editorial model for future encyclopedias. He spent most of his time writing and studying nature. His nephew, Pliny the Younger, wrote about him:

"For my part I deem those blessed to whom, by favour of the gods, it has been granted either to do what is worth writing of, or to write what is worth reading; above measure blessed those on whom both gifts have been conferred. In the latter number will be my uncle, by virtue of his own and of your compositions."

This brave man, Pliny the Elder, (it has been recorded) died in AD 79 in Stabiae while trying to save a friend and his family by ship from the eruption of Mount Vesuvius, which had destroyed Pompeii. A huge wind caused by the volcano's eruption disallowed his ship to leave port. All aboard died. He is remembered for his wisdom and courage.

Late this afternoon, we were blessed to be back home, where the heart is. But I'm wondering, "Where to next?"

Cruising to Vancouver, British Columbia

Sunday May 8, 2016

Happy Mother's Day to All

We were in our pool exercise class a few weeks ago when Mary and Essau bounced over to us and said, "Hey. We're going on a cruise. It's cheap. A repositioning cruise on a ship that needs to get back to Vancouver, British Columbia. Wanna go? I think we can talk our teacher, Ron, and his wife Mary to going with us. Cece and Dick are going." Hmmmm. It took us ten seconds to decide it would be fun to spend five days traveling with our pool buddies. So we signed up.

The Jewel of the Sea docked in San Pedro after a winter of Mexican Riviera trips and needed to get back up to Vancouver to prepare for a summer of Alaskan cruises. So on Sunday, May 1st, the Jewel was gently nudged out of the harbor and we began our journey north. The custom for cruise travel is to provide guests more food, drink, entertainment, comfort, and luxury than is possible to absorb. And in this we were not disappointed. But because the Jewel's goal was to get to Canada, port stops along the way were few.

Our first stop was Astoria, Oregon on the Columbia River, which divides Oregon and Washington. Astoria is famous for housing Lewis and Clark over the winter of 1806 when it was way too cold to be outside. They stayed in Fort Clatsop, hoping to find a ship to take then home. But, eventually they returned to the east coast the way they came: on foot. No cruise ships for them.

Jewel of the Sea

The Flavel House

Astoria's Flavel Museum is a beautiful home, built in 1885 by George Flavel, a wealthy businessman. In 2014 a group of local businessmen bought the house, restored it and it is now a prime tourist attraction. Covering an entire city block, the home is 11,600 square feet. Nice size for a guy with a wife and two daughters.

Our highlight port visit was Victoria on Vancouver Island where we had all day Thursday to tour. We visited the sunken Butchart Gardens, once a gravel pit, now repurposed as a world-class park. The short bus ride from our cruise ship brought us to the Italian Gardens, the Japanese Gardens, the Rose Garden, the Ross Fountain, and the Star Pond. There are ornamental birds all over the gardens. The statue of a wild boar had a very shiny nose. It seems visitors can't resist rubbing his face. Fifty full-time gardeners care for the 55 acres, which contains 900 plant varieties and 26 green houses.

The King and I in Butchart Gardens

Back on board the Jewel, we spent our final night savoring the bounties, packing and settling up accounts. Friday morning, after a short overnight cruise to Vancouver, we say our goodbyes to friends old and new and head out onto the streets of Vancouver. Because we were flying to visit family in Texas the next morning, we had arranged—sight unseen—a one-night economy hotel stay. We spent a night in the "armpit" of Vancouver in the midst of homeless town at the Patricia Hotel on East Hastings Street. It has been said that East Hastings Street is the magnet for the meth addicts. The street is lined with bodies, cigarettes, and trash. Steel bars protect businesses from invaders. Young women prostitute themselves, luring customers with boldly displayed breasts and thighs. The local soup kitchen busily serves those who need feeding.

All along the way, I'm reading "Lunch with Buddha". Richard is reading "Dinner with Buddha" and our friend Roger has been reading "Breakfast with Buddha". The main character, Rimpoche is teaching us love and tolerance toward our fellow human beings. He's reminding us that each person is on her own path, which is a very good thing to remember as we travel through life.

During my early morning walks aboard the Norwegian's Jewel, interesting thoughts occurred to me: What if everyone on the planet who could afford a vacation donated a cruise to a Syrian refugee. The ships could pick them up and bring them to safety. All that food, clean rooms, a library, room service with clean towels, two swimming pools, and three Jacuzzis. Plus the private spa, private dining area, private suites for families. Medical services.

We made it through that night, got a taxi to the airport and enjoyed our quick stop over in Texas. And now we're back home from that trip. What a week: an abundance of food, money, room key cards, and excursions into prime attractions. We've been in Texas visiting family. Pizza with grandson Billy and wife Christina and their three girls: Claire, Joselyn, and Genevieve.

On Mother's Day, we met and meditated with daughter Dianna's AA group and son-in-law Bob in Dallas. Jim, who led the AA meeting this morning, told me he fears for his daughter, who is going through hell: using, abusing, causing painful feelings for her family. Love and tolerance are needed now, more than ever, not judgment or hatred. Stress. Anger. Misunderstandings. They have no place in our hearts.

The Dali Lama reminds us: "The purpose of life is happiness. The way to happiness is through service." For those who serve: Never give up. For those who suffer: never give up. For those who wonder, wander, or weep: never give up.

After the meeting, we took a drive to Weatherton, Texas for Claire's Statewide Gymnastic Competition. Out of seventy 10-11-12 year olds, Claire came out 3rd. Congratulations Claire! Later we had a beautiful BBQ with granddaughter Jennifer, her husband Joey and their girls: Zoe, Chloe, Tabatha, and Bailey Grace . . . and Joey's mom Susan and her husband Ricky.

Claire with Great Grandma Sue

Then, Bob and Di whisked us away to Dallas Fort Worth Airport, where as parents of an American Airline employee (thank you Di) we caught an almost free flight home.

Ron, our fabulous pool Kinesiology instructor tells us every Tuesday and Thursday that "Attitude and Gratitude equal Gladitude." At the end of each class, he has us all shout out, "It's a beautiful day. Wooooo!"

We feel so blessed to have all these wonderful opportunities to met people all around the world. We are blessed with a beautiful family, and so many amazing friends.

What's next?

Ireland – July 2015

Travel Itinerary Richard and Sue

Ireland – July 13 – 29th.

Day 1 Monday July 13: Leave LAX at 8:00 a.m. and fly to Newark, New Jersey on United Airlines flight 1556. Leave N.J. at 7:30 p.m. on United Airlines Flight #25 and arrive in Galway 7:00 a.m. on July 14th.

Day 2. Tuesday July 14: Hotel: Galway
Day 3 Wednesday July 15: Hotel Galway

Day 4 Thursday July 16: Hotel Killarney
Day 5: Friday July 17: Hotel Killarney
Day 6: Saturday July 18 Killarney
Day 7: Sunday July 19 Kilkenny
Day 8: Monday July 20 Kilkenny

Day 9: Tuesday July 21 Dublin
Day 10: Wednesday July 22 Dublin
Day 11: Thursday July 23 Dublin

Day 12: Friday July 24 – 28 Harding Hotel (just us, rest of group flies home on 24th)
Harding Hotel: Copper Alley, Fishamble Street, Christchurch, Dublin, Ireland
Telephone: 353 (0) 1-679-6500

Return home on Wednesday August 29th on United Airlines Flight #22 out of Dublin at 9:00 a.m. to Newark, then on to LAX on United Airlines Flight #1140, arriving at 3:41 p.m.

Dear Family and Friends,

We're home from a lovely 17-day trip to the Emerald Isle of Ireland. Yes, we are, and a fine trip it was. Just lovely. Fifty of us traveled from Orange High School to LAX to New Jersey and right across the Atlantic Sea to

Shannon to perform five lively concerts in such glorious venues as Saint Nicolas Collegiate Church in Galway, Saint Canice Cathedral in Kilkenny, Saint Mary's in Killarny, Saint Patrick's Cathedral in Dublin, and at Saint Joseph's in Glasthuly.

American gospel, spirituals, folk tunes, and a few Irish Ballads we did blare out across the landscape, even performing several "drive-bys" where we popped into such places as the Waterford Glass Factory and Showroom, the Nox Hotel Lobby, the medieval church of Kevin's Cross and Kitchen, often singing Jester Hairston's Amen, flashmob-style.

Special thanks: Thea and Shirley for driving us up to OHS at 3:30 in the morning, the Friendliness of the Irish people, the wonderful singers on our bus who loaded and unloaded the Rascal at least 50 times, the strong young busboy and cute young woman at The Silver Moon Café in Howth who caught Richard when he lost his balance, the DART attendants who quickly set up the ramps for us to enter and exit the trains, Mike Short, Orange Community Master Chorale director and Charles Stephenson, Master Chorale of Saddleback Valley for their expertise in guiding us through Ave Marie and Magnum and (my favorite) Salmo 50 – la la la la la la la la la. Love it! All of our amazing and beautiful singing friends. And a huge thank you to our dear Linda who drove up to LAX in the afternoon traffic to bring us back to our little bungalow on the creek. We are so grateful for all of the reminders of what a wonderful world we live in.

Memorable moments: Walk'n rollin' along the rocky western coast at the Cliffs of Moher (south of Doolin) in the sunshine, stepping over 4-inch long slugs, taking lots of pictures of the sea and the screeching kittiwakes, and then enjoying tea and pastry in the Long Dock restaurant with the big picture windows.

Bussing our way around the Dingle Peninsula, the westernmost tip of Ireland where the Gaelic language is mandatory in the schools, where fishing and farming still matter.

The echo of our voices as we sang in the Cathedrals. The energy of music. The awakening of our spirits. The sight of James loving his dream-come-true (thanks to many of you) and his strong tenor voice as he sang in perfect pitch with a blessed energy.

The purple heather growing on the hillsides, the sheep with their spray-painted butts in shades of red and blue, the black cows and white cows and brown cows, the seagulls, the colorful horses with their young colts, the gray-vested black jackdaws.

Visiting the Writers Museum with original works of poor poet W.B. Yeats, and the prolific James Joyce, and George Bernard Shaw, and Oscar Wilde, and Samuel Beckett, and my favorite: Jonathan Swift (A Modest Proposal: "For preventing the children of poor people in Ireland from being a burden on their parents or country, and for making them beneficial to the publick" - 1729.) The greens of Ireland - 50 shades for sure. The night at Citywest Hotel just outside Dublin where we learned drumming and two Irish dances: the set and the ceili. The night we were entertained by the outstanding Merry Ploughboys, a quartet of Irish Ballad singers. We sang and clapped and laughed.

Five days on our own in Dublin after most others left for the U.S. The night we decided to go to the movies and see Inside Out and because of the many steps up to the theater we could not get Inside and had to stay Out. The excellent meals in great little Bistros where we could take our time and relax. The Chester Beatty library and the Silk Road Mediterranean restaurant.

Trinity College in Dublin where we viewed The Book of Kells with the motto "Turning Darkness into Light", the Old Library with its 200-foot long main chamber of 200,000 books dating from as far back as 1732, the Brian Boru harp from the 1400's, Dublin's Castle, Grafton Street shopping mall, Dublin Maker - a display of inventive ideas of creative thinkers from around the world.

The Harding Hotel on Fishamble where the window in our room gave us a perfect view of Christ Church Cathedral across the street. We watched the rain, snacked on leftover salad and trail mix, enjoyed coffee and tea, tromped up and down the elevator dozens of times, got to know the staff from Ireland, Turkey, China, Brazil, other places around the globe.

Facts: Ireland was under British rule until the revolution in 1922. Northern Ireland is still part of Great Britain where the pound is the currency while the Republic of Ireland uses the euro. In 1973 the Republic of Ireland joined the European Union and was granted a huge amount of money to build roads, buy trains, purchase sheep, and to further invest in tourism.

Ireland was the first nation to welcome all people the freedom to marry whomever they love regardless of anything.

The farmers spray paint their sheep's rear ends in different colors in order to identify them.

Many fortifications were built for the purpose of defending the homeland from a possible Napoleon's French invasion in the early 1800's, which never happened.

Five million folks live in Ireland and six and one-half millions sheep live in Ireland.

The Irish Pride of land-ownership and the miles and miles of family-built heather-covered rock walls sometimes running right down to the sea. The government owns the national parks but little else in the way of land.

Once, the Musical, at Olympia Theater in Dublin was a feast of singing and a great reminder of the many facets of love. Never doubt the power of the muse.

There are about 25 ways to prepare potatoes. Our favorite is in the soup. We consumed at least a dozen bowls of veggie soup and it was wonderful.

It rained most days on our trip. The temperature ranged between 54 and 64, cloudy with moments of light showers and the occasional sunbeam.

Miles of cars--at least a thousand cars--lined up on the two-lane highway to get into Kilarney to watch the highly competitive Irish Football game between County Kerry and County Cork.

The Blarney Castle, Waterford, the walled city of Viking origins, Kilkenny Castle, hiking Glendalough in the Wicklow Mountains. Wow! You've just got to go to this wonderful country. We loved it. You'll love it too.

Many blessings to all of you for making our lives so great. You've given us a great "Attitude of Gratitude."

Sue and Richard

P.S. Always "mind the gap" and "bin your gum."

Summer Road Trip - 2016
July 17 - August 5, 2016

1. July 17, 18, 19 San Francisco
2. July 20 - Eureka Area
3. July 21 - Albany & Keizer Area, Oregon
4. July 22 - Tacoma, Washington Area
5. July 23, 24, 25 - Victoria on Vancouver Island
6. .July 26 . . TBD . . .
7. July 27 - Kamloop BC @
8. July 28, 29, 30, 31 - Deer Lodge @ Lake Louise
9. August 1,2,3,4 - Glacier National Park in Montana @ St. Mary's Lodge
10. August 5 - Head Home .... ☺

North to . . . #1 (written July 19, 2016)

"Take a risk today. Go out and live your life.
Let the joy of life flow through you!"

Judy Morley

Sunday July 17, 2016

What could be better than singing along with Willie "On the Road Again" and "If You're Going to San Francisco, Be Sure to Wear Flowers in Your Hair" written by John Phillips of the Mamas & the Papas, singing along with Scott McKenzie? And when you're at the rest area north of Bakersfield be sure to fold your hands and say "Namaste" to two beautiful sari-begowned Indian Ladies in the Women's Restroom.

We listened to Janet Evanovich's "The Heist" about FBI Special Agent Kate O'Hare as we drove up the 5 through miles of dry hills and the occasional pistachio grove. The prominent stacks of bailed hay, which, since our last trip through England, we call "Hay Henge." On through the fog across the Bay Bridge as room #482 awaits us.

Evening: One of Sue's brilliant brainstorms comes into fruition at the Boudin Restaurant, upstairs overlooking Alcatraz and the Bay Tour boats. Here's the story:

A couple walks into a restaurant and are seated. Wine is served. He notices a sexy young woman standing in the corner. As she twinkles her fingers at him, he looks away and smiles at his wife. The next time he looks up, SYW is holding a sign: "Take her hand. Look into her eyes. Smile." Whoa! OK. Good idea. Fifteen seconds pass. Again he looks toward the corner where SYW is holding up another sign. This one reads: Say "I love you as you kiss her hand." Mentally, he rolls his eyes. Without pause, SYW holds up another sign. "Do you want her attention later this evening?"

He's getting the idea: women want attention, commitment, to feel adored. Again, he glances over at SYW. This sign reads: "Do NOT look at the Dodger game on the big screen TV." He thinks: OK men want food, affection, and baseball. I guess women are just different. After the wine, the chowder in a bread bowl, the rock-cod tacos, and a bit more handholding, they leave the restaurant. Unnoticed by his wife, he hands a $20 bill to SYW. By the end of the evening SYW has collected over $500, which she shares with the waiter who seats all the men facing her and all the women, facing their men. Stand by for another great brainstorm.

Next day: Monday July 18th. Walking 4.7 miles and seven hours took us through all the best of Golden Gate Park. First stop: California Academy of Science. Isn't it amazing that years of scientists studying the universe helps us all to understand evolution, the comets' contribution to life on planet Earth, and then it all gets computerized and animated so we can all enjoy this brilliant knowledge? Veggie chili soup for me. Chicken wrap and salad for The King in the Academy Café.

Next: The Japanese Tea Gardens with their pagodas, flora and fauna, winding pathways where we traipsed back and forth looking for accessible trails. We laughed. When Richard wondered if his rascal could make it across one of those very narrow concrete bridges across the lily ponds I reminded him to just close his eyes and step on the gas. Only a few times did I doubt the wisdom of those words. He never tumbled in. No tea for us in the Tea Gardens – too many steps.

Today was the last day of "12 pianos" being played throughout the San Francisco Botanical Gardens. As we strolled through the grounds we'd hear music. First we came upon a group of young men creating the sounds: one on trombone, one on drums and one seated at the piano – in the Australian Gardens. Next we found ourselves sitting down listening to a young woman play soothing classical music. As she gave up the bench, a young man sat down, removed his right tennis shoe, and played his favorite piece. Next, a ragtime player entertained us with several pieces. Wow! Redwood trees, Japanese maples, music, sunshine, happy little kids chasing each other around.

In Orange County we could have driven the distance from the park to the Marriott in 20 minutes. In San Francisco, because of the plethora of "no left turn" signs, buses and trolleys having the right-of-way, bikers and walkers and segue riders, one-way streets suddenly becoming one-way the other way, and all the construction, it took us a couple of hours. We finally figured out that we'd have to make three right turns to equal any left turn we needed. Ah. City planners.

The day ended with Trader Joe scones and leftover chicken-wrap and a Barbara Streisand and Ryan O'Neal movie (wasn't he "hot" back then?) "What's Up Doc?" Lots of great memories and laughs.

Tuesday, July 19, 2016

By 1:00 today we'd walk 'n rolled 5.7 miles. Walked to Pier 39's shops and restaurants and decided to split a veggie-omelet at Eagle Café. Our waiter Gabrielle brought extra plates; kept the coffee hot and said thank you when we pointed out the little gnat who was swimming in the maple syrup.

Up the hill in Chinatown we spent a few minutes in St. Mary's Square – a little park on the edge of homelessville, then were amazed at shop after shop of trinkets from China – and so many restaurants. A typical menu sign would announce: Come insaid for chicken-leg soup, hollow vegetables (when in season), sea slug with lettuce and frog leg in clay pot.

Imagine our excitement when we realized there was a noontime concert in St. Mary's Catholic Church. Only problem was they couldn't get the lift to work, so after much maneuvering, Richard backed out of the lift and we made a quick, but sad, exit.

Outside of Chinatown we came upon several streets lined with Italian restaurants. Needing an early-afternoon break, we headed back to room 482. Lucky we had fresh apricots and Trader Joe's whole grain crispbread with us.

The plan for tomorrow: rise early and head north to Eureka for lunch with friends Vicky White and Victoria Light. More news as it happens . . .

Love and blessings, to all. Sue and The King

North to . . . #2

Wednesday, July 20.

Happy Birthday to our son John. We love you!!!

Up at 5:15. Packed and on the road (again) to Eureka by 6:30. Over the Golden Gate, while sharing a banana. Farewell to the City by the Bay. We loved every moment. Traffic coming south into the city backed up for 6 miles. Northbound wide-open, except for about 12 spots on the 101 and 5 where construction crews were improving driving conditions while earning a decent living. Our taxes well spent.

At 11:30 we stopped for gas in Fortuna, across the street from Fortuna Wheels and Tires. Wow! Carmina Barana! Another quick phone call to Vicky White to say "almost there." She reserved a table by the window at the Café

Waterfront in Olde Towne Eureka. The Café Waterfront is a former brothel for fishermen and miners. Leave it to our friends to pick the most interesting places. Hugs and kisses and laughter. We hadn't seen Vicky White and Victoria Light (yes, the publishers of White Light) for two years when we all gathered up at Tahoe City for Rev. Liz Luoma's installation.

We enjoyed halibut salad and catching up on family history. Hard to believe their little granddaughter Stella is 11 years old. Harder to believe we have seven grandkids, eight great-grandkids. They took us on a little walk 'n roll in the harbor and talked about the highlights of Eureka. We will be back some day.

After lunch, we drove and drove and drove, listening to the latest escapades of Special FBI Agent Kate McHare. At 9:00 p.m. we were in Albany, 450 miles from San Francisco, checked into the Rodeway Inn and slept like a couple of senior citizens who'd been on the road most of the day.

Thursday, July 21, 2016.

Happy 4th Birthday to our Great-Grandson Sylas. We love you!

Before meeting Cousin Jim and wife Diane, we stopped off at the Williamette River, which is notorious for homeless characters hanging out. One of these characters, Lorin Dante, offered to take our pictures, which we paid for with 20 minutes of listening to the mysteries of life. He's a "solar designer on wood artist." Apparently not too unusual in this neck of the woods. They say if the police get a call, it's usually Bowman Park on the Williamette.

Photo of us by Lorin Dante

Lunch with Diane and Jim was such a kick. They are involved in preparations for their daughter, Courtney's, August 6th wedding. Cousins talk about what great little kids they had been and wonder where the time goes. Christian, the owner of Sam City (a Vietnamese restaurant in Albany) reminded us three times that if we stopped talking and laughing he could take our order and start cooking. The veggies and tofu were perfect.

Cousin Jim and wife Diane - me and The King

Spent the evening with Matt (Richard's college buddy) and his wife Kenda. If you want to know what your husband REALLY did in the 70's this is the way to find out. Much fun laughing and sharing stories in their beautiful home in Keizer right on the lake, then halibut dinner on the other side of the lake at Delaney Madison Grill on the shore of Staats Lake. So, tomorrow, on to Port Angeles in Northern Washington.

Matt and Kenda with me and The King

Funny street names and signs along the way: Skoomchaka, Nisqually, Puyallup, Steilacoom, Congestion on Relief Project, and Kitchen-Dick Road.

Friday, July 22, 2016

After being turned away from four hotels in Port Angeles, a kind hotel clerk, Randy, offered to phone a few and finally located the ONLY vacancy, the Flagstone Motel just a few blocks from the Black Ball Ferry Line. Someone had canceled his reservation moments before. It was cheap and funky and perfect.

Saturday, July 23, 2016

The next morning we took a walk n' roll through Olde Town Port Angeles and had a huge surprise! We had just crossed the street and heard a familiar voice,

"Richard is that you? What are you doing here?" It was Trish Burson-Johnson whom we knew from Center for Spiritual Living Costa Mesa. What a miracle! She and husband Will and her parents have lived in Port Angeles, Washington for a whole month. They bought seven acres with lots of buildings for their new home and spiritual center. After standing on the sidewalk chatting for 15 minutes we decided to share fig and fennel scones at a little café. We're always amazed at what happens when we travel.

The Black Ball Ferry takes 90 minutes to cross from Port Angeles to Victoria on Vancouver Island. I drove on and Richard rolled on with passengers because once you park your car on the ferry you get to hike up about 40 steps to the deck, which the Rascal does not do well. Fortunately for us, we'd made reservations for the ferry two weeks ago.

Once in Victoria we checked into the Marriott then spent a couple of hours checking out the place. We walked by the Empress Hotel, which opened for business in 1908 and is famous for serving High Tea in the afternoons, the Victoria Bug Zoo, the Royal BC Museum, the International Busker Festival which happens every July at the Inner Harbour. Lots of street performers juggling and balancing and dancing, food and drinks. Also happening this weekend is the Deuce Classic Car rally. 150 old cars lined the main streets while hundreds of middle-aged men walked around in either pride or envy. We contemplated one little 1932 white Ford coupe that was for sale for $40,000.

Sicily, our waitress at the dockside Steamship Grill and Bar brought Richard salmon and veggies while I feasted on beet and feta salad. We shared a beer and lemonade and nearly fell asleep at the table. We are so out of practice. We laughed about how fun it is getting old. We are so grateful that we get to travel and see the world. I often wonder how this little farm girl got to this amazing place in life. It's incredible. I'm so grateful. Ron Hastings, retired Kinesiology instructor at Saddleback College taught us: Attitude = Gratitude = Gladitude. It's all true.

Blessings to all, Sue and The King

North #3

"Above all, do not lose your desire to walk.
I have walked myself into my best thoughts
and know of no thought so burdensome that one
cannot walk away from it."

Buddha

Tuesday July 26, 2016

Royal BC Museum in Victoria on Vancouver Island, British Columbia is full of beady-eyed woolly Mammoths known as giants of the ice-age. The most precious creature we've ever seen is named Lyuba, meaning love. She's a perfectly preserved baby Mammoth who died in a muddy pond in Siberia about 40,000 years ago. Apparently she fell in, died and froze. A Siberian farmer discovered her in 2007.

We walked through a rich collection of fossils, casts, preserved flesh, immersive media and engaging interactives. We marveled at the Proboscidean family tree, from woollies to mastodons to dwarves to modern-day elephants. Sometimes standing more than 14 feet tall, mammoths and mastodons towered over the lands of Europe, Asia, and North America from as long ago as 1.8 million years in the past to as recently as 10,000 years ago, during the Ice Age. And now they're here at the Royal BC Museum. We saw the 3-D iMax movie about creatures of the Ice-Age, narrated by Christopher Plummer.

Victor Wells III entertained us with his guitar strumming and singing Blue Grass, as we enjoyed High Tea at Victoria's famous Embassy Hotel. While we feasted on organic cream tea, scones, teeny veggie sandwiches and chocolate-mousse he sang "Harvest Moon" and "My Dog Blue" and "Sunny Afternoon." What a treat. What a connection. His sister has had MS for 35 years and is also a very inspiring survivor.

Here we are in the famous Empress
Hotel enjoying High Tea

Tomorrow we ferry across the sea to Vancouver on the mainland and head for Kamloops 477 kilometers east.

Thursday July 27, 28.

Kamloops' desert-like territory heated things up a bit; wonderful salads at Mittz in old part of town, folk singers in the park on the Thompson River, then a quiet night at Fairfield Inn. Drove through kilometers and kilometers of forested mountains, ooohing and aaahing all the way.

Friday July 29:

Ah! Lake Louise! Named for Queen Victoria's otherwise anonymous fourth daughter, Lake Louise is famous for its teahouses, grizzly bears, Victoria Glacier, and countless hiking trails. This morning we walk 'n rolled along the lake for almost two miles - with about 100 other tourists. We offered to take pictures of others; they took pictures of us. Everyone was happy, friendly, and awestruck by the color of the glacier water, the stand-up paddlers and canoers, the warm sunshine. So many of you told me this was the most beautiful place ever, and now we believe it.

The King and I at Lake Louise

Lake Louise Village's Pipestone Quarry sells dinosaur bones, petrified wood, beautiful stones, and ammonites of all sizes. To add to his frog collection, Richard purchased a gorgeous ammonite. Meanwhile I perused the Viewpoint Book Store and found "The Walker's Anthology" by Deborah Manley. More than one hundred literary figures contributed to this compilation, including Mark Twain, Agatha Christie, Barack Obama, Henry David Thoreau, and (a fave of mine) Bill Bryson. (See quotes above.)

According to our iPhone 6, we've been walkin 'n rollin' at least six miles a day.

"Excuse me. There's a grizzly bear over there," said the young woman to the two old folks standing outside their 2005 white Dodge Caravan.

Yikes! We scurried back into the van and closed the doors. Thanks to the young woman in the parking lot on the way to Banff, we were not bear meat this evening. We'd been warned about the bears but thought they'd be out in the wilderness, not at a roadside stop. When we left, there were about a dozen vehicles stopped for picture-taking.

By the time we realized we were hungry for dinner the restaurants were all closed. We had apples, crackers, and almond butter with granola for dessert. Life doesn't get any better. And so to sleep . . .

Much love from Richard and Sue

North to . . . #4

"If you're walking down the right path and you're willing to keep walking, eventually you'll make progress."

Barack Obama

(From "The Walker's Anthology" by Deborah Manly)

July 30 and 31, 2016

Another day, another bear, a herd of antelope, several golden mantled squirrels, dozens of glaciers, the ice-fields of Banff, lakes, rivers, the call and shrieks of several Clark's Nutcrackers, moth moss and moss moths, little kids speaking Dutch, German, French, Italian, Spanish, Mandarin, Japanese, Vietnamese, Urdu, and, of course, the Queen's English; strangers asking,

"Do you want me to take your picture?"

Handing over iPhones and expensive cameras. Richard bouncing along the Lake Louise trail in his Rascal, people dodging as he flew over rocks, mud puddles, slabs of granite, up steep slopes, and down steep hills with his warning call, "Hee Haw."

(An aside: After dating Richard for two months (1993) I told him if he wanted this relationship to work, he'd need to find a way to take walks with me. The next day his dad bought him a Rascal (battery-powered scooter). We've been walkin' 'n rollin' ever since.)

Lunch by the fireplace in Deer Lodge: apple slices dipped in almond butter, Trader Joe's crisp bread, and rice crackers.

Gratitude for Raj, a student from India for serving yesterday's late lunch in "Something Else" Greek restaurant in Jasper. (Greek salad and spanakopita for me and minestrone soup and turkey sandwich for Richard). We exchanged "Namaste," packed up half of the meal and later took it to our Lodge for dinner.

Gratitude for Vicky, a Mandarin speaker, for keeping room 10 at Deer Lodge in reasonable order. She said she'd love to take a road trip but doesn't know how to drive.

Gratitude for Deanna, a geolocation student from Newfoundland, serving breakfast in the Lodge dining room. Someday she'll be directing Google Maps.

Gratitude for Peggy Bassett for channeling our special parking space in tourist-riddled Jasper Village while dozens of busses and hundreds of cars searched.

Gratitude for iPhones, email, Facebook, and texting for keeping us connected to family and friends.

"Not all who wander are lost."

J.R.R. Tolkien

North to . . . #5

Monday August 1,

Drove from Lake Louise in Canada to St. Mary's Lodge right outside Glacier National Park in the good old USA. First night in our little creek-side cabin with Richard's sister Jerri. Much joy at seeing each other and unpacking and old memories.

Tuesday a.m. huge breakfast: sautéed onions, potato, zucchini, bell pepper, tomatoes, lettuce and scrambled eggs. Off for a drive and a hike. We drove north to Many Glacier Lodge. Joe, the attendant in the hotel, guided us down to the basement and out the "employees only" back door and pointed us toward what he thought might be a fun trail for us to try. We walked 'n rolled the semi-accessible trail part-way around the lake. When we got stuck, a lovely strong angel named Jessica stopped her hike to help tug and push The King and his Rascal over a few bumps. At the kayak launching area we took off our boots, rolled up our levi's and walked into the cool refreshing water. The air was about eighty-six degrees. On our way back we ran into Jessica and her family - a husband and three adorable little kids. We talked for fifteen more minutes about the wonders of nature and their amazing life in Montana.

Then it was on to Logan's Pass at the summit - 6646 feet. The information center was accessible! The sun was shining. People were happy! The trail around the Pass was accessible and we saw a family of Mountain Goats. Dad had on a huge collar as the group is part of the Mountain Goat Study. We stopped off at 'Nell's (probably named in honor of Mr. Grinnell who helped establish Glacier National Park.) Richard and I split a Black Bean Burger. We walked and rolled almost five miles today.

Wednesday: Jerri went off for a tour on the Red Jammer bus. The King and I drove our 2005 white Caravan on Going to the Sun Road. We so looked forward to high mountain peaks and high mountain glaciers and high mountain waterfalls and lakes and high mountain everything. As we approached the summit, the temperature dropped to 38 degrees. The drizzle and fog and clouds were unexpected, but just as every time we keep our spirits up, knowing life is going to get better, a rainbow appeared in the valley below us. We pulled to the side of the road with several other cars and took a few pictures. Because of the fogginess, we only got a peek at Heaven's Peak. Still it was all beautiful.

The rest stop at the Avalanche Picnic area was also drizzly and cold. I hopped out of the van to take a few pictures and came back to tell Richard the good news/bad news. Good news: there's a completely accessible .7-mile trail. The bad news: you're going to get out of the nice warm van, get into the Rascal and we're walking 'n rolling the trail. Hats, gloves, jackets, a fuzzy warm blanket and two umbrellas and we were off to see what an avalanche had done to the hillside of Trail of the Cedars. Wow! Wow! Wow!

I love this picture because it shows how this incredible man—my husband, my lifemate follows me even when it's freezing cold. He's always happy after.

Next we stopped off at Eddie's Café for a Black Bean Burger, where all the helpers wore tee-shirts announcing:

"Almost Everyone Eats at Eddie's."

Then back to our cabin on the creek by 6:00. Jerri's making veggie soup for dinner. How good can life get?!

North/South #6

August 8, 2016 (8 & 8 = 16)

Dear Family and Friends,

We're home!! And there ain't no place like it. As we cruised through Gate 3 into Laguna Woods at 10:30 Saturday night Richard said, "This is where we belong." We tried to find a place in Vegas at 4:30 on Saturday. No rooms, so we drove on home. We came from Top Hotel right outside of Burley, Idaho to Laguna Woods in fourteen hours. 804 miles. Whew!

We're unpacked, the wash is done, everything put away. Time to plan another trip. Our friends Carlos and Tanya just dropped by and talked about their family trip to Yosemite this past week. That sounds like a GREAT idea. Will let you know.

Love to all, Sue and The King

Carnegie Hall - May 2017

SAVE THE DATE . . . .

Dear Lovers of Music, especially Carmina Burana,

Here's the DEAL OF THE CENTURY. If you'd like to see yours truly, along with other members of the Orange Community Master Chorale and the Saddleback Master Chorale and the Irvine Community Orchestra perform Carmina Burana in Carnegie Hall on Saturday, May 27th at 1:00 p.m. you may purchase tickets online for a mere $125 (plus $6.50 service charge, plus $475 air flight, plus $1150 hotel for the weekend plus $250 for meals for a total of #2,006.50).

OR, you may wish to see the same fabulous performance on Sunday, May 7th at 4:00 p.m. at Santiago Canyon College in the city of Orange for a mere $20. That's right folks! $20 . . . . with FREE PARKING.

Let me know if you'd like tickets for the Sunday May 7th performance. I'll begin picking them up Monday February 27th. If you're flying to NYC you may order tickets online for $125, plus $6.50 service charge.

Sincerely, Sue Snyder, Alto I

NYC May 24 – May 28, 2017

Day 1. Wanna sing in Carnegie Hall? We've all heard those words "Practice Practice Practice." So true. Here's how I did it. Joined Orange Community Master Chorale in January of 2005. Sang Carmina Burana in 2009. What a challenge. Wednesday May 24 had friend Linda drop me off at Long Beach airport. Met up with 23 members of OCMC. Jet Blue was an hour late so pilot speeded up on the way to JFK. Struck up a conversation with a little girl in line at check-in line. Her mommy had her arms full with her bag and the stroller. I helped kick her bag along. They'd spent several days at Disneyland, meeting other Princesses and were on their way home to San Francisco.

As I approached Gate 8, I spotted my three roommates: Maureen, Gale, and Mary quietly sitting in those comfy airport bench seats. After hellos I asked a question: "Did I tell you that I snore like a freight train?"

Wish I'd had my iPhone on video mode and recorded their faces. My next wish was that I had not said that. After their assurances that they'd be

OK, I had to tell them I was just kidding. I decided then and there, since I asked if I could room with them I would tone down my "Living in Hallelujah fun-loving energetic" self. That turned out to be a good idea. The flight was smooth because I brought myself a bag of veggies and a bag of trail mix. Read all the articles in SOM magazine. Did two Sudokus: a Loco and a plain. We arrived at JFK at 11:30, got to the hotel at 12:30. In bed by 1:15.

Day 2. Up at 6:25 Thursday. We strolled down 42nd Street to Delmonico for breakfast. The $10.00 per pound buffet offered raspberries and strawberries and mango along with scrambled eggs with veggies. The $6.00 per pound buffet offered egg dishes of all kinds and bread. Coffee was $1.49. Guess which buffet I picked? We got back to the hotel ballroom for the 9:30 rehearsal with full orchestra OMG! Amazing. Had time to meet with and talk to the gang from OCMC. Sat with James and gave him one of the bills Richard sent for him. He was very grateful.

All went well except that it rained all day. Riding atop the Hop-on Hop-off bus wasn't the most brilliant idea I'd ever had. With a poncho on the seat and another on our bodies, we still got very wet. After two hours we landed at Battery Park across the Hudson from Statue of Liberty, which we observed through the fog. The local Deli welcomed us with a blast of hot air.

Gail, Mary, and I enjoyed hot tea upstairs and finished off my bag of veggies (love them snap peas) and dug into my bag of Trader Joe's little chocolate chip cookies. Back out into the rain. My two sensible buddies rode inside the bus for the trip home to Grand Hyatt. Back up into the storm I go to observe the high-rises, the people, the sights. My Iceland Boots kept my toes warm. Everything else got wet. Thank goodness I'd packed extra Levi's and tees. Dropped Levi's over tall floor lamp in our room and socks over elongated night light. Spirits High.

Thursday evening I had dinner in bed: Greek salad from one of the Grand Central Station delis. Got up, invited Mary downstairs. It was prom night for the local High School. The girls and boys were all lavishly dressed and coiffed and made-up. They looked like models and were so happy to be seen and even_happier when I offered to use their iPhones and smart phones for picture-taking. None of the kids turned down my offer to photograph them. Most of the guys had elaborately-styled Afros. Many were quietly following their dates around holding up their long flowing dresses. (Especially important when riding up and down the escalator.) All of them were excited and had such a good time posing. What a wonderful connection.

Day 3. Friday a.m. Living in Hallelujah. Left Grand Hyatt around 7:00 and headed for my favorite spot in NYC: Central Park. Stopped off at Rockefeller

Center. Fountains and flowers. Five young Chinese men taking pictures. I spoke no Chinese. They spoke little Californian. iPhone sign language and more picture-taking. One funny selfie and I was on my way. CP was quietly and sparsely alive with unleashed dogs, mommies with babies in strollers, and a few joggers. A quiet walk. Buddha offered me a wooden beaded bracelet and asked for money for Peace Effort. One $. Two $. Five $. He pointed at $20 on his chart. I smiled and bowed and headed off down the trail.

Ah! Strawberry Fields and the amazing "Imagine" mosaic as viewed from Yoko Ono's parkside home. John will never be forgotten. A young man sat across from me. Opened his guitar case, set up a money-collector and began to sing Beatle songs. So much love in this world. Gave him a tip and strolled on.

The path under the bridge. Greensleeves on an erhu, a Chinese violin. Talk about Living in Hallelujah. I think I'm in heaven. Then I turned west on 77th and stopped for eggs and a croissant with strawberry jam. (Note to my sister Jeanne Reed: It was better than we feared and worse than I'd hoped for.)

My next stop was the NYC Historic Center, which could have been named the Women's Center. History of U.S. wars. History of construction of NYC in the 1600's. Built by slaves: African and Irish. Learned that there are now 168 languages spoken in NYC. Bar immigrants from entering the U.S.? Don't get me started. We're all immigrants. I viewed an 18-minute documentary film while sharing the auditorium with about 200 Elementary school kids - 99% of them of African descent. I had no idea it was built by slaves. Never thought about it. Poverty everywhere. Apartments in the 1900's often housed up to eight families. One bathroom per building. Wow!

Posters of Women's efforts during WWI lined the hallway. From nurses in France, factory workers, cooks. Visited the gift shop. Lots of children's books regarding Women's inventions, women's right, women's brilliance, all to encourage young girls to be the best - which reminds me of Hillary's new intentions to help young women get involved in politics and her reminder to vote, to encourage everyone to vote.

Wandering through Central Park again I found more opportunities to meet world travelers. This time I met a young couple from Ireland. Of course I offered to take their pictures and then they took my picture by the pond. After walking 6.8 miles, according to my "health app" I got back to the hotel at 1:10, took a shower and was down in the ballroom for 1:30 - 4:30 rehearsal.

Friday evening Mary and I strolled down 42nd Street to Bryant Park. Chairs were set up for a free production of The Merry Wives of Winsor, which was delightfully performed by fifteen Drilling Company actors. Slang mixed with Shakespearian words of wisdom. A riotous comedy. Great way to end a very long Friday.

There are quite a few homeless people in NYC. Veterans, druggies, runaways. We spoke with Joe. He'd been in the Vietnam War and was affected by Agent Orange. He'd lost most of his teeth, broke his shoulder and got whacked in the head by a three-story fall off a construction platform. He receives $75 worth of food stamps and $271 in cash once a month for living expenses. He has no job but lives and pays rent to stay on a little farm.

A young man slept behind a sign. "I need $16 to get home to Long Island." I woke him up and gave him a $20. He teared up and said nice things. He's going home to mom. His part-time job ended and little company couldn't pay his last paycheck. As we walked away I wondered if he had enough to eat. Who knows which stories are true, if drugs, alcohol, or oxyconton are involved. Spirit guides me.

Day 4. Saturday, May 27, 2017. Carnegie Hall presents: Up early. Blueberries and mango on Greek Yogurt. On the bus at 8:00 a.m. Arrived Carnegie Hall 8:30. Rehearsed until 11:00. Irvine Symphony musicians arranged themselves on stage about 1:45. Master Chorale of Saddleback Valley, Orange Community Master Chorale (my group), and two Children's Choirs followed. As I climbed up the risers and turned to face the audience my brain asked,

"What's this little farm girl doing here?"

Our audience of 2500 sat in anticipation. I tuned into the passion and confidence of our director Mike Short, an amazing Orange High School music teacher. At that moment I knew all the practice, all the rehearsals, all the energy that went into getting into this place, at this time, were worth it. I love a challenge and wow oh wow did I find one this time!

Carmina Burana, composed by Carl Orff, is basically 24 poems written by a group of de-frocked monks in the 1300's. So, of course it has to do with gambling, drinking, and lust. Mostly sung in Olde German. The first song "O Fortuna" has been the theme song in countless movies. Not only did we receive a standing ovation at the end of our performance but the audience insisted we bring back our director and the three soloists THREE times. Back on the bus and onto cruising, eating, drinking, dancing on the Hudson. The Children's Choirs loved the loud music and dancing on the ship.

Day 5. Sunday morning we sang parts of O Fortuna to our taxi driver, Hill from Haiti. He seemed to enjoy our enthusiasm. JFK Airport is about an hour outside of NYC through a maze of streets and highways that he knew very well.

Our flight home took us over our cousins in Nebraska, the snow-capped Rocky Mountains of Colorado, and the deserts of Southern California. Our flight attendants Carolina and Lewis were so kind and thoughtful, we could tell they loved their jobs: serving Jet Blue customers.

Richard came to pick me up. I met a new friend May Lan, also from Laguna Woods, in the Baggage Claim area. We gave her a ride home and she took us out to Wahoo's for dinner the next night. It's a beautiful world. Home is where the heart is - and the husband - and the zucchini - and peace 'n quiet.

Yosemite #1

September 10, 2017

Here they go again! Remember the summer of 2016 when we returned from a 4700-mile road trip and 21 days of seeing amazing things like San Francisco, friends in Eureka, cousins and friends in Oregon, then Victoria Island and Lake Louise and Glacier National Park and . . . whew! Upon our return to our little condo on the creek at 907-O, I said, "I'm done traveling. I'm tired. Never again."

Well, two days later Carlos and Tanya came to visit and told us of their fabulous week of camping with their four kids in Yosemite. My little squirrel brain went: "Yosemite?" In November we booked Yosemite Valley Lodge for five nights in September. So, we're leaving early tomorrow morning and returning Sunday evening.

If we have the energy at the end of days of long hikin' and rollin', we'll send out fabulous stories about snakes and bears and other creatures we are sure to meet along the pathways. At this point we are full of enthusiasm, energy, and excitement. The three E's.

Love and Blessings, Sue and The King

Yosemite #2 – September 12, 2017

"It is by far the grandest of all the special temples of Nature
I was ever permitted to enter."

John Muir
Scottish-born American Naturalist

We left home at 4:15 a.m. From 907-O to Yosemite Valley Lodge is 359 miles, about a 7-hour drive at an average of 50 mph. We drove up Highway 5, then veered onto 99, until we hit highway 41, which took us right into Yosemite Valley. Sharon greeted us at the gate with maps and booklets, a special accessible attractions packet and a warm smile. Yahoo! We're here and it's only noon. Our first stop was Bridalveil Falls, first named Pohono by the Ahwahneeche people. "Spirit of the puffing wind."

Bridalveil has a 620-foot drop. We found a handicap parking spot and unloaded the Rascal for the steep, but paved, climb to the falls. There we had a fun conversation with a young family from Michigan. Three kids ditching school to see the beauty of California. They blamed it on their Grandpa. We told them we're retired teachers and understand their reluctance to head home. We joked about excuses to give their teachers. Kidnapped by Grandpa. Sick. Tired. Flat tire in California? They happily told us they'd be two weeks late starting school this year.

Back in the van we headed for our room at Yosemite Valley Lodge—right across from Yosemite Falls. Wow! Queen-sized bed, TV, Wi-Fi, roll-in shower, and our own little meadow right out the back door—a tiny patio in the woods. We immediately set out our green salad, a container of egg salad, and crackers for lunch. Before heading back out into the wilderness again we took a 30-minute nap. The first step on our next destination would be Lower Yosemite Falls. The trail to the Lower Falls is completely accessible. Not so the Upper Falls. The three sections drop a total of 2,425 feet. We heard many languages: Swedish, French, Spanish, and saw license plates from all over the U.S. Would the world be better if we all got outside everyday? Everyone seemed happy, content, and friendly. By the end of the day we'd walk 'n rolled four miles.

Dinner: Yogurt and cantaloupe topped with granola for me. Salmon burger for The King. And so to bed, remembering the words of the poet Gary Snyder (no relation to us): "Nature is not a place to visit. It is home." Ah, yes.

Yosemite #3 - September 13, 2017

Left room 3514 in Maple Lodge at 9:00 a.m. and caught the free shuttle to Mirror Lake. Our driver, Antonia, let down the ramp, rearranged seating for several fellow adventurers, and invited Richard to rascal up the ramp. By the time we got to Stop #17 at M.L. the bus was jammed full of people, mostly standing and hanging on. At this time of year, Mirror Lake is more like a puddle meadow—or grass sprouting in a big puddle. Beauty everywhere. Cool crisp air. Birds singing. It was only a 1-mile walk along the Tenaya Creek to the Lake. We marveled at the variety of flora and fauna. California Black oaks, Incense-cedars, Ponderosa pines with puzzle-type bark, and (we think) the Pacific Dogwood with little clusters of red berry-looking thingys. (Sorry to get so technical.)

We collected a few of the tiny acorns that were scattered everywhere. As we stood oohing and awing at Half Dome, across the lake, along came a couple from London, England. Sean pushing Hillary in a wheelchair. Naturally, we struck up a conversation about the thrills and challenges of traveling. They'd been visiting the natural wonders of California and would be leaving for Monterey and San Francisco. We learned that she had MS also. We sent them on their way with a copy of Richard's book. I mean, what author does not carry around at least one copy of his latest book when he's out walk 'n rollin'?

We left Mirror Lake and found a trail that led us to Yosemite Valley Store and Visitor Center. The history of the Europeans destroying Native Americans' homes and taking their land, the volcanoes that formed Yosemite Valley, the History of the National Parks: it's all there. We learned that Half Dome just looks like there used to be another half. It's 8,836 feet tall. North Dome is 7525 feet tall. By now the temperature was 81 degrees—15 degrees higher than predicted. So we headed for our little home in the meadow. Ah, another long nap. This could become a habit. We walked 5.2 miles today.

Out to dinner: we shared Chili verde rice with veggies and a small salad in the Y.L. food court. So nice to have someone fix dinner for us. Tomorrow: Hetch-Hetchy.

Love and Blessings to all.

Yosemite #4 - September 14, 2017

Happy 16th birthday dear sweet Granddaughter Rylee "oink"

When Richard taught 6th grade science and took his students up to Arrowhead area camping and studying nature, he asked if there would ever be a time when he could get up to Hetch Hetchy and introduce his students to the wonders of O'Shaughnessy Dam. So, today we made it happen. But without the students.

We drove over Big Oak Flats Road and Evergreens and Hetch Hetchy Roads, a 40-mile trip from Yosemite Lodge, over narrow winding roads and steeeeeep cliffs on one side and jagged rocks on the other. Fortunately, speed was limited to 25-miles per hour and there were plenty of turnouts to let the impatient pass. John Muir described H.H. as "a grand landscape garden, one of Nature's rarest and most precious mountain temples." We agree. It's like Yosemite with a lake in the middle. The dam holds the water supply for San Francisco and surrounding areas. Another of our conundrums: population of people versus nature.

Upon arriving, we unloaded the Rascal and walk 'n rolled across the dam. Wow! Wow! Wow! The view! The cascading water! The bright blue sky! The domes and falls! Sometimes all you can say is "Wow!!!" After walking across the dam, where we photographed the domes and cliffs and Wapama Falls, we entered a dark rocky-bottomed tunnel. Richard bumpity-bump-bumped through 150 feet of tunnel as I tried to determine a good path, never mind the brilliance of such a feat. We made it! After traveling on another 150-feet beyond the tunnel, we realized the Rascal was not going to make it any further. Too many rocky trippers on the trail. We stopped in the shade for a water and trail-mix break and determined that I should travel on by myself while Grandpa (also known as The King) relaxed and greeted other hikers who braved it through the tunnel. After ½ mile of an uphill very rocky pathway, I decided to sit on a ledge known as Lookout Point. It overlooks the reservoir so I took pictures and listened to the wind. This must be what heaven is like. I wish I'd had the time to hike another mile and a half to Wapama Falls. Next time I will.

When hikers saw Richard in his Rascal at the foot of the trail, he told them The Queen was hiking up the trail. When people saw me alone they told me they'd seen Richard enjoying the view and the shade of a California Black Oak. There are not a lot of creatures around at this time of the year, just a few squirrels, some mule deer, and several Lorquin's Admirals fluttering about, which I thought were California Sisters.

More snacking, hiked back through the tunnel, loaded up the Rascal, instructed a young couple to turn their car around and not drive the wrong way on a one-way road, offered the driver several Kleenex tissues when he motioned that he had a runny nose. Hey! Ya do what ya can to make the world a better place.

Beautiful scenery as we traveled back to Yosemite Lodge. Visited the office for Wi-Fi instructions, which have not been much help. Ho ho ha ha ha. Caught the shuttle up to Yosemite Valley Village for a quick dinner and the 7:00 one-man show. Lee Stetson is a John Muir impersonator and has performed all over the world, mostly in Yosemite Valley for the past 35 years. He has finally gotten old enough that he no longer needs stage make-up. His outstanding and believable performance made me wonder about male testosterone. Why do guys do such crazy things? Leaving the theater we purchased Stetson's book: "The Wild Muir" and went outside to get his autograph.

Although we were warned that the lights on the handicap ramp were burned out, Richard decided to cause some excitement by driving the Rascal off the curb, so he crashed to the ground, head first. I screamed, "Somebody please help." Five strong men (testosterone-fueled, I'm sure) came to our rescue. They righted the Rascal, put the batteries and baskets back on and reconnected them, picked Richard up off the concrete and helped him sit back in the Rascal. Before the Y.V.E.R. crew arrived, he tested the Rascal and it worked fine. The two lumps on the right side of his head are just a bit bloody and Richard says they are nothing to worry about, although his right shoulder is sore. He was questioned by Kay Lloyd, part of the ranger staff. Craig, emergency crewman, arrived right before Joy came by ambulance. It was highly recommended that Richard go to the emergency center for an examination but he just wanted to get back to "home" at Yosemite Lodge. So, that's what we did.

Love and Blessings, Sue

Yosemite #5 - Thursday September 15, 2017

Up early—had the office connect me, by phone, with an Australian-accented Wi-Fi connection helper. After much ado, and patience on both our parts, we got connected. Hope it stays.

So, we had breakfast in the food court: scrambled eggs, potatoes, coffee, and a croissant for me. Packed in a lot of energy for the upcoming challenges of the day. By the way, Richard seems pretty healed up today. In good spirits. Scratched-up right arm, two little bumps on head seem smaller. He had no qualms (well, not too many) about Rascalling about the Valley. Thank you for your prayers. They really worked. In case we do anything else crazy, please keep us in your thoughts.

We walked all around the meadows just outside our back door—crossed the Merced several times, saw a huge buck lying down chewing the grass. He looked quite bored with us. We traveled on and decided to use the Yosemite Shuttle to take us up the road to Happy Isles. The first shuttle we attempted to ride didn't work out. The driver didn't or wouldn't or couldn't lower the bus so the Rascal couldn't climb. We waited a few minutes until Delores' Shuttle picked us up. She lowered the bus, put down the ramp and off we went. A young couple got on the bus. I asked her if they'd hiked today. She blushed and said, "Just a little." I then noticed that neither of them was sunburned and they seemed much happier than any of the other riders. Shiny new wedding rings. Hmmmm. Newly-weds.

We arrived at Stop #16. Happy Isles, Mirror Lake, Vernal Falls, and Nevada Falls. What's so fun about hiking with Richard is that he names all the plants and trees and birds and butterflies and the huge rock formations. Such a scientist. Oh, the choices this morning! We decided on Vernal Falls. The paved trail was mighty steeeeeep. Richard went about a block and decided the uncertainty ahead might not be worth the risk so he parked alongside the path. I put a large rock under the front wheel and off I went. The sign read 1.8 miles to Vernal Falls. There were lots of hikers but few my age. Seventeen. Oops! I forgot. I'm not 17 anymore. Yet she persisted. I took pictures along the way of beautiful scenery, the Merced flowing at a mighty pace. I actually had to stop and breathe several times but it was all worth it. Vernal Falls was stunning. People taking pictures. Laughing. Snacking. A sign beside the bridge told of an accident that occurred at this spot in August of 2012. In a young mother's words, "They weren't swimming. They were playing in a pool by the edge." Both of her young sons were pulled under by the swift current and drowned. So sad.

The little market and the grill in Half Dome Campground were open so we picked up cranberry-walnut salad and two boiled eggs and shared them out on the deck in the cool breeze. After our late lunch decided to forego the crowded Shuttle and hike back to 3514 in Maple building at Yosemite Lodge. I could feel my energy seeping away. But we traveled on. We got almost back when we ran into Tina, the table cleaner at the YVL Foodcourt. She told me her name and that she was from Modesto. There are so many young people working here—mostly seasonal. Yosemite is open in winter for skiers but many of the facilities are shut down. Tina said, "I'll see you at breakfast tomorrow." She left with a big smile on her face.

Just before I collapsed in a sweaty heap on our bed, I checked my Health App. I'd hiked 8.4 miles today—and have yet to go out in search of dinner. Maybe we'll have Granola and soy drink for dinner tonight. And now for a nice long nap.

Yosemite #6 - Saturday September 16, 2017

"Non Nobis Solum Mati Sumus."
(Not for Ourselves Alone, are we born.)

Marcus Tullius Cicero

We left for an early morning walk along the Merced and thought maybe we could hike west to El Capitan. Soon the bike path turned to gravel, then sand, then rocks. We cruised across pine needle trails through the forest and found ourselves in a beautiful picnic area with a lovely sandy beach along the river. Sandy beach. We watched two young cowgirls (if they ride horses, why don't we call them horsegirls?) unload two beautiful horses off their trailer.

Maybe Richard was following me without thinking or maybe he was thinking about the cowgirls. Well, anyhow, next thing I knew he'd sunk the back two tires of the Rascal into the sand. Deeply. So, remembering what Cicero advised, I tried pushing, then realized that was not gonna work. We got the crutch and Richard off the Rascal and helped him walk a few feet away. From a kneeling-in-the-sand position, I pivoted the front of the Rascal over a few feet (seemed like miles at the time) and squirreled the back wheels out of the abyss. Standing alongside, I gunned the motor and viola!! Freedom! I've become quite the expert at digging Richard out of sand pits and rocky trails (that I've led him into). I suppose it'll happen again some day.

After two miles of wandering the valley it was time for a café mocha break. Ah. Quiet time with books and notebooks and Rev. Michelle Medrano's daily guide, which was all about forgiveness. She quoted Nelson Mandela, words which are particularly poignant in today's world.

"As I walked out the door toward my freedom, I knew that if I did
not leave all the anger, hatred and bitterness behind that
I would still be in prison."

Back on the trail we heard, then located a beautiful little Western Bluebird. With every chirp, his tail flipped up. I felt another nap coming on.

After that we shuttled near the old Ahwanhee Hotel, which was recently renamed the Majestic. We decided to walk the last half-mile and found ourselves just in time for a wonderful one-hour tour of the hotel. Zack, our guide, gave us the history of the hotel as two different weddings were being performed out on the massive back lawn. We decided to have late lunch/early dinner in the Majestic Hotel Bar. Great salad for me—chicken sandwich without the bread for Richard. Wow, I never thought I'd get to eat in such a beautiful place. When I questioned a young clerk in the hotel lobby about room rates, they were just as I'd thought: the sparest rooms go for $600 a night. Guess we'll stick with our little lodge in the valley.

Next stop: the 8:00 p.m. program in the Le Conte Memorial Lodge, which was built by the Sierra Club in 1892. Lee Terkelsen, a retired high school teacher narrated his 45-minute hiking video called "Along the Muir Trail, from Whitney to Half Dome." Lee told us that he'd done that same hike 8 or 10 times. Some years there was still snow on the mountain trails. This trail is 211 miles long and he would take 30 days for the trip. Ironically, there was a young man named Daniel (age 41) in the audience who had just walked the Muir Trail in fourteen days. He was a slim energetic guy from Switzerland. We had the privilege of riding the Shuttle with him after the program. He told us he's an IT worker and is sent to Las Vegas once a year in late summer for a conference. He spent the last year planning his 14-day 211-mile hike and wants to hike it again next year.

Early tomorrow (Sunday) morning we'll be heading home through Lee Vining and down highway 395. Yahoo. More adventures.

And so to bed . . .

Sunday, September 17, 2017

We're home!!! We left Yosemite at 8:15 this morning and traveled down the 395, 15, 91, 241, and 133. Got home at 5:30. When we left the Yosemite Valley Lodge we decided that we'll go back there next year but the day we leave, we'll be up at 3:30 and beat the traffic. So HAPPY to be home.

Love and blessings, and thank you all for your words of encouragement. The Wi-Fi thingy didn't work for long so couldn't send our notes out from Yosemite.

Road Trip - October 2017

What's the first thing that comes to your mind when you receive a wedding invitation from Cousin Tyler and girlfriend Mikaela in Lincoln, Nebraska? Right!

"Road trip."

We received the news in May about the October wedding and decided to drive to one of our favorite places on the planet: Bryce Canyon in Utah. We kept track of the weather: low 20's in the morning. Mid 60's in the afternoon. Great! Pack the gloves, warm hats, and jackets.

Next: What's halfway between Bryce and Lincoln? Right! Colorado Springs and the Garden of the Gods.

Next: Send a message to granddaughter Jennifer in Irving, Texas about discounts at "her" hotel chain. Our "hotel angel" Jennifer got us great discounts in Colorado and Nebraska so we decided to rearrange all obligations between October 14th and 28th – not an easy task for two hyperactive retirees. But we did it!

October 2017 Wedding in Nebraska . . .

"On the Road Again."

Willie Nelson

Saturday, October 14th.

Up at 3:15 a.m. Dressed. Backed van out of Mili's carport. Parked at the edge of walkway outside our condo at 907-O. Twenty minutes of loading van with all the doors open. Four a.m. Richard hops into passenger seat. I drive his Rascal back into the breezeway. I hop in, buckle up, and turn the ignition key. Click-click. Click-click. Click-click. Oh, oh. Dead battery. Again? It died two weeks ago and we were told it was a good battery.

Whipped out my iPhone 6. Pressed "Roadside Farmers" which is Farmers Insurance Rescue Team. Explained our situation to nice young lady – how can anyone be that nice at 4:00 a.m.? She assured us someone would be on the way to 907-O. We drank coffee (café mocha for Richard). Munched on our avocado on toast and read Dr. Ernest Holmes message for the day. The message seemed to be something about being positive, looking on the bright side, and practicing patience.

George arrived at 4:45 a.m. and hooked up the battery charger and viola! Our 2005 Grand Caravan with 169,000+ miles on it was revived. George warned us that the battery has a malfunctioning cell. We need to replace it. We were on our way. Yippee!!!

Due to recent and current wildfires in Anaheim Hills and East Orange, parts of the toll roads 133 and 241 had only one lane. The 91 Freeway was pretty busy for 5:30 a.m. but we cheerfully traveled on. Gusty winds across our desert. Air temperatures in the 40's. At 2:00 p.m. mountain time we arrived at our destination at Bryce Canyon Lodge – we thought. Oh, no.

When the desk clerk looked at my printed confirmation sheet I'd printed out two months ago, he said, "Oh! Those people! You shouldn't trust them. They tricked you." Huh? We were in the wrong place. We would not be staying right at the edge of the canyon but six miles back down the road. Boo hoo! Our reservations were for Bryce Canyon Lodge PINES. Not Bryce Canyon Lodge. Remembering Dr. Holmes suggestion to be positive, look on the bright side, and practice patience, I walked back out to the van in tears. I felt like a fool for being tricked.

We drove back out of the park. Found BCLP and showed our confirmation printout to the desk clerk. She said, "Oh! Those people! Not good." Huh? O.K. We'll just stay here. You have an accessible room?

"No. They didn't ask for one. Our one-and-only is not available."

Sweet Linda and Sweet Cheryl, the office clerks, offered sympathy. We'll be staying three nights. Huh? I thought it was two, but three is even better. We'll just stay two in Colorado. Positive, bright side, patience.

So, we unloaded our bags into BCLP room 138 quickly – no more dead batteries thanks. Opened little black cooler and noticed olive oil and balsamic all over everything. Washed the apples, plums, tangerines, and four plastic dishes. Dried with nice white towel. Soaked towel in sink. Scrubbed out balsamic spots. Dried all the fruit and dishes. Collapsed. Short nap! Almond butter and sliced apples for dinner. L.A. Dodgers beat the Cubs. I think they were also practicing being positive, looking on the bright side, and patience. End of Day 1.

Day 2. Sunday, October 15th. A note of advice. "Mosquito repellant will never replace sunblock." Look, 75-year old females have so many bottles and tubes and containers of lotions and potions and blockers and moisturizers that it isn't any wonder I got some things confused. But the day was great! We started the morning with breakfast at Ruby's Inn and Diner where we had stayed three years ago on another road trip.

Hiking in Bryce Canyon is beautiful, stunning, and otherworldly. About 9:00 a.m. I started down the Navaho trail from Sunset Point. After hiking about two hundred feet down the narrow winding path (corkscrew style) I realized that I really didn't want to wear my heavy jacket so I walked back up and dumped it into the van, being careful not to use up the battery. As it turned out that was a really good idea. By the end of my 3-mile hike down Navaho Trail, through the canyon, up to Queen Victoria's Garden and back up to Sunrise point, I also had stripped off my sweater, rolled up my pants and rolled down my socks. I met people from all over the world: India, Korea, China, Indiana, Maine, and Washington. Walking among the hoodoos is magical. So much ooooohing and awing. Everyone taking pictures.

Excited, exhausted, and exhilarated, I found Richard relaxing in the sunshine, reading a book on the deck of the REAL Bryce Canyon Lodge. He offered me lunch in the beautiful dining room where I saw several fellow hikers. I ordered the Queen's Beet Salad. Oh, yum. Richard had the fish tacos. He ate all of his lunch. I ate half of my salad, which we later shared and called it dinner. Also devoured two of our famous gluten-free veggie cupcakes. Then we watched Justin Turner, the Dodgers top batter for the year and third baseman hit the homerun that won the game!!! And so to bed.

Day 3. Monday October 16th.

Spent today driving the rim of Bryce Canyon, stopping to capture the sights from such spots as The Amphitheater - a 17-mile drive. At the end of another joy-filled day, we packed up and set the alarm for 5:00 a.m.

Day 4. Tuesday October 17.

Left BCLP at 6:00 a.m. Temperature 21 degrees. As we traveled Highway 89, the temperature dropped to 13 degrees. The car heater did not respond. Hmmmmm. We were icy-cold but not too worried, as we'd packed three little blankets and a large quilt and a pillow in case something unforeseen happened. The heater continued to malfunction, to worry us. At 2:30 we stopped at Café 163 in Edwards. I had a veggie omelet and Richard had the usual - a turkey sandwich without the bread. We saved half of everything for dinner. Back on the highway, we drove over 600 miles as the temperature gage zoomed upward. The red light came on. Scary. Through Denver the outside temperature was in the low 80's. In order to bring the temperature of the radiator down, we turned on the car heater full-blast. Traffic slowed.

We got off the freeway and found a gas station where we refilled the radiator. Assisted by a young man who'd just stopped for cigarettes, and a beautiful young blond woman who rushed over to help as we lifted the hood. Richard got out of the van. We dumped all of our water into the radiator. The engine cooled. We drove on to Colorado Springs, another 50 miles.

We made it to the Fairfield Marriot just off Highway 25 by 8:00. With tons of gratitude to our Texas Granddaughter, Jennifer, we get a nice discount when we stay at Marriott. (Thank you, Jen.) Mike, the check-in clerk, after hearing our tale of woe, referred us to TJ Auto. Once in our room, we finished off our leftover lunch, left a phone message for TJ Auto, and went to bed, kinda tired, a bit apprehensive. By 8:30 Wednesday morning, we'd contacted TJ's and then delivered our van to his shop down on Mount View Ave. Terry, at the front desk, was most kind. Because it would be a couple of hours before the mechanics would have time for us, he offered to deliver us to Colorado Springs "Garden of the Gods," our destination in C.S. "Wow! You'll drive us over there?"

We spent an hour in the Visitor Center, watched an 11-minute video about the formation of the various "gods" in the park, and met people from all over the states. My favorite rock formation is "The Three Graces." All this with Pikes Peak in the background. Then we hiked almost four miles of paved trails and roads. In her 1858 letter to her mother, Julia Archibald Holmes wrote from Pikes Peak,

"How I sigh for a poet's power of description,
so that I might give you some faint idea of the
grandeur and beauty of this scene."

Back at the Visitor Center, we enjoyed black-bean burgers (minus the bread for Richard) with an astounding view of Pikes Peak. Tim phoned to let us know our "block" was cracked and beyond repair. They could possibly overnight the new equipment from Kansas, maybe dismantle the van on Thursday, and put it all back together on Friday, working overtime, which the guys were willing to do so we could make it to Lincoln, Nebraska in time for Saturday's 7:00 p.m. wedding. We discussed renting an "accessible" van and leaving Colorado Springs on schedule. That way, the mechanics wouldn't be stressed, we wouldn't be getting up at 2:00 a.m. on Saturday, driving over 600 miles, hoping to get to Tyler and Mikaela's wedding by 7:00.

Terry spent hours on the phone hunting down an appropriate rental for us. When he found a deal, he actually thanked us for the opportunity to learn how and where to find specially equipped vans for especially wonderful guys like my Richard. We spoke with Holly Mills in Denver who promised to deliver a rental at 8:00 a.m. Thursday morning.

Day #5

Holly was right on time. She backed into a parking spot, pushed a button and the rear side door opened. A ramp unfolded, the van lowered. We loaded in our suitcases and other valuables, we drove the Rascal up the ramp. I ran back into the hotel to thank the morning desk clerk for a nice stay – and there was Richard's suitcase. No problem. I rolled it out to the van and loaded it. No one's fault. Remember positive thoughts, look on the bright side, and patience?

After Holly's assistant Al pointed out everything we needed to know about our "new" van, we were on our way. We left the Marriot Fairfield at 8:44 and drove for ten hours, stopping only to fill up the gas tank and purchase a few snacks.

My sister, Jeanne and her husband Curt, meanwhile were flying from San Diego to Omaha and being limo-ed down to Lincoln. Cousin Roger, father of the groom, kept in touch. Cousin Julie kept in touch. Julie and her husband Ken greeted us at our Lincoln Fairfield and helped us get all our stuff into our - wow! Suite! Thanks again to Granddaughter Jennifer. We all went out to dinner at the local FireCracker restaurant, then when home to bed. We were VERY tired. But HAPPY.

Day 6.

Richard and I kept talking about all the Angels that just seem to appear in our lives. They all come to help us; to share our joy. There was George, sent to us Saturday morning from Farmers Insurance and recharged our batter. There were two special Angels in Bryce Canyon - Linda and Cheryl - who calmed me down when we didn't get into the Bryce Canyon Lodge. There were all those waiters at Ruby's Inn: Samantha, especially was helpful. Chad at the REAL Bryce Canyon Lodge took care of us at lunchtime. The young man who stopped at the gas station to buy cigarettes and came to help us get the hood up on the van, the beautiful young blond woman who offered moral support.

Angel Mike at the Colorado Fairfield who linked us to TJ Auto. Terry at TJ Auto, Tim, the owner of TJ Auto, who drove us to and from Garden of the Gods. Connie, who oversees the Breakfast Room at the CSF and came rushing to put out the fire I started when I tried to toast an English Muffin. Holly and Al who delivered the rental van. All these Angels who just appear. Just to make our lives better.

Day #7

Up early Friday morning for breakfast with Jeanne and Curt. Enjoyed a walk in Pioneer Park with Ken and Julie. Ken left for work: college professor of educational law. At 12:45 we met Cousin Roger at the most amazing Speedway Motors Museum of American Speed. I could feel our brother Andy's spirit in this place. He was into "Race Cars" and loved many aspects of the industry, as a mechanic and racecar driver and businessman in his short 48 years. He left this planet December 27, 1987.

Julie went off to enjoy Garth Brooks with her husband. Roger went off to set up and enjoy his son's wedding rehearsal. Jeanne, Curt, Richard, and I went back to hotel for naps. We later enjoyed a wonderful Chinese dinner at China Wall Restaurant, spent time shopping in - Walmart!?? - and went back to hotel to rest up for another adventurous day.

Day #8

The BIG DAY is here! Saturday, October 21. At 7:00 this evening we will all witness the wedding vows of Tyler and Mikaela at First Plymouth Church. Jeanne, Curt, Richard and I decided this would be a good day to check out The Capitol of Nebraska: Lincoln. We walked several miles admiring the architecture and eventually got to the University of Nebraska at Lincoln: UNL where Curt immediately climbed into one of the hammocks set up for tired students.

Jeanne and Richard went off to the bookstore in search of . . . . things. I sat at the fountain guarding my beloved bro-in-law as he took a little nap. Then it was time to get back to the hotel for a nap, an early dinner of leftover China Wall Café veggies and tofu.

Rev. Dr. Jim Keck guided the ceremony with joy and love and knowledge. Mikaela's sister Rachel read from St. Paul's Letter to the Corinthians:

"Love is patient, love is kind. It does not envy,
it does not boast, it is not proud, it is not rude,
it is not self-seeking, it is not easily angered,
keeps no record of wrongs, does not delight in evil,
rejoices with the truth, always protects,
always trusts, always hopes, always perseveres."

Mikaela's sister Laura was her maiden of honor. Tyler's brother Ross, his best man. There were seven bridesmaids and seven groomsmen. Everything about the wedding--and the reception at the Lincoln Country Club --was perfect.

One of the great joys of getting together with cousins Julie, Roger (father of the groom) and Barb is getting to know their kids better - and their grandkids. Isaac is a 5th grader, Trip is in 3rd, Trey, five, is in kindergarten, and Collier, three, is spending lots of time helping his parents with the cows and dogs on the farm. Landry, the only little girl among the bunch is four, almost five, and in preschool. We enjoyed watching the boys tackle each other and laugh. Reminded me of football players. Such joy!

Day #9.

Up early for breakfast, then took Curt to Urgent Care. Cold & sore throat & earache. Drove around and around looking for the Walgreens for prescription and cough drops. Positive thinking, bright side, patience. Again. Since Curt was hungry and wanting fish, we drove back over near the University to the one and only Wahoos for tacos. In the meantime, Richard spent the morning chatting with Ken. Then it was naptime again. At 5:30 we headed over to Cousin Julie and Ken's for a delightful get together with family.

OMG! With mimosas for the big cousins and orange juice for the little ones, Roger toasted the bride and groom and the California Cousins. (That was nice.) The food was amazing. Chicken noodle soup. Tomato soup. Biscuits. Cracker. Cheese, Salsa. And to top it all off . . . . . wedding cake.

Thank you Julie for spending your day in the kitchen and thank you Sharla (Roger's wife) for bringing the mimosas and cake. Twice, Isaac, age 10, clinked his glass to get our attention so he could practice toasting the occasion. I think we've got a politician in our midst. And so back to the hotel for a few hours of sleep.

Monday, October 23. Day 10. Up at 5:00. Packed up the rental van - with the amazing push button ramp. Love it! We left the hotel at 6:00 a.m. and arrived in Colorado Springs at 2:00 p.m. Checked back into the Fairfield hotel. They remembered us from last week. Stopped at Mimi's for late lunch, then headed over to TJ Auto to pick up our van. It wasn't quite ready so arranged for the owner, Tim, to bring it to us by 9:00 tomorrow morning after they do a bit more work. Holly will be here about the same time to pick up the rental. And then? Yep! We'll be heading up the hill to visit Pike's Peak National Park. Good thing we brought lotsa warm clothes. OK. Time to watch the Football game: Washington Redskins vs. Philadelphia Eagles. Gotta get in the mood for tomorrow's beginning of the World Series: Dodgers vs. Astros. Peace and love to all.

Tuesday, October 24 Day 11

We never knew Pikes Peak was so beautiful and majestic and COLD. After driving 12 miles up the twisty turny winding corkscrewy road we arrived at the top. The wind was blowing 40 miles an hour. The temperature was 21 degrees. With the wind chill factor, it felt like 0 degrees. Richard (the smarter of the two) sat in the car while I chanced a walk through the gift shop and out onto the edge. Woohoo! Amazing sights for miles and miles and miles. And

COLD. The wind was so strong I could barely stand up. After ten minutes outside I ran back to the van and hopped in. Brrrrrr.

Came back down from Pikes Peak and stopped at the oldest hotel in Manitou - The Cliff House. It was built in 1883. Another angel - Layne - appeared to get Richard and the Rascal up to the front porch. Because of street repairs we couldn't get up the usual ramp. It was blocked by a large cement truck. Positive thinking. Bright side, Patience. Layne opened the gate to the closed restaurant next door and brought us up their ramp, took us to an elevator, and walked a maze of hallways and viola! We were on the front porch of this picturesque old hotel with a view of the mountains and the setting sun. How good can life get? And then: YES!!! The Dodgers beat the Astros 3-1. And so to bed.

Day #12. Wednesday, October 25.

Left Colorado Springs and the Fairfield Marriott after saying goodbye to the staff. Drove out of Colorado, into Utah, heading for Moab. Around 5:00 we settled for the Holiday Inn Express where we get no discount. Well, a $5 per night discount for being over 60. So we registered for two nights, tuned into World Series Game #2 (Dodger vs. Astros), then headed out to dinner at The Peace Tree Café where we shared a salmon dinner. The veggie of the day was Brussels sprouts. Richard thought I'd like them because they were grilled. I ate a half, then another quarter just to be sure they were as bad as I thought. Yep. Pretty bad. Not a convert. The rest of dinner was delightful. Back to the hotel to finish up watching the WS. Oh! Oh! The Astros won in the 11th inning. Yikes!

Day #13. Thursday October 26.

Richard's dad would have been 99 today. He was the best dad: kind, inventive, knew lots of good jokes. He left us December 29th of 2000.

We stopped at the local market and picked up snacks for the day: Kale salad for me. Chicken salad for The King. Also a bag of Snapea Crisps and a bag of chocolates. Oh, and a carton of watermelon squares. Moab is about six miles south of Arches National Park. It was 46 degrees when we left our hotel and warmed up to 65. It was a perfect day for hiking. We checked things out in the Visitor Center by watching an amazing 15-minute video on how hoodoos and arches and potholes (the kind of potholes on the side of a monstrous rocks) are formed. We started on Park Avenue Viewpoint and Trailhead. It was mostly accessible and, as usual, Richard was the only hiker bumping over rocks and beds of sand. Also the only one who knew the names of the layers of rock and all the plants and trees. I don't know why but everyone was smiling at him. I guess it's true: he's a love magnet.

When we got to "The Windows" we went as far on the trail as we could before we ran into steps. Richard sent me off on my own. When I got as far as Turret Arch, I met two couples from The Netherlands, Amsterdam specifically. They're on a two-month trip around the US. They asked if I'd take their pictures. Of course, I did. Then they took mine. At that point I saw a sign that read,

"Primitive trail leads to parking lot.
One mile."

Heck! How hard could that be? I only met one other person on the trail. He was young; walking opposite directions from me. When I got about ½ mile into the hike I remembered there are rattlesnakes and mountain lions out here somewhere. Aside from scrambling up and down the sides of a couple of cliffs and losing the trail a few times and having to traipse up and through one of the huge arches, it was a darn good hike - and only one mile. Richard was waiting for me near the parking lot when I got back. So we traveled on.

Imagination is a wonderful thing. Millions of monstrous rocks out here, most of them with names like: Parade of Elephants, Sheep Rock, Three Gossips, Tower of Babel, Courthouse Towers, Balanced Rock, Garden of Eden, Elephant Butte, Broken Arch and Dark Angel. It was WOW everywhere we went. And I only loaded and unloaded the Rascal 12 times today. Thank goodness for our old van (which now runs beautifully) and the Rascal lift.

My best-ever hiking buddy

So, early tomorrow morning we head for someplace near the Arizona California border. We plan to be back at 907-O sometime Saturday evening. Home sweet Home. When you start thinking about home, it's time to head back.

Day #14.

Up early. Drove to Jean, Nevada just west of Las Vegas. Beautiful drive. Easy. No problems. After gassing up in Beaver, Utah, I helped Richard and the Rascal out of the van. He traveled over to the front door of the little gas station market to go inside to use the restroom. Three people rushed over to open the door for him. People are so nice. Everywhere. Always people are asking "How can I help?" Sometimes I'll hand them the crutch and say, "Just make sure he gets into his seat OK." Then I busy myself with loading up the Rascal. If I just say, I can do it all, they look disappointed. Richard says, "Thanks and don't stop asking people if they need help."

I'm learning Chiara Ferrau's song "Nella Fantasia." It's in Italian and pretty much says, I fantasize a world where everyone feels cared about, where everyone is peaceful. Watch Jackie Evancho sing it on Youtube. She's much better than me. Much. The world needs more love. More peace.

We'll be home tomorrow where there's no lack of zucchini or kale or avocados or mangos or blueberries. Ooooooo. Can't wait. We are so grateful for all our family and friends and a big wide world waiting to be discovered. So grateful we were able to attend Cousin Tyler and Mikaela's wedding. Already planning the next trip.

Ciao.

Love and Blessings, Sue and The King

Saturday, October 28.

Got home at 12:30. Unloaded. Washed up dirty clothes while Richard took a much-needed nap. Cooked zucchini, eggplant, onion, lentils. Heaven.

Firenze, Italy April 16 - May 17, 2018
Story #1

If you're thinking about taking a travel-companion with you to Florence, Italy for 30 days, and he's in his 51st year (at age 69) of dealing with the challenging effects of MS, here are some things you need to know.

1. Be willing to push his Rascal—up and down cobble stone streets--for a couple of blocks when it runs out of power.
2. Have five Euros ready to bribe a young African, living in Italy down-on-his-luck guy named Peter to push your traveling companion to the best place to use an electrical charge.
3. Don't crow too much when you finally beat him at cribbage while you drink "American" coffee with a chocolate croissant as you await his Rascal getting charged up again. That'll take two hours.
4. As you approach the Uffizi Museum of Art and the Rascal is slowing down again, be willing to approach one of the handsome young workers and ask if they have a wheelchair to use for a few hours. When he says "yes" and tells you he will get your tickets (free for the differently-abled, and a care-giver) try not to cry tears of joy. Accept his hug like a lady.
5. Offer the worker an extension cord and adaptor to give charging the Rascal another try.
6. Enjoy an incredible afternoon of pushing companion in borrowed manual wheelchair through six centuries of the finest art ever produced.
7. When the announcement is made that the Uffizi is closing at 6:35 and you really have to pee, leave your beloved companion (in borrowed wheelchair) in the cafeteria and hike down four flights of stairs to the toilette.
8. Keep up your spirits when the sign in front of the toilette says, "Closes at 6:15" and it's only 6:11 according to your iPhone6.
9. Ask five non-English speaking workers if there is another toilette. When you are directed to go down another floor and are told the only other toilette closes at 6:45 and it is 6:23, hurry down two more levels.
10. Keep smiling and saying "grazie" to all the people who tried to direct you.
11. After you are relieved, phone your beloved and discover that a few nice ladies are taking him back to the entrance where his Rascal is being charged.
12. Keep looking for him as you stand outside the door of the gift shop—the door with the sign that says "Do Not Enter".

13. When a pretty, middle-aged lady steps outside the door and looks around, approach her and ask if she has your husband.
14. Realize he is your favorite person in the whole world when she takes you inside and he's sitting there in his Rascal. Thank middle-aged lady for her help. Accept another Italian hug.
15. When the Rascal still isn't working properly, keep up your spirits by pushing again. After all, you're only going to be 76 in a couple of months.
16. After pushing him over the Ponte Vecchio, stop off for a dish of chocolate and coconut gelato. Convince him all will be okay. In tandem take in three deep breaths and release each with a smile, knowing you are both okay.
17. Encourage him to phone Skip—who lives in sunny southern California--and is the prince of motorized scooters--and discover that the problem is we need to use the transformer when charging the Rascal. See? Simple!
18. Sit in the living room of your apartment and admire the Arno as it flows by. Listen to the young guitar-player sing "Imagine" and Leonard Cohen's "Hallelujah" and a song by Cat Stevens, on the Old Bridge (Pointe Vecchio) as you sit by your favorite person in the Universe.
19. Thank Allah, Spirit, Divine Mind, Mother-Father God for feeling so loved and so blessed. Know that you are always in the right place at the right time.
20. Thank heavens for all the Angels who have helped in so many ways as you journey through This Thing Called Life.

Love, Richard and Sue

Story #2 April 23, 2018

Warning: Today's story could make you cry.

A Good time In an Old World with Angels Galore.

Angels Everywhere. It started like any ordinary day in Firenze, Italy. I got up about 7:00 and took a two-mile walk along the north edge of the Arno River, heading west. I noted the variety of birds: pigeons, seagulls, moorhens, and one hungry grebe. Got back home about 8:00 and fixed an easy breakfast. Then. Then. Then. Because the Rascal still wasn't running correctly, I pushed Richard over a mile, across cobblestone streets, and with the help of several

Angels got up and down walkways without curb cuts. The Rascal weights 130 pounds so only the bravest volunteer. Angels everywhere.

We were looking for Ricardo's Electronics Shop when a tiny man with an amazingly bent body, riding along in his electric cart noticed me pushing. Mariano is from Romania. He speaks some Italian and some English. He is deaf. He reads lips. He offered to help by pointing us in the direction of Spinelli Motors. He guided us there, dodging buses, cars, and bicycles in the street. Claudia, Thomas Spinelli's wife and Mariano had a long loud excited talk. She called forth her husband Thomas who helped Richard into their only chair. I showed Thomas how to dismantle the Rascal and he checked all plugs and converters and wires and other mysterious stuff.

Meanwhile, Mariano is waiting out on the street to see what's going to happen. He waited about twenty minutes then took off for his painting class, taking our contact info. He said he'd text later to make sure we're okay. We kissed on both cheeks, which is a really cool custom here. We thanked him and offered him money. Instead he insisted that we take his two bottles of Fruitti Fresh to get us through the day. He told us that very often people help him and he's passing on the love. Angels everywhere.

I offered to go with Claudia to Ricardo's Electronics to get a cord with a special plug to fix our problem. I'm glad she told me "No, you stay." She hopped onto a large motorcycle and took off. Meanwhile. At 12:30, Thomas suggested we call for a cab, go out to lunch, and come back at 17:00 o'clock (5:00 p.m. American time). Matao, our cab driver blasted around town, narrowly missing about 50 pedestrians, 25 bicyclists, and several buses. He dropped us off at a luxury hotel with a luxury restaurant. $71 later and three attempts at beating The King at cribbage, we were ready for another exciting ride around Firenze.

Wanna know what we had for our 3-1/2 hour lunch? Okay. We split a huge chunk of herb-encrusted salmon, a small salad, and a plate of the most delicious roasted eggplant, bell peppers, onions, tomatoes, and tiny zucchini. Then came the "American" coffee: one plain, one with chocolata served with the best Tiramisu on the planet.

As we were leaving the restaurant, we were stopped by a pretty young lady named Katherine (from Florida.) She offered to pray for The King, which she did as she anointed him with "Biblical oil." She asked for total and complete healing of all nerve cells and thanked Jesus for removing all effects of MS. Then she hailed down a taxi for us. Angels everywhere.

Upon our return to Spinelli Motors, Thomas took out Richard's card. "Oh?" He pointed at Richard's book title. I told him we're also on YouTube. In an instant we got to see, on a large screen, the ten-minute replay of our week at Freebo's songwriting workshop. We all laughed. I cried. What a life we have had together! We asked for the bill. Thomas wrote on a piece of paper. Six Euros. That covered the cost of our new electronic cord.

"But for you?"

"No, no."

He didn't want to take any money for his excellent diagnosis of the Rascal's problem and his hours of labor. I couldn't hold it any longer. I burst into tears. People here are so wonderful, helpful, kind, loving. After several days of wondering where the next miracle would come from, we found it. We gave Thomas 50 Euro and said,

"Please take your wife out to dinner."

So after 4.6 miles in just 13,922 steps, I'm going to sit out on our balcony over the Arno, watch the paddlers, the tourists taking selfies, the birds, and wait for this evening's entertainment which magically appears every evening.

Love peace and joy to everyone everywhere. Caio caio.

Sue and The King

Story #4 - April 27, 2018

Walk an' roll a mile to the Autobus Station. Seven Euros one-way to Sienna please. Wait for the "handicap" bus. Ride through the most beautiful countryside to Sienna. Thirty-five miles. Vineyards. Olive trees. Villas. Villas. Villas. Little villages. Big villages. Two old farmers feeding the chickens; a shepherd herding his sheep. Beauty everywhere.

Sienna, situated atop three hills. At the center and bottom of these hills is the main attraction on Piazza del Campo, the Main Square, the ever-popular and ever-beautiful Fonte de Gaia. (Gaia, of course refers to the primal Mother Earth Goddess, the Mother of all life.) In English: the Fountain of Joy. Because this fountain was the gathering place for all who came to fill their water jugs there was great joy; life was good.

The Fountain of Joy was created in the 15th century by Jacopo della Quercia. One part of the scene is of God creating Adam and helping him to his feet, which inspired Michelangelo when he painted his Sistine Chapel ceiling. The center sculpture is of a Mother holding a young child. Could be "Mother Earth and Us" or "Mary with Jesus"?

Other sculptures on the wall of the fountain are representations of Lady Justice with her scales of "Faith, Hope, and Peace." She also holds a sword. Two wolves adorn the fountain. Water trickles from their snouts and is often gulped up by the ever-present and persistent pigeons. More joy.

Because the Piazza is like a giant bowl, people feel free to sit or lie on the ground, as if they are on some sandy shore. Some are sleeping or just resting. Many are slurping gelato. The smart ones are the little boys chasing pigeons: laughter from the kids and the birds. Delightful laughter sounds the same in every language. It's kinda like being in Laguna Beach.

Smoked salmon and fennel salad for Richard and tomato salad with buffalo cheese for Sue at the La Casta orl for 36.50 Euros, including three Euros each coperto, which is cover charge, or, as we'd say in the US, the waiter's tip. 4.5 Euros for a bottle of water, still. If you don't ask for water still, you'll get water with bubbles. Later, as we sat on the piazza, one of us got a vanilla gelato, which was delicious but too much. The gelato servers seem to fill the cups and cones to overflowing with their creations. It's not unusual to see people with chocolate noses or pistachio chins; children with their "I Love Italy" tee shirts covered with sticky blobs of gelato. Joy.

Today, Saturday, we're just hanging at "home" catching up on laundry, cooking, sleeping, writing, reading, and watching the paddleboard races on the river. King Tut, our visiting Egyptian Goose, is still down there on the shore, balancing on his leg with the foot. He's happy. A little girl—about three years old--just dumped a plate of crumbs for him.

Ciao. Ciao. Sue and The King

Story #5

The Uffizi Gallery in Florence, Italy holds the greatest collection of Italian paintings, anywhere. Dignified. Historical. Centuries of man's highest accomplishments in the World of Art and Creative Thinking. The works of Michelangelo and Rosselli and Perugino and Lorenzo di Credi are on display for the entire world to admire. Scores of tourists—many of them art students--enter with thoughts of educating themselves on the lives and works from medieval times (1200-1400) through the High Renaissance (1500-1550). Philosophers, scientists, writers, and patrons come to contemplate the rise and fall and rise of mankind.

So, if you're a Laughter Yoga Leader and Teacher, you may want to have a serious talk with yourself before entering the Uffizi. Just because you see the famous "bust of Marcus Vipsaniuns" you don't have to think it looks like Mark Wood, famous singer and guitar player in Orange County. The bust of Socrates may look like Skip—our Rascal repair expert—but that is no reason to burst out laughing. The vipers curled around the picture frame of another famous work may remind you of geese, so if the phrase "goosey-faced snakes" comes to mind, just keep the thought to yourself.

When you come upon the bust of Commodus and you think of Rev. Jim T. hold that thought until you are alone. And, no, those are not broken-off penises the male statues are holding, but scrolls. (It was Pope Pius IX, 1857, who commanded the breaking-off of . . . male genitals.) Usually, when I have a laughter-seizure, Richard can roll away from me in his Rascal and pretend he doesn't know me. This time, I was pushing him in a manual wheelchair, so he had to endure. Poor guy. He must wonder what's he's gotten himself into: a mate that makes him travel and try new experiences and laughs for no reason. Ho ho ha ha ha.

Excuse me while I go laugh some more.

Love and Blessings, Sue and The King

Story #6

Sunday May 6, 2018

We visited the Pitti Palace yesterday. It is the most sumptuous place we've ever seen. It holds eight museums and acres of gorgeous Boboli Gardens. Pink roses everywhere. Birds: we spotted house finches, ravens, European Starlings, and of course, pigeons. About 100 steps up a steep hill there is yet another museum full of the Pitti Family china dishes and teapots and hundreds of small porcelain figurines. The view encases miles and miles of olive groves and huge villas. The vista is stunning.

Near the top of the hill is large fountain with Neptune standing in the middle atop a small island. Perched right behind Neptune is a Great Blue Heron, which I suppose is part of the fountain décor until she moves her head my way. Of course, I whip out my iPhone6 and snap a few shots. Other tourists do the same. She looks at me. Could this be our friend Amorra Raa coming to visit? To tell us heaven is in Boboli Gardens?

Our beautiful friend, Amorra Raa, passed from this life in December. Her memorial service was held in January at the Center for Spiritual Living in Irving. Amorra Raa was a beautiful free spirit who spread love and joy wherever she went. Her kindness and caring and her sense of humor are legendary. At her service we were honored with a small bag of her ashes. We brought the ashes with us to Italy, knowing her perfect placement would be revealed to us.

I trotted down the hill to find my Knight in Shining Armor (also know as The King) waiting for me in the shade of a giant Italian Cedar tree. Upon viewing my stunning video of Amorra the Heron, we decided Boboli would be honored to receive the ashes of this great lady. I sat on the ground by an acre of purple lupine and yellow daisies and little white flowers. Sitting in his Rascal, Richard read aloud about Amorra's life and the poem composed by her Grandson Ramon. We ceremoniously spilled her ashes onto the ground knowing she will be blown about, nourishing the flowers.

And so ends another beautiful day in Firenze, Italy.

Ciao Ciao

Sue and The King

Story #7

There's a saying here in Firenze:

"Life is harder here, but it's easier.
In the U.S. life is easier but it's harder."

Some examples:

1. Many people in Italy use bikes—rentals from the city. No need to gas up a car, pay insurance on a car, wash it, or loan it to your teenagers. BUT. How much can you carry on your bike? What's the weather like? In the U.S most of us have cars so we don't think about how many bags of groceries we can carry. Ten bags? Okay. One bag? Okay. Remember to pay car insurance, keep track of mileage, gas-up, oil-change?
2. In Italy there's no need for a clothes dryer. Wash your clothes and sheets and towels in the sink or in a tiny washing machine. Capacity: one sheet or three towels. Hang wet items on portable clothesline. (Remember those?) Or hang items over the railing of your balcony. In the U.S. wash huge loads of dirty items at a time, toss all into the dryer.
3. Health Insurance in Italy. Health insurance in Italy is primarily organized on a regional level through the nationally established Servizio Sanitario Nazionale (SSN), which provides universal coverage, including the full funding of public doctors and prescription drugs. (I Googled this for accuracy.) In the U.S. the average individual pays about $6000 a year for coverage, not including prescription drugs.
4. Public Universities. Average tuition fees for a higher education in Italy are between €850-1,000 per year, depending on the university and program of study. In the U.S., According to College Board, tuition fees for 2017 and 2018 at state colleges are an average of US $9,970 for state residents, and $25,620 for everyone else. This compares to an average of $34,740 at private non-profit colleges.
5. In Firenze there are many little "mom and pop" pastry and gelato shops, leather-goods stores, clothing boutiques, and kiosks selling souvenirs to tourists. Many of the shop owners live in apartments above their businesses. In the U.S., think 405 Freeway at 8:00 a.m. on a weekday. Stress?
6. In most of Italy, museums, shops, cathedrals are open from about 10:00 a.m. to 1:00 and from 3:00 p.m. to 6:30 or 6:45 p.m. Most people

go home for a two-hour revival time, enjoy lunch and perhaps a nap. In the U.S. Two-hour lunch? What's a "nap"?

7. The state guarantees a leave period of six months for each parent, with a maximum of 10 months per child. Parental leave in Italy provides qualified workers with 30% of their monthly salary in the first three years of the child's life. Parental leave varies in the U.S.
8. Mondays: most museums and shops closed. A day of rest. In the U.S. you can shop until you drop—everyday.
9. Law 104/92 in Europe. If you are disabled physically or mentally, admission to museums, cathedrals, and busses are "Gratuito" and you are escorted to the front of the line—even if there are 500 people in line. In the U.S. be patient. Get out your cash.
10. In Italy: no smoking in the autobus or train terminals or in museums. Okay everywhere else. In the U.S. smoking restricted in most indoor venues and many outdoor venues.

So, life is easier and harder in Italy and in the U.S. One of the coolest things in Italy is the many different languages heard on the streets, in museums, and in restaurants, kinda like in Laguna Beach. Because the U.S. is a newer country, we have more modern conveniences. None of our buildings were created in the 1300's. What a wonderful world!

Blessings from S&R

Story #8

The Iris Garden, A Vivaldi Concerto,
The Three-Tenor Concert, The Monet Experience,
Galileo, and Picking up Trash.

South of the Arno River—in Oltrarno—and up the hill—Piazzale Michelangelo offers breath-taking views of Firenze and a chance to view a couple of acres of the most spectacular Iris Garden. It is simply magical. Maintained by the Italian Iris Society, it's a terraced garden overlooking the city of Florence and contains the widest variety of this enchanting flower. It is only open for three weeks a year—in Maggio. Steep and stony pathways lead down to a calming pool encircled by a dozen benches, filled with "chillaxing" (a Costa Rican term) tourists.

I left Richard at the top of the hill where he could view the wonders of Tuscany, the Ponte Vecchio, and munch on a bag of pistachios. He kindly sent me on a one-hour tour of millions of iris. A cute muscular handsome happy young gardener was collecting buckets of weeds, for indeed, they had taken over in some spots. At this point I think the only thing I miss about home in Laguna Woods is digging in our veggie patch. My instinct is to grab a few weeds but I constrain myself and take 50 pictures instead. To view the gardens you can go online.

With the help of several very strong angels who pushed, tugged, and lifted The King up five huge steps, we were able to enter Santo Stefano Church last Wednesday evening and attend the Concerto presenting Pachelbel's Canon, Mozart's A Little Night Music, Bach's Air, and Vivaldi's Four Seasons. All performed by the Orchestra da Camera Fiorentina, consisting of four violins, one viola, one base, a cello, and a keyboardest on the harpsichord. The musicians were mostly local folks: we shared a few moments with the viola player after the concert as he was unleashing his bike for the ride home. I know my sister Jeannie remembers the night four years ago on our trip to Venice how—when we heard about a Vivaldi Concerto as our tour group was having dinner—we quickly left the diners and jogged over to the local church for a delightful concerto. Vivaldi is my fave.

Last evening we were again hoisted up over the steep steps into Santo Stefano's for the Three Tenors concert. Angels everywhere. These three amazing vocalists entertained us with songs from several operas, including: Puccini's Tosca, Verdi's Il Trovatore and Rigoletto, and of course, Luigi Denza's Funiculi Funicula. At the end when we, the audience, insisted on an encore, they repeated Funiculi Funicula as we all clapped our hands together. It was a beautiful experience. At the end of the concert, the ticket-taker, Pablo from The Ukraine, helped us down eight steep steps to a special side room where we'd stored the Rascal.

Yes, we count our blessings, every day.

The Monet experience is a virtual reality production put on by Cross Media. It's hard to explain: it's a sensorial immersion inside the masterpieces of several impressionists and their great works. First stop: put on a pair of Oculus VR to access an enchanting experience of being completely immersed in the paintings of the masters. For example, you're actually on the hill where Monet painted Woman in a Garden.

Wearing the Oculus VR you can turn around and see the hillside. You can look down where you think your feet are and see, instead, the flowers beneath you. After that, you lie on the floor of the sanctuary with lots of other viewers and watch the landscapes being reinvented and painted by Claude Monet. All accompanied by lovely French musical sensations. The 50-foot high walls, the floor, and the ceiling were a continually moving piece of art. If it comes to a venue close to you—go. No one could not love it.

If you're an English major (such as I) and you tour Galileo's Museum, it's a good idea to have a Science major, former Sci Teacher (such as The King) to help you understand Galileo's (and other early scientists') experiments and inventions. For example: the Tellurium invented by Charles Francois in Paris in the 1800's. The Volta Hydro lamp/electrophorus. The double pendulum to illustrate the damping of oscilliation invented in 1386. The armilliary sphere created by Antonio Santucci in 1588. Huh? I did kinda understand the Apparatus for showing stable equilibrium and the telescopes. Measuring instruments of all types were displayed in the museum—the work of brilliant minds.

Galileo was tried by the Church—the Roman Inquisition—found guilty of heresy because the Bible taught that everything revolved around the Earth. He was sure that the planets revolved around the sun, which we now know to be true. Even English majors understand that. Galileo spent the rest of his life under house arrest where he wrote one of his best-known works: "Two New Sciences," in which he summarized work he had done 40 years earlier on kinematics and strength of materials.

Richard and I often pick up trash, just to make the world a little better. The last piece of trash I picked up this morning was an empty Lucky Strikes box from the Tobacci Shop. The manufacturer? R.A. Patterson Tobacco Company Est. Rich's Val USA. British/American Tobacco Group. The warning on the front cover reads: il fumo aumenta il rischio di cecita. Il fumo uccide—smetti subito. Il fumo del tabacco contiene oltre 70 sostanze cancerogene. More than 70 cancer-causing elements? Yuck. Why are all these young people here smoking? Pretty long-legged blonds. Dirty old men. Chubby Americans. Skinny Chinese. Yo no comprendo.

There are few smoking restrictions here in Italy. Mostly in museums. It's okay to light up in restaurants, gelato shops, when walking down the street. We've witnessed people walking out of eateries, lighting up, tossing a lit cigarette into a trash bin or onto the street. Why? Why? Why? E-cigarettes are also popular. Hopefully, the people we see smoking them are trying to quit. Hopefully. It's no Laguna Woods, where few people smoke, or Laguna Beach where no one is allowed to smoke except in their cars or in their homes. It's a different world. Most mornings we see workers sweeping butts off the sidewalk into the street—they are followed by small vehicles that vacuum them up. ("Weet Weepers, as son John called them.)

Life continues to be beautiful, amazing, and a challenge. We love it here.

Love and Blessings, Sue and The King

Story #9

"Away, away from men and towns,
To the wild wood and the downs,
To the silent wilderness,
Where the soul need not repress its music."

Percy Bysshe Shelly

How to navigate the vicissitudes of life with Spirit--no matter what happens. This is about the highlights of the lowlights. What is it they say about lemons? Read on.

Plan B. Today's plans were better than yesterday's plans. We thought! For the second day in a row we walk 'n rolled a mile up to the train station thinking we'd be heading for Lucca. The only way we knew to get to the train station was to walk through the underground mall and take the elevator up to the ticket office. Ha!

Plan A. Yesterday the elevator was non funzione, (non-functional) so I traipsed around the mall, went back outside and discovered the way into the train station from the street. Yay! At the corner of S.M. Novela Cathedral and MacDonalds was the grand entrance! More yay! By now it was a bit late to start off for a day in Lucca. We walk 'n rolled 4.6 miles. Decided to go back to our apartment and rest up for the next day's adventure. Homemade tonna (tuna) salad for dinner. After getting Richard back up the elevator, I took the Rascal back across the street. Greeted by Alisio—nice guy who works in the Parking Garage—he took the Rascal back to its room and plugged it in. "Domani." I ran back across the street. Took fragalo gelato out of the freezer for dessert.

This morning we had it all planned perfectly! I went across the street to the Parking Structure, paid 20 Euro for overnight parking and battery charge. Drove the Rascal across the street to our apartment. Elevated up to 3rd floor (which in America is the 4th floor) helped my mate into the elevator, picked up the Rascal's basket full of maps, bottled water, fanny pack, and our jackets. We left at 10:30, plenty of time to walk the 1.1 miles to the train station. Got there at 11:15. Bought tickets in the machine. Boarded the train to Lucca, we thought. Other passengers said, "No, this train goes to Pistoia." We de-boarded then discovered Pistoia was just a stop along the way to Lucca. Yikes! Too late. The train took off without us.

One of the assistants in the terminal pointed to the "Blue sign with the White top. They will help you." There were half a dozen folks in wheelchairs, waiting for help. Seems you need to let it be known ahead of time when you travel in a wheelchair. We'd already paid for our tickets so we were directed to return to the ticket terminal and have the assistant in there scribble something on our tickets so we can use them tomorrow. All we need to do is show up 30 minutes before we want to board, report to the SalaBlu office with the Blue sign and the White top.

Plan C: When we stood in Eisenhower Park in the City of Orange on March 11, 1995 and said, "I will," we never dreamed we'd be spending our 278th month-a-versary in Lucca, Italy. This morning we reported to SalaBlu at 10:45 at the railway station Santa Maria Novella. A special attendant came to the office and got us. He was carrying a folded up ramp for the Rascal. Helpful guys directed us onto the train. Richard hopped (figuratively speaking) out of the Rascal. Got ourselves into two little seats that shared one large tangled seatbelt.

We couldn't figure out how it fit together. We tried several combinations but none made sense, so we decided to laugh ourselves silly. What better way to spend an anniversary?

Laughing ourselves silly over seatbelt mystery

The train ride was just over an hour and cost about 10 Euro each way. Lucca is a beautiful quiet little town just north of Firenze. It's famous for the big wall built to keep out the enemy in the olden days. The town made the thick wall into a big wide path 2-1/2 miles around the town for biking and hiking and walk 'n rolling. From the wall we saw another amazing botanical garden built under the guardianship of Maria Luisa of Bourbon in 1820. It includes the arboretum, the hill, and the lake. Also a few greenhouses.

Just up the street from gardens we spotted a 3-story building with a caved-in roof, broken windows, and missing doors. With a little imagination and some money we could create our own bed-and-breakfast complex. We'd live in Lucca, of course. We'd put in a large elevator, a viewing deck for guests, a big kitchen for baking cookies and sautéing veggies from our veggie garden, private bathrooms for each guest. But . . . The King wouldn't even discuss it. Strike that one off the bucket list.

The yearly Festival of Volunteers was happening. We met Croce Rossa (Red Cross) workers, the Volunteer Rescue Squads, Special Olympics promoters, Auser Comprensoriale Lucca—volunteers who organized, we think (none of them spoke English) the local senior center. We watched twelve kids—standing in a circle—stick their swords into the ground as they held tightly onto the top. When the instructor yelled "1,2,3" each kid released his or her grip on the sword and tried to grab the handle of the sword on the right. If you miss, you're out! The group was soon down to three kids. They were having fun and at the same time, learning concentration, balance, and lively competition. This organization was named Euro-Fencing.

Lucca is the birthplace of famous composer Giacomo Puccini. You know, the guy who wrote his most famous opera Turandot (daughter of Turan). There's even a big statue of Puccini in Cittadella Square. Our granddaughter, Rylee, along with a few children of the San Diego Children's Choir, sang the Chinese folk song Mo Li Hua (Jasmine flower) when Turandot was performed in Southern California several years ago.

At this time of the year, groups of students from kindergarten through high school are touring the museums and other historical sights in Firenze. There's so much lively chatter, laughter, and (one would hope) learning happening. We hear many languages here: Dutch, Spanish, Farsi, German, English, and Italian. We love it here because it's interesting and challenging and because I've always wanted to spend a big hunk of time here. We are SO fortunate and grateful and happy and amazed. Life is totally awesome. Tomorrow we pack up. Early Thursday morning, we'll be heading for home.
Love, Sue and The King

Story #10

It is every Romantic's dream to sit outside, while bathing in the Tuscan Sun, enjoying an authentic Italian croissant and a cup of espresso while gazing into the eyes of her favorite guy—to bring to a close a dream of living in a distant country--experiencing untold adventures and untellable communications. To gaze, one last time at the landscape of beautiful gardens, of a clear-flowing river, to complete a dream vacation. To know, for sure, that this person, this lovely, loving person is forever true and solid and wise.

Prime example of a Romantic Couple

Wow! That sounds pretty good! Well, that was the idea and I think it would have worked out that way except that it was raining and cold and several times we had to turn around on the cracked sidewalk because one end of the walkway had a curb cut and the other end didn't. We stopped a bunch of times to let crabby tourists pass by and we got a bit wet. Most restaurants were closed and the few that were open were only serving early lunches. By 11:00 we were pretty hungry and I just had to have a croissant and a cup of coffee, American style coffee. Weak.

We finally found a pastry shop where, although a bit crowded with hurried Italians, did have croissants and coffee. All we had to do was park the Rascal outside, get The King to a chair at the back of the restaurant where we shared a table with an older woman and her daughter (who was attached to her phone). I paid for what we wanted, took the receipt to the pastry bar where I was informed that "No. You did not pay for a croissant, you paid for this." Okay. Two apricot pastry-thingys. I took the apricot pastry-thingys over to

Richard and went back to get our coffee at the other bar—the coffee bar. We had to laugh at ourselves. Is this romantic?

Just then a little house finch landed on our table and began gobbling up the crumbs. I was too slow to get a photo but the young woman next to me got a beautiful picture of the sweet little bird. He acted like he owned the place and perhaps he did.

After enjoying our brunch we arrived at Santa Croce, the church that holds the remains of Michelangelo and a long list of other artists, sculptors, painters, and musicians. Santa Croce is, perhaps, one of the most beautiful places on the planet. Long after his death, Galileo's remains were allowed in the church. Remember, he's the one who defied the pope by saying that the Earth revolved around the Sun. Tombs of Rossini and Machiavelli decorate the courtyard outside the church.

Inside Santa Croce, left of the altar is my favorite piece of artwork: The Pieta. So sad to see a mother holding her dead son. I think of friends who have lost their sons to early deaths. You know who you are. My heart goes out to you. There can't possibly be anything more difficult than losing a child. The Pieta is a reminder.

Okay, we're packing up. The Taxi will be here at 7:15 a.m. We'll arrive at LAX at 4:25 p.m. That's Thursday, May 17th at 4:25. Swiss Air Flight 040. Linda!!! Thanks for picking us up.

Love and Blessings, Sue and The King

Travelin' With The King to Idaho – May 20, 2019

We woke up at 4:00 this morning and decided to get on the road nice and early. The traffic was terrific heading up the 133, out the 91 and Oh! Oh! The carpool lane on the 91 east does not connect with the 15 north, so we sped across the lanes, got off at the next off ramp and got onto the 91 going the other way for about a block, then hooked up with the 15 north, finally.

It's after 8:00 p.m. now and we're safely ensconced in Jackpot, Northern Nevada's premier nightspot: Cactus Pete's Hotel and Casino. We drove an astonishing 800 miles in 12 hours. Only had four official stops: one rest stop, two filling stations, and the ADA port-a-potty in the rainy parking lot in the new almost completed McDonalds's in Ely, Nevada. That was fun!!! A nice construction crew guy named Mike offered help and asked where we were from. "California? You must be liberals!" We smiled.

We experienced every kind of weather today—except earthquakes and thunder strikes—we had sunshine, drizzle, light rain, heavy rain, and light hail which turned into snow. Our new Chrysler Pacifica Hybrid, whom we call Big Red (like my '99 Miata is called Little Red) has a bejillion fancy gadgets that we have yet to figure out. For example, when the weather gets misty, the windshield wipers slowly wipe off the wetness and when the heavy rain and snow come down, the wipers go faster—without us touching anything.

After we shuffled through the rain in Ely so Richard could use the ADA porta potty, and we got back into BR and started it up. We were surprised when the steering wheel and seats were WARM!! Don't know how that happened but it felt really good because it was 33 degrees and drizzling again. So another find! Heated seats! Such luxury. Also, the wipers don't work as automatically when the front lower radar-sensors are covered with snow. For a period of time big chunks of snow would fly off the front of the van, smash into the windshield, then the wipers worked better. Also, the headlights know when to go off and on, and when to go from bright to normal.

Sirius xm streams in the Beatles, and bunches of other rock stations via satellite. We have a new lift in the back of the van for Richard's Rascal. We are getting better at working it every day. At home we could plug in and charge up so we were getting about 50 miles to the gallon of gas. On the road, only 35 miles to the gallon.

The best thing today (besides being together) was the scenery: the clouds in every shape and shade of white and gray drifted over us, sometimes blessing us with sprinkles, other times, drenching us. Snow-capped hills and mountains and roadside puddles of white surrounded us. Going up the 93 towards Idaho we felt like we were in a giant postcard of beauty—a postcard that kept changing. If I had four hands, I would have taken pictures, but I diligently kept my eyes on the road and my two hands clasped onto the steering wheel. Only twice did I accidently call Siri when my left thumb touched a tiny green dot on the steering wheel.

And why, one may ask, are we going through all this? Well, our precious friend Beth said "yes!" when her boyfriend Troy popped the big question and they are getting married next Saturday in Garden Valley, Idaho. We've been following the weather for the last month. Up until a few days ago, GV was in the 80's. Perfect for an outdoor wedding! Now: rain, rain, rain. For some reason, which we will understand better when we see their new home in GV, they decided it would be a good idea to move up here from sunny So. Cal. Something about their kids being nearby.

Tomorrow we're heading for a two-night stay in Boise where we'll visit the Snake River Birds of Prey National Conservation Area. One of us is crazy about bird watching and the other is a very scientific thinker, so this will be a good thing. After that we'll head for the yet-to-be famous Garden Valley Motel, which has an astonishing 12 rooms!!!

Thursday May 23, 2019

I am always amazed at how life brings unexpected joy: Angels that offered to help and restaurant chefs and waitresses who accommodate our diets. Then, there is Shawn whom we met in Julia Davis Park yesterday. I saw this handsome young man (probably a mere 50 years) taking a photo of a memorial tablet telling the history of Tom and Julia Davis who were the first settlers along the Lewis and Clark Trail who offered assistance to all who passed along the road. The park was created in 1907 with a land donation from Tom Davis who was one of the founders of Boise, Idaho. He played a prominent role in attracting visitors and pioneers to the valley. He dedicated the park to his wife who had died of typhoid in 1906.

So, I say to Shawn. "Hi. Would you like me to take a picture of you looking at that?" One of the things I do to make the world a better place is offer to take picture of tourists all over the world, of course with their iPhones and cameras. Shawn introduces himself to Richard and me. He owns a small bike tour company and acts as a tour guide all over Boise. Naturally, he gives us a 20-minute lesson on this amazing place and tells us how to get everywhere and even leads us down to the Boise River. What a gift! One of the places he thought we'd really like is called Freak Alley Art Gallery. So we strolled along the Boise River and then stopped on our walk 'n roll to see the

Anne Frank memorial. Not only is there a bronze statue of Anne, but an elaborate display of war heroes and war stories. Many touching stories about numbers of Jews murdered and people who tried to hide them. And the reminder to not let this happen again.

This morning we parked near the Capitol Building and went down the ramp to the underground Gift Shop. Dianna, the manager, gave us a booklet on the "Capitol of Light." As we began to thumb through the pages, we heard a tour guide (Jim Clark) begin his talk. We drifted over and noticed that the 30 women he was speaking to were dressed nicely, high heels and all. I asked one of the young women if this was a class from Boise State University? She introduced herself (Sandy) and told us this group was young women interested in becoming legislators and were touring the Capitol as part of their program. This was a private tour, but their leader (Kathy) invited us to join the tour and told us these young women were from all over the country.

We heard the history of the creation of the building; we were invited into the governor's office and the Senate Chamber. We also got to view the JFAC—Joint Finance-Appropriations Committee. Jim explained (as did Shawn yesterday) that everyone is invited to look around the Capitol Building, no questions asked, no security check. Firearms are not banned, whether concealed or not!!! And since Abraham Lincoln signed the law that created Idaho Territory in 1863, there is a beautiful statue of Abe welcoming all to the Capitol of Light. Boise is the Center of Lincoln County.

Hanging out at the governor's desk

Next: Freak Alley. This is a block-long alley where all the walls of buildings on both sides are painted in cute, funny, crazy, spooky, ribald, interesting, and scary artistic visionary murals. My favorite is a doorway painted with bright yellow sunflowers and the truism: "Focus on the things that bring you joy." And this definitely was a day filled with joy.

We discovered the Eureka Restaurant in the Old Town Boise District. We found outdoor seating and enjoyed fish tacos (for The King) and a BIG green salad for me. About the time we finished, the wind came up, sprinkles descended, and we called Robbie, our waitress over to box up the salad and hurried back to Big Red. The wind began blowing over signs but did no real damage. Unlike Sunny So. Cal., the weather here can change in an instant.

We are ever grateful to our granddaughter, Jennifer, who arranges Marriott Hotel stays for us all over the country. We love you Jen. You are a treasure. (And happy 10th birthday to little granddaughter Tabatha last Tuesday.) Jen: You make the cutest babies.

After an amazing day viewing and learning about Boise, we drove northwest to Garden Valley, about 50 miles from Boise. The scenery is beyond beautiful. Green. Rivers. Mountains. Trees. Mountain roads are one-lane each way and they are very twisty so we used just about every chance to pull over and let the speeding Idahoans pass us.

The Garden Valley Motel

We parked in front of our home for the next three nights and as I ascended the ramp to the office, I found a Pine Processionary moth. Or, it could have been an Emperor Gum Moth. They look quite a bit alike. He appeared lifeless but when I moved him he flashed bright pink tail wings at me. Although beautiful, these little guys seem to do a lot of damage to the forest, so I am told.

Emperor Gum Moth or a Pine Processionary Moth?

After meeting Laurie (manager) at the Garden Valley Motel, (usually $80 a night, but since the TV was not working it was $70 a night for cute accessible room with queen bed and single bed and great kitchen) we checked in; then decided to drive up to 26 Quail Run where the wedding of the year will take place tomorrow! We're praying for the rain to go elsewhere and the sunshine to make it a joyful time.

The Motel turned out to be really fun. It was actually in the midst of a lumberyard, a junk yard, and a dirt parking lot. We loved it. Everyone was really nice. We had a kitchen, a great bed, and a pretty good shower setup. The owner parked big lumber-hauling trucks around the motel. There were heaps of boards—enough to build a decent sized house—and several broken-down cars and trucks. Plus it was only a few miles from the wedding. What's not to love about that?

As we drove towards Quail Run, we began to understand why people move here. Lotsa land and water and fresh air. There are many new homes, most in small neighborhoods. There is even a gorgeous brand new golf course. Aha! We found the wedding spot: a field where the family of Beth and Troy had set up a wedding venue. There were many cars parked at the house. We decided not to bother. See you tomorrow kids.

At 10:30 I stepped out the door of our motel room in search of stars. I didn't see any but a man carrying a suitcase came up the steps and looked at me. "Hear those robins singing? That means no rain tomorrow." Don't you love it when angels tell you good news?

The Wedding Story

Beth and Troy live on a 5-acre parcel in Garden Valley Idaho, near the Payette River, surrounded by tall green mountains. A small area near the house is fenced in for the Tortoise, Crumpy, and the dog, Jedi. Nine colorful chickens cluck and peck in their near-by coup and all around the yard. They produce about nine eggs a day. The biggest white one is named Queenie. Then there's Princess, Waffle, Pancake, Cinnamon, Nutmeg, and three others that don't seem to have names yet. One of those manly John Deere lawn mowers has sheared the acres of lawn down for the wedding. Several dozen cars are parked out in the field near the "chapel" and the "dining and dancing" area. About eighty people awaited the "wedding of the year." People arrived from eight places in California, two places in Colorado, Oregon, Florida, Wyoming, South Dakota, Nevada, Washington, and a whole bunch of folks from Idaho. And one couple flew in from Australia.

The nuptials were scheduled for a May Day, expected to be in the mid-eighties. And that promise seemed clear until the weather turned days before the wedding. The tempest that flooded the area continued in earnest until just days before when the deluges became showers, black skies lightened to gray, and temperatures rose into the 50's. But forecasts wouldn't assure the sun's return. Hours before the event the skies were still unclear of their intentions. It's not raining now, so here we go . . .

The King and I at the Wedding

Six beautiful young women, including Beth's sister Kelly and Troy's daughter Arlin, walked up the aisle in low-cut sleeveless baby-blue gowns. The handsome young men included two of Troy's sons Austin and Grady, and

Conner (Beth's son-in-law). The men wore nice jackets and ties and their best Levi's and tennis shoes or boots. Troy and his mother, Donna, walked up the aisle next. Then we all stood as the bride—wearing a full-length white strapless wedding dress with a long train—was escorted forward by her daughter Regina. Promises and rings were exchanged under a cloudy, but dry sky. We all cheered as the longest recorded "you may kiss the bride" kiss went on and . . .

Beth and Troy May 25, 2019

Catered dinner. Country music by cute young DJ named Toby. Perfect weather. No rain. Reconnecting with friends and neighbors old and new and young. Congratulatory speeches by Beth's sister Kelly, and Troy's best friend Phil, and Beth's daughter Regina. Troy stood, walked about the dance floor looking, in amazement, at the crowd of well-wishers. He liked us all being there—a lot. Love all around. We all agreed: most beautiful wedding ever. (Except for the one in Eisenhower Park in Orange, Ca. on March 11, 1995.)

Today—Sunday May 26—many of the guests went back to the house to help eat up the leftovers and say goodbye. A few of the young daredevils were racing around the property on Quads. About eight fruit trees in big pots stood on the porch awaiting planting day. Two cherry trees. A Fruit Cocktail (apricot, plum, peach, nectarine). Oysters were steaming on the BBQ. 'Twas an afternoon to be remembered. A wedding to be cherished. So many memories, old and new. A love feast. Thank you Beth and Troy for your friendship and for hosting a totally amazing gathering of family and friends.

June 4, 2019

Ha Ha! We're home. Yes. We've had so many people contact us and ask, "Are you home from your Idaho Road Trip?" The answer is "Yes!" We're home." We (I, Sue) drove 2077 miles.

We arrived home last Tuesday evening at 7:00. We unloaded Big Red, washed up dirty clothing, emptied all the snack containers, put the suitcases back into the carport cupboards, and went to bed. We didn't get up until 5:30 the next morning, which would be 6:30 in Idaho.

We had a wonderful time together! Saw so many beautiful sights and met so many angels. We are filled with gratitude, with love, with feelings of being blessed.

And so, what's next? We leave for Scotland, England, and Wales trip on July 8th. Stay tuned.

Love and Blessings, Sue and The King

Total UK Trip Notes #1 through #9

Orange Community Master Chorale (directed by Mike Short) and the Master Chorale of Saddleback Valley (directed by Charles Stevenson) will be singing beautiful music (we hope) in several venues in the next two weeks. Sue has been a member or OCMC since January of 2005.

New adventure: we are sitting in Business Class on Lufthansa Airlines anxiously awaiting our 10-hour trip to Frankfurt and then on to Glasgow. Wow! Business Class. We are VERY excited. After flying home from a month in Italy last year, Richard said, "No more air flights." But when Ashley with Music Celebrations International found us a deal, we said, "We'll take it."

Salvador, our shuttle driver picked us up right at 11:30 this morning—took us over to Mission Viejo to get another passenger, Roz on her way to visit family in Turkey—and onward to LAX. Salvador had interesting stories about growing up in Long Beach, being part of a gang for a while, playing football, helping with campus security and finally feeling grown up when his English teacher convinced him to write about his life and take a good look at it. Yay for English teachers!!!

I no longer need to remove my shoes for security in airports so zipped right through but Richard was interrogated for 40 minutes including a trip to the private security department and the emptying of his backpack and fanny pack. Then it was discovered that the security guy had something on his glove that kept setting off the alarm. It's a good thing our plane left 30 minutes later than planned. This morning's Affirmation in our Daily Guide came in handy: "I am choosing patience, kindness, and understanding." Also, Rumi reminded us: "Out beyond ideas of wrong-doing and right-doing there is a field. I'll meet you there."

So we're flying across the beautiful USA toward our destination when I spot Utah, whose State Bird is the California Gull. My lovely attendant brought me a glass of white wine—a Reisling, I believe. Now I need a nap. Later I watched the movie Bohemian Rapsody, which I loved. A well-deserved Academy Award winning actor. And so to sleep in my own reclining chair/bed with pillows and blankets.

Are there any downsides to Business Class? Yes! One huge one. The King and I are three feet apart. For 292 months we've sat side-by-side holding hands. However, due to the lovely table between us we could only gaze across the distance. Otherwise all was quite nifty. (Google that one grandkids:

Jennifer, Billy, Courtney, Brandi, Olivia, Tristen, and Rylee.) Oooo. Here comes breakfast. Gourmet meals: all vegetarian. Lots of fruit and veggies.

It was about 5:00 when we finally got to Glasgow and met our tour guides: Janet C. and Janet S. Our "coach" driver, Neil took us to Edinburgh's Marriott West. Lovely dinner, lovely hotel and off to bed. Tired . . .

UK #2 Wednesday July 10.

Fabulous breakfast at hotel. English breakfasts always offer eggs, tomatoes, and beans. We love it! Steve, our new bus driver, dropped us off. Well, dropped us off is just a silly term. Several people hopped off the bus when we got to Edinburgh Castle carrying our jackets and backpacks and pulling Richard's Rascal out from underneath the bus. The guides at the Castle were extra helpful, taking us to elevators and ramps. Honestly, I don't know where all of these angels come from but we are grateful and often brought to tears by the people all over the planet that help us get around.

We visited Edinburgh's (pronounced ED'n-burah by the Scottish) Royal Mile with its medieval and Georgian districts, which are just below the volcanic sill of Arthur's Seat and Carlton Hill. Edinburgh is the political capital of Scotland. The motto of the warriors? Nemo me impune lacessit, which roughly means: "No one messes with me and gets away with it." Our bus stopped at the bottom of the Royal Mile and we hiked up up up the hill to the castle at the top. Our tour guide JC—Janet Cameron—was ever on the alert for accessibility. She is a treasure! There were rooms full of swords of war, which made us wonder why there were so many many many memorials built in admiration of humans who had murdered other humans. Something's wrong with that. The King (Richard) and I took a break in the tea room overlooking a colorful labyrinth of cobble stone streets, medieval skyscrapers, and beautiful green gardens of the valley below.

The chorale gathered below the Castle and above the Palace to sing a tune. This time it was O Magnum Mysterium. The crowd of tourists cheered and clapped for us.

Then we all hiked down down down to the Palace of Holyroodhouse where we viewed Meghan's wedding dress. How many of us said "I do" in a boat-necked, three-quarter sleeved white gown designed by Clare Waight Keller, artistic director of Givenchy and paid for by the queen of England at the cost of L250,000? In American dollars that is about $311,000. Honestly, it was stunning. Her veil was lifted by seven of the royal children, as it was 200 inches long and quite wide. A copy of Harry's tux was off to the side and barely noticed. Also on display were pictures of the royal family dressed in all their finest. This was much more appreciated than the shields and swords and cannons, suits of armor and pistols and hammers and so many sharp-edged weapons of war.

Richard and I met Adam, one of the guides at the Castle, who gave us an explanation of the river running below. It's called the Firth of Fourth and further on that river is the Fife. The River Fourth flows into the North Sea. All this landscape was built by volcanoes, and carved down by glaciers. The locals say it's a city formed by fire and ice. The history of this area includes the story of the 300 "witches" who were accused and either burned, or bound and dropped into the sea. If they floated they were pronounced guilty and burned in front of the castle. If they drowned, they were considered innocent. Thank you Adam.

We were "on your own" for lunch. Richard and I walked 'n rolled along the many souvenir shops and pubs until we came to the Yum Yum Kurdish Food café where Mark, the cook prepared falafel, veggies, and salad for us. He came from Kurdistan in Turkey in 2002 with some of his family and established this tiny 10-seater restaurant for the tourists. The food was THE best. Our friends Maureen and Gale popped in the door and pronounced, "We'll have what she's having." Good choices. Most of the customers were students who had ordered take-out with simple text messages.

Forty-four of us on this 2-bus trip form the Orange Community Master Chorale and the Saddleback Valley Master Chorale. Plus, we have our entourage of about 45. This evening we sang at St. Giles in Edinburgh. We started with Morten Lauridsen's "O Magnum Mysterium," telling of the birth of Christ—in Latin. Beautiful and touching. After that we sang "Ave Maria" and a few lively American Folk songs. My favorite is "The Drinking Gourd," which refers to the Big Dipper that guided the slaves away to freedom.

And so to bed . . .

UK #3 - On Friday, July 12.

We cruised Loch Lomond—meaning Lake of the Elms. No monster appeared. Our amazing tenor David Williams led and we all joined in performing the Scottish tune "Loch Lomond":

"By yon bonnie banks and yon bonnie braes, where the sun shines bright on Loch Lomond, Where me and me true love were ever wont to gae, on the bonnie bonnie banks of Loch Lomond."

It's a sad song about Bonnie Prince Charles' men who were killed and captured in the uprising of 1745. One man is executed and the other is set free. According to Celtic tradition, the condemned man's spirit would return to his homeland via the "low road". And his spirit will reach his homeland before his comrade get home on the high road, but sadly, he will never meet his true love again.

As we de-boarded our little cruise ship I noticed five of our younger members skipping rocks on the shore so I decided to show them how it's really done. I ran up the ramp, leaving Richard to fend for himself. I bounced down the steps to the beach. Not to brag, and remember, I've been skipping rocks much longer than any of them, I won the championship rock-skipping contest. SIX skips. Sam claimed that he also skipped six times but had no witnesses. Besides, he's only 28 years young.

So we scurried over to the buses and were on our way again. (We did sing "I'll Be On My Way." Several times.) We made a brief stop at a church. Richard stayed on the bus and I promised to bring back a few photos and a story or two. First I met Evan, a young Chinese man who was a volunteer guide for the summer. "Oh, yes," he informed me. "I have been to the United States. Wisconsin." Then, I met Hazel, the woman who arranges the flowers for the church. She politely asked where we were from. I told her we're singing all about the UK but not here. She graciously allowed me to take her picture for Richard. Ten minutes later I rushed back over to let her know we were about to sing one song. I think it was "O Magnum." Again. Afterwards she said, "It was <u>low</u>-vole-ee." And 'twas.

Lunch (on your own) was at an Italian Restaurant in Princes Square, a 4-story building with an open center, and a glass ceiling. About a dozen restaurants looked down upon an interesting vision. As we enjoyed salad (me) and pizza (The King) we giggled at the signage on the spa below: CoolSculpting Non-invasive fat removal THAT WORKS by Dr. D. McK. We won't give out his full name because we don't want to embarrass him—or her. I said, "That's funny." Richard said, "That sucks."

That evening we performed at St. Mary's Cathedral in Glasgow. Of course we sang the traditional "A Welsh Lullaby:" "Hush my dear one, sleep serenely Mother rocks you humming lowly; Close your eyes now go to sleep." Altos sang some words and did lots of ooooooo-ing. And we sang "Salmo 150—Psalm 150" where the altos sang lots of la-la-la-la's, sometimes 14 times in a row. The song was composed by Ernani Aguilar, of Brazil.

We're having a jolly good time.

UK #4 - Saturday, July 13

Oh! That King Henry VIII. He was a bad boy. In the 16th century he had his men destroy monasteries—anything that was Catholic. The Church of England was to be the new "true" church, ruled by him, ushering in the "divine right of kings." When the pope refused Henry an annulment from Catherine (first of six wives) he decided to rewrite history. He was an author and composer. As he aged, however, he became severely obese and his health suffered, contributing to his death in 1547. He is frequently characterized in his later life as a lustful, egotistical, harsh, and insecure king.

But I digress. The 73-mile long Hadrian's Wall was built by the Romans in about A.D. 122 during the reign of Emperor Hadrian to keep out the "barbarians" to the north. It took 20,000 troops to build and defend it. At each mile-mark they built a castle. The purpose of the wall was not entirely clear, but we enjoyed our time there. We hiked about the ruins of the Housesteads Roman Fort, climbed up into a reconstructed fort, and visited the gift shop.

Sunday July 14

We took a "morning walking tour of York" which was not enough time to see everything. We stopped in York Minster for a look, visited the Shambles Market Place. Although the butchers have now vanished, a number of the shops on the street still have meat-hooks hanging outside and, below them, shelves on which meat was displayed. The shops currently include a mix of restaurants and shops as well as a bookshop and a bakery. Five "snickleways" lead off the Shambles. Shambles Market operates daily and is situated between The Shambles and Parliament Street. The market was previously known as Newgate Market after the street on which it is located, but was renamed in 2015.

As we passed through the Market, we spotted a little boy about three years old, standing alone. He looked lost. I got down beside him and said, "Are you okay? Where is your Mommy?" He started to cry. So did I because I thought about my own children and the times they got lost. So, I stood up and held his hand. We found his "mum" who was only 30 feet away, standing in a crowd of people watching a street musician. She picked him up and he cried some more. Smile.

Because Wimbledon is such an important event to most of England, attendance at our 3:30 afternoon performance was quite low: 30 of our entourage and ten members of St. Lawrence's Church. I kept my eye on the old white-haired minister who was obviously not fond of American Folk music and a bit befuddled at 18-year old Sophia's performance of Carmen's Habanera. Yes, it was a bit sassy. As it should be. The attendees we spoke with afterwards were very happy with the music. We thought we were low-vole-ee.

Monday July 15

And on to Liverpool. Our handsome, physically strong and healthy, super caring coach driver, Stewart (former bomb detonator for the army) played Beatles music and sang along to "Hard Days Night" and "Ob-la-di" (which our chorale sang in concerts) and "Blackbird" and "Come Together" and others . . . A word about our bus (oops! In England they are coaches, not buses) drivers. Every one of them was patient and caring as they unloaded the scooter (Richard's Rascal) from underneath the coach. So many of our fellow singers and entourage helped by carrying our things off the bus, handing over the crutch, and guiding Richard's feet—foot patrol. Charles, Frank, Mark, Dan, and especially Dennis made things easier and doable. Carolina and Connie were always available for holding our stuff and getting "the butt into the seat." Thank you one and all. There are angels everywhere.

Liverpool is where the Beatles began singing in The Cavern Quarter. After we located the "lift" and got Richard downstairs, we donned headphones and were treated to a fascinating tour of "Beatlemania" the world's largest permanent Beatles exhibition. I believe it was an old bombed out shelter, patched back together after the war. We enjoyed watching an old video of police trying to calm down young women who were screaming and attempting to touch one of the young singers. Remember the first time they were on the Ed Sullivan show? 1964?

We later learned that the big shopping center at Mersey-side Albert Dock in Liverpool is owned by The Duchess of Westminster. More on her later.

Driving towards Chester's Mercure Abbotts Well Hotel—our home for the next four nights—we drove through miles of green hills where cows and sheep roamed. All were grass-fed. We read in a newspaper that every second 19 liters of ice-cream is consumed in England and, sadly, the sheep produce babies that are eaten when they are young and tender. The wool of the ewes is not fit for much of anything as they are out in the open most of the time; their wool is kinda rough.

Our tour guide, JC, informed us that many of the shops in this town—and across the UK—have shut down because of high rents and the inability to compete with online shopping. Many of the little shops are rented out to non-profits. Ox-Fam has a used book store. Other shops have become "used-items" stores. As we walked 'n rolled down a quite street a man on his bicycle stopped us and asked, "What has happened to this place? It used to be lively and busy and there were no empty shops. It's sad." We repeated the story JC had told us.

Chester—and many other cities in the UK—depends on tourism to survive. Many of the older hotels do not have air-conditioning. Global warming is a big threat to these little places. It will be interesting to see what happens in the coming years.

More stories later . . .

UK #5

Tuesday, July 16

Caernarfon Castle is in Wales. While the castle was under construction, the town walls were built around Caernarfon. The work cost between £20,000 and £25,000—about $35,000--from the start until the end of work--in 1330. It would cost a bit more in 2019. Actually, it was never totally completed and no one ever lived in it for very long. We had a great time climbing the narrow rounding steps up to the top of the castle, taking pictures, and yelling down at the smart tourists who did not go up to the top. Several of our younger members donned capes, shields, and swords for playing war. Silly. But fun. We did get to sing a couple of songs as we stood out in the center of the castle grounds: "A Welsh Lullaby". Carolina's voice is so beautiful I had tears running down my face. "Hush my darling, sleep serenely. Now my lovely slumber deep." Lots of applause from other tourists.

Here we are in the yard of Caernafon Castle

Wednesday July 17

A wonderful day exploring the town of Chester in northern England where we briefly performed one of our "drive-bys". Again, we sang "O Magnum Mysterium." This time in the Chester Cathedral. We were bused—or coached—back to our hotel to have our "farewell" luncheon, then clean up and change into concert attire. And back on the bus—I mean coach—for a ride back to the Chester Town Hall. We performed a shared concert with the Chester Male Voice Choir.

The Chester Male Voice Choir traces its roots back to 1941 when it was founded as a works choir at HECO, the Hydraulic Engineering Company. Several of the performers are in their 90's. All had beautiful voices, smiled a lot and seemed to love what they do. Their director, Rodney T. Jones has been conducting them for over 30 years. His love of music and his energy guided them through really cool songs like "Carrickfergus," an Irish Folk Song, Leonard Cohen's "Hallelujah," a couple of African pieces: "Senzenia" and a trilogy.

Our group sang "Dirait-on" ("Abondon, en toure d'abondon, ten-dress touchant aux ten-dresse") by Morten Lauridsen, "Stomp Your Foot" ("Stomp your foot upon the floor, throw the windows open, Take a breath of fresh June air, and dance around the room"), "Ob-le-di Ob-le-da" ("Desmond has a barrow in the market place, Molly is a singer in a band) Beatles song. At the end of the performance we all got on stage together and sang "You'll Never Walk Alone" ("At the end of the storm is a golden sky, And the sweet silver song of a lark.") As we were singing I noticed a very tall, pretty lady sitting with our tour guide JC. I supposed it was one of her friends. During intermission I had a chance to speak with JC so I scooted over to her and her friend. Her friend was introduced as The Duchess of Westminster. Whoa. Duchess?

Later, JC told us that The Duchess owns the huge shopping center in Liverpool and Westminster and is worth billions. Her real name is Natalia Grosvenor but we call her The Duchess. She's a young vibrant 60 year old. During intermission JC took her over to meet Richard, yes, our Richard, The King. She said it was "lovely to meet you." Richard said he felt very honored. They talked about the tiring of touring.

After the concert we went back to our hotel about 11:00. Everyone but The King and I was leaving about 5:30 in the morning. We spent a restful day at the hotel sleeping and reading and writing. So nice.

UK #6

Friday July 19

The first taxi came to the Mercure Hotel at 9:30 a.m. but was not big enough for the Rascal, so we waited 20 minutes for a bigger van. Sebastian arrived, set out the ramp; loaded us up and off we went for the 27-mile drive to the Crewe Train Station. As it was raining hard, we got a wee bit wet. Still can't get used to these amazing folks who drive on the wrong side, I mean the left side, of the road. Many of the streets we flew down were so narrow our driver slowed, sometimes stopping, for opposing traffic to squeeze by. Big bushes on both sides of the road. We closed our eyes a lot.

Once at the Crewe Station, Sebastian unloaded us and we were off to the Booking Station. We'd made reservations 24-hours in advance, as that is the correct protocol for people who are amazing and handsome and differently-abled. A pleasant train-station helper took out his key and opened the closet on the train that held the ramp. We got great seats because the train was totally empty. Then 18-month old Freddie and his mommy Sam hopped aboard. I helped her fold up the stroller and we tucked it in front of the Rascal. They sat in seats across the aisle from us and, although he only knew one word, little Freddie and I had a great conversation. He was on his way to visit Grandma who works with autistic adults and lives in London. I taught him some Laughter Yoga exercises. He loved our mantra: ho ho ha ha ha. As the train stopped in seven stations along the way and became more crowded, I moved across the aisle to sit with them. Freddie loves doing the fist-bump and the high-five.

Two hours later we arrived in Euston, the main station for London. A very nice passenger let us know that he was available to assist us with our bags and the Rascal. A train-station assistant put our bags—and me--onto a big cart so Richard followed in the Rascal. The nice old volunteer who possessed the key to the handicap restroom emptied her big purse searching for the key and, at last, discovered it underneath her wallet and packet of Kleenex and set of plastic forks and spoons and a few tired rubber bands. She was fumbly but pleasant. We smiled, as we recalled advice from Paramahansa Yogananda: "Know that this universe is nothing but a dream bluff of nature to test your consciousness of immortality." PY is always right. Several men helped us get into a ramp-enhanced van and we were off to the luxurious Amba Charing-Cross Hotel in London, our home for the next six days. Our driver Gary talked all the way to the hotel.

Checkout time is 12:00 but the people who had our room wanted to stay until 4:00 so Clive escorted us to the private lounge where we were offered beer, wine, and champagne. We settled for tea and latte. In the meantime, Michael from Wales entertained us with his strong opinions on everything. He'd graduated from Med School the night before, as did his girlfriend. They are preparing to explore the world of medicine before making final decisions on which area of the healing world they feel most passionate about. He explained the education system. It seems medical students do not have to repay their student loans until they make over L25,000 a year and are given an allowance for room and board as they go through school.

Brexit seems like a really bad deal for the UK, as he explained. He felt like it was the uneducated that voted to leave the European Union because they thought the immigrants would go away. But, in fact, so many jobs will be gone. There will be no one to clean houses, wait on us in restaurants, or sweep the streets. The education system will suffer. More homelessness. Not a good idea.

Michael told of a three-week visit to the US a couple of years ago. He and his dad were in Nashville when they heard Tennessee had just voted that it will be legal to carry concealed weapons into bars and at the same time were voting to do away with Obama Care. His dad had a fit, as he reasoned that "if you get shot in a bar, it's not your fault, but you will have huge medical expenses to heal." He also ranted, just a bit, about advertising in the U.S. Pharmaceutical companies tell people to inform their doctors about what kind of medicine they should receive. And we pay big bucks for medicine here to fund the advertising of that medicine. "Makes no sense." Then Michael was off to change his short pants and flip-flops for a proper suit for tonight's celebratory dinner.

Finally, at 17:00 our room was ready. Upon arriving at Room 214, Asit, the hotel food manager offered us beer, wine, or champagne. We settled for bananas, apples, and tangerines. Then we strolled down the street in the rain looking for dinner. Falafel sandwich for The King and salad for me. At Pret-a-Manger.

Thought for the day:

"If it's funny later, it's funny now."

And so to sleep.

UK #7 Sunday July 21

Happy 7th Birthday Sweet Sylas our precious great-grandson. We'll hug you soon.

When your "Health App" records 4.6 miles (12,383 steps and who knows how many spins of the wheels on the Rascal), it's time to sit down and have a Greek Salad and a plate of Falafel at the Blue Garden Restaurant on Strand Street in London. So we did. And because we promised Riad (who immigrated from Iraq) we'd write a nice review about the meal, we were comped a latte for The King and a bowl of Lebonese pudding. I think he called it Riz B Haleeb, which means rice in milk. It was topped with strawberries and crushed pistachios.

We had seen signs all over this part of London that roads would be closed for several hours today. On our early-morning walk we spoke with three women wearing "Multiple Sclerosis" tee shirts . Others were wearing tee shirts supporting meds for psoriasis, cancer research, and celiac intolerance. The goal for over 1,000 participants was to run the 10K down major streets, past Westminster Abbey, across the Thames and back to the starting place.

Richard got in free to the Churchill War Rooms. E17.60 for me. We walked 'n rolled through the underground War Rooms which were the British government's WWII headquarters for the fight against the Nazis. This was the most important part of the underground emergency accommodation provided for Winston Churchill's Cabinet and its chief military advisors during the war against Germany, Italy, and Japan from 1939—1945. Bedrooms, meeting rooms, a kitchen, a map room, all highly protected by massive amounts of steel overhead. We saw pictures of bombed out structures: public buildings, churches, and homes.

As a young war correspondent, Churchill was captured and held for six days in Pretoria, South Africa until he escaped by climbing over a wall when the guards turned their backs for just a moment. He jumped onto a train and hid under many feet of coal sacks for sixty hours as the Boers searched for him. As there was a huge reward—L25—offered for his arrest, lots of people tried to find him. He persevered. He returned to England.

We had visited St. James Park yesterday and found ourselves back there again as we tried to get around the 10K race. The lake in the park is home to swans, Graylag Geese, herons, pigeons, coots, moorhens, Egyptian Geese, and white pelicans. There must have been 1,000 people lying on the lawn in the sun. The line at the café was long.

UK #8 Important Miscellaneous: Friday July 19 - Wednesday July 24

Gretna Green is a parish in the southern county of Dumfries and Galloway and is situated on the Scottish side of the border near England. It was most famous for the many wedding ceremonies performed there. According to English law created in 1754, a person may not marry without parental consent if under the age of 21. Furthermore, anyone could perform the wedding if there were two witnesses. Because Blacksmiths were important figures everywhere many of them performed weddings.

There had to be one in every village, town, farming area, and monastery. After all, who else could supply folks with nails, bolts, tools, weapons, kitchen equipment, wagons, and all the structural equipment to build a castle or house or palace or cathedral? The Village Blacksmith Richard Rennison performed 5,147 weddings so his anvil became the lasting symbol for Gretna Green weddings. Gretna Green is still a popular spot for weddings.

Iceland is not the only place with the following saying; it's also a popular quote in Scotland. "There is no such thing as bad weather just bad clothing." We prepared with rain gear, boots, ponchos, and warm headgear. Also shorts, tank tops, sandals, hats, and sunglasses. We've used everything.

Temperatures have been from 45 degrees to nearly 100. Almost every person we talk with asks about the "perfect" weather in California. There are no climate-change deniers whom we have met—yet. There is a lot of worry about climate change in Europe. Most structures are ancient, and to install air-conditioning will be very costly.

Hop-on Hop-off coaches are busy in London. We bought 24-hour passes and were able to use them from Monday morning at 10:00 through Tuesday morning. That way we only walk' 'n rolled about five miles a day and still saw most of London. We've decided that our favorite places are the parks full of flowers, families, and friendly people. The best spot is Lady Diana's Memorial Fountain in Hyde Park. Yesterday's temp got up into the 90's so the "fountain" which is really a speeding circular river was busy busy. Hundreds of toddlers and their parents and nannies were running, falling, sitting, and splashing in the water. Laughter, screaming, water-powered squirt guns, little kids and their new friends having so much fun. And these beautiful little creatures spoke many languages. Some had straight hair, some kinky. Parents were of every mixture of religion and culture and nationality and skin-tone, shape and size. Everyone was happy, just as Lady Diana would want.

LDMF is way better than Disneyland. It really is the happiest place on earth.

The Isle of Anglesy is in northern Wales. We stopped in the village of (see name below) to spend a few pounds in the supermarket-café-clothing mart-souvenir shop-bakery-hat-shoe-everything store. Above the front of the store was a word—a giant word. The giant word is the name of the village.

The Welsh claim that this is the longest word in their Language—58 letters!!!

Llanfairpwllgwyngyllgogerychwyrndrobwllllantysiliogogogoch

For the phonetic pronunciation:

Lian-vire-pooll-guin-gill-go-ger-u-queern-drob-ooll-llandus-ilio-gogo-goch

What does it mean? Simple:

The church of Mary in the hollow of the white hazel near the fierce whirlpool and the church of Ysilio by the red cave.

Please check Wikipedia for more information. ☺

UK #9

There are times when I ask myself: "What is this little farm girl doing here? How did I get here?" I first had this thought in 2007 when Richard and I attended a very posh wedding in a mansion in San Francisco. Another time: singing Carmina Burana in New York City's Carnegie Hall with the Orange Community Master Chorale in front of 2500 people. And again right now as we enjoy the Business Class/First Class lounge area at the London Heathrow Airport. I mean it: there are people here who know how to look intelligent, well-to-do, sophisticated and important. There are five kids here under the age of 8. I feel more like one of them. Having perfected the art of Laughter Yoga and having lost the ability to take much of anything seriously, I want to run and jump with the little kids. But . . . Richard is keeping a knowing eye on me. Oh, pooh!

We're catching the 9:30 a.m. to Frankfurt, the 2:00 to LAX and should arrive about 5:00. Super Shuttle is standing by. What I want most to do when we get home is go check our tomato patch in the Laguna Woods Community Garden. Thank you Linda for taking care of things. I hope you didn't eat all of the tomatoes.

Love and Blessings to all.

Later: 9:00 p.m. California. Home at Last. All is Well. Tomatoes on the kitchen counter. I ate 12 of them.

And a Few Other Stories

Not recorded in this book are numerous trips to visit daughter Dianna, son-in-law Bob and their family in Irving, Texas. We did a couple of Road Trips east, but more often flew on American Airlines. Did I mention that our daughter works for American? Did I mention we get—mostly—free flights when there are available seats? Did I mention that one of our granddaughters works for a big hotel chain and gets us amazing discounts, often? We get down to Oceanside to see our son John and his wife Tanya, their three kids and their grandson. Our daughter Brenda and her husband Mike and our other granddaughter live in Orange County. In case you're counting, that's three kids, seven grandkids (of which two are married), and eight great-grandkids.

From 1999 to 2005, we made summer trips to Idaho with my little red kayak and our big—two-seater—yellow kayak strapped to the roof of our Dodge Caravan. Our dear friends Kathie and Jack had a second home in Ketchum. We'd spend a week or two with them, rise early in the morning, drive up to Lake Alturas and spend the day cruising about the lake. Usually, Jack and Richard fished—with Jack at the "helm" and Richard in the back seat. Kathie often took the day off to enjoy the quiet of home. That left me free to paddle up the lake to the creek that connected Alturas to Lake Perkins. How I loved that trip! I'd leave the guys to fish while I talked to the otters and deer and other creatures. Once I even spotted a moose in the meadow. Never did I meet anyone else crazy enough to navigate that connecting route between the two lakes. It was so shallow in spots that I often would get out of my little red kayak and drag it across the rocks. We loved going to Idaho.

We enjoyed free concerts out under the stars at the Sun Valley Resort. On one trip, we were fortunate to be in the presence of Supreme Court Justice Sandra Day O'Conner and listen to her stories of growing up in Arizona and her days in court. We were once gifted, another time, with a pair of very expensive tickets to an Authors Convention and met Frank McCourt and Mitch Albom, and we were out-of-towners rubbing shoulders with some of the jet-setters who summered in Sun Valley, Idaho.

Several times during the summer months, I'd leave home in Olde Towne Orange before daybreak, drive to my sister Jeannie's home in Escondido, and we'd be on the local reservoir by 7:00 a.m. We'd paddle around the edge of the lake taking pictures of everything: mostly the Great Egrets. We called ourselves "wild life photographers." But all that fun ended when the dog thingy happened.

I could no longer do strenuous activities. Gave up my roller-blades, my bicycle, my snow skis, and my kayak. The grandkids have inherited the kayaks.

The first four years of our marriage we'd spend a week each summer up at Asilomar, two miles south of Monterey. Friends from our Spiritual Center, along with other like-minded folks from across the country would gather for a retreat along the Pacific Ocean to hike in nature, stroll along the beach, and attend lectures by some of today's great Spiritual speakers and authors: John Grey, Wayne Dwyer, Jessie Jennings, and Swami Beyonanonda. Which may be the reason Richard is so full of adventure. You see, we'd only been dating for ten months our first time up to Asilomar together. One morning we decided to ditch the conference and find a kayak for some fun out on Monterey Bay where the Sea Otters hang out. We did, indeed, find a little shop that rented kayaks. We picked out a double, got Richard into a wetsuit, drove over to the bay, helped Richard walk down to the shore, stood over the kayak, and after all that commotion, he looked up at me with his beautiful blue eyes, and made the following statement (in a concerned voice):

"I can't do this."

People with MS don't have total control over their bodies. That is, the brain and the body have a disconnect, so I understand that one may feel a bit apprehensive about being out on the ocean and having no control over life and death. Yes. I do understand, so I responded.

"Shut up and get in the kayak."

This may have been a "make it or break it" moment in our relationship. With nerves of steel, he acquiesced and let us put him into the boat. I hopped in with the paddle, shoved us out, and headed for the seaweed and the otters. We had a wonderful, magical, adventure. Now, almost 25 years into this adventure called marriage, he's game for almost any of my crazy ideas. (See story on Peace Pilgrimage.)

I'd purchased my little red kayak several years before we met. I would put the top down on my little yellow 1977 VW convertible and drive down the 55 Freeway towards Balboa Island or Newport Back Bay with it jammed into the passenger seat and sticking up into the air. Now, just to be clear, Richard's parents were extra special wonderful people and sometimes a bit protective of their eldest son, the one with MS. I'd be the same way with my son: cautious of whom he dated. When we had been married two years, their Christmas present to me was a check for $500. Wow!!! I was flabbergasted.

I knew, without a doubt that this money was meant for a very special gift, something I had wanted for several years. "Do you know what I'm going to do with this money?" I asked, as I thanked them, "I'm going to buy us a double-seated kayak." Mom's gasps were heard for miles across Whittier. Maybe she now wished she'd just given me a nice red sweater or a gift card. Well, as the years went by, they got used to me introducing their son to one adventure after another.

Also early in our years together, before we discovered motels, we did a bit of camping. I remember camping up in the Bishop area near North Lake. We set up camp but slept outside under the stars. One dark moonless night, after counting 60 falling stars—really meteorites—tiny particles of debris that get caught in the atmosphere—we fell asleep. The next morning I announced that I was going to hike up the mountain and Richard said he'd drive his Rascal down the road a ways and fish. I asked how he planned to do that since the river was down a steep hill where the Rascal could not go. His response was that someone would help him. He got his fishing gear together, I packed some snacks, and he motored away. I went hiking.

Upon returning from my hike, he told me that two young guys saw him above the river and asked if they could help. See? Angels everywhere. These strong men helped him get down the hill, carried his gear down, and set him up for a morning of catching dinner. I know, me too. I'm always delighted to hear his stories of how he connects to people and how everyone wants to help him.

Then there is the time-share Richard purchased some time before I met him. Lagonita Lodge is on the south shore of Big Bear Lake. We've been up there probably a dozen times over the years. We used to take our kayaks in the summer and paddle all the way down to the dam and back before the wind came up, usually on the lake by 6:30 and back before 10:00 a.m. The Lodge has a nice indoor swimming pool, an indoor spa and an outdoor spa, a huge recreation room, meeting rooms, a dock with rental boats and fishing. Recently we spent an October week up there editing this book. We took one day for walkin' and rollin' the six-mile round trip on the north shore to the Discovery Center, another day at the zoo and, of course, we joined 200 other trick or treaters in the Old part of Big Bear on Halloween. The rest of the week Richard edited "Travels of The King and I" and I plugged away on my little MacBookPro.

The first weekend of every October we join the Universalist Unitarians (also known as the UUers) up at Camp de Beneville Pines near Jenks Lake in the San Bernadino Mountains. We hike. We eat awesome vegetarian food. We play with little kids. Craft lessons are available and we often volunteer to be part of the "No Talent Talent Show." Our favorite contribution has been our rendition of "Do Wa Diddy Diddy Dum Diddy Do."

What's next? Well, we just put a down payment on a Holland-America cruise to Alaska in July of 2020. Several friends have expressed interest and say they'll be signing up for the trip, which includes three nights in Denali. More adventures to come . . .

Part of Our Texas Family

The King getting ready to fly over Bryce Canyon

Richard's Travel Stories

I've become aware there is one most important skill the Rascal traveler must develop: "Keep your eye on the road." Read on to find out how I learned the hard way. The consequences of letting this job slide can be shattering.

In the last 25 years, I've had dozens of opportunities to journey the world, almost always tied with my loving, healthy wife Sue, as well as what has become my main mobility—my Rascal electric scooter. For me, the optimal ride is the three-wheeled scooter, allowing short, easy turning. Because my weight doesn't approach 200 pounds, this model suits me best. Sizes, weights, and battery life are all issues to be weighed before purchasing any scooter. But in my opinion, the joys of travel with our Rascal have been nothing short of amazing.

Travel by Air

The Americans with Disabilities Act made flying with my Rascal a snap. It's treated as baggage, stowed in a special luggage compartment and delivered to the arrival gate, all without charge. Because I can't walk through the TSA screening stations, I get a "special" individual pat-down, as does the Rascal. While it can be annoyingly detailed, it's worth it to be able to "ride the range" in the airport, awaiting departure. I can usually motor down the Jetway where airline crew takes charge of getting my wheels down to the tarmac. As I step onto the plane, I can watch handlers carefully (usually) load my ride on board.

Note: Airlines are primarily concerned with two factors in scooter transport: first, the weight of the vehicle and more importantly, the type of batteries it has. NON-SPILLABLE-SEALED (OR GEL-CELL) batteries are a must. Before any trip, I print out and attach labels to the Rascal, listing weight and battery composition. And because airline ground crew aren't always aware of the special handling each scooter needs, I also place colorful stickers on key lift points as well as edges that cannot be used in transport.

The more we travel, the more beat-up my Rascal becomes but it's such a relief to arrive at the destination, watch from the plane as they unload my ride then be met at the gate with a scooter that's ready to go. And these precautions are an important way I can assure this success. (International flights can be a bit more intimidating but with enough advance planning accessibility issues can be met.)

Keep Your Eyes on the Road, Part I Spring 2018

Our travels to Europe have been the most rewarding as well as the most challenging. Three weeks in France and Holland, 18 days in Ireland, 2 weeks touring Italy, two weeks in Scotland, Wales and England. Our current adventure is a dream my Sensational Sue has had in her bucket for as long as I've known her: spending a month in Florence, Italy, renting an apartment on the Arno River, overlooking the famed Ponte Vecchio (that's Old Bridge) and exploring Italian life in detail.

A month? Me? I don't know. We've shared a lot of dreams in our 25 years but 30 days negotiating the furrowed crotchety streets, bouncing helplessly along sidewalks that end abruptly with no exits, feeling trapped in a beautiful 4th story apartment without Rascal access, yelled at in Italian by neighbors who refused to even allow us to rest Rascal overnight inside the doorway at the foot of impenetrable steps ..... My dream? I think not. But over the years we've had so many challenges so many opportunities to meet and overcome the unexpected, even the unwelcome, and this is no different. So we roll on.

Our 10-1/2 hour redeye from LAX to Zurich was uncomfortable at best. Swiss Air had battery issues for the Rascal and I couldn't convince them worry was unnecessary. The same issues were raised on the Zurich to Florence leg but after 15 elapsed hours (LAX to FLR) and 9 more hours lost to the sun, we made it to Firenze and the Rascal worked swell. What could go wrong?

It was after 7:00 p.m. and still light out when we jumped to the front of the cab line at the airport (some sour faces in our rear window) and had Simone hoist the Rascal onboard with our other luggage and give us a 50-Euro ride to 54 Via Dei Bardi, our digs for the next 30 days. Like so much of Italy, Via de Bardi was under repair, reduced to a single lane: west to east. And laced with heavy metal portable blockades and gouges and gapes in the pavement preventing passage from one side of the street to the other. We would soon become aware that bicycle, taxi, politzia, and even bus traffic could be heard day and night. Each morning at around 4:30 or 5:00 street workers and supermarket deliveries begin off-loading materials for that day's jobs, dragging and scraping the blockades to new more useful sights, filling the supermarket with new food with the backhoe and jackhammering usually beginning around 7:00 and often still going on at 7:00 that evening. Anyway, we were able to get the cab out of the traffic and unload. Simone helped haul stuff to the wooden doorway marked 54 and soon a bike with Francisco arrived and welcomed us to Firenze and 54 Via de Bardi.

In the many places we've walked 'n rolled, one truth always seems to find its way to our side; there is no end to the Angels who come to our rescue. Just in the last 24 hours I needed and received help, seldom asked for, but freely offered by people nearby. Getting up eight massive steps last night, one crutch, one wife, no handrails, two men became my guardrails, each lifting one of my stray feet up to the next step. As we reached the top and I was grabbed by Sue and handed my crutch, I turned and graciously gave thanks to them; both as proud as could be. "You're my heroes," I said. "No, you're the hero," one said to me as I thanked the long line of lookers waiting the completion of my ascent so they could make their entrance. Wow! As we were leaving, after a fabulous violin performance, two equally strong and generous guys supported my downward steps. Magicians, I called them.

These are just two examples of the gifts I know I'm here to provide. I've learned to give myself permission to ask for and receive help, not to let my body's low-level of functionality deprive me of all the wonders I can find. And by giving people, even those who could be considered strangers, the chance to give, to help, to contribute, to serve, I'm giving them a gift equal, or even greater, than the gift I'm getting. Does that make sense?

Keep Your Eyes on the Road, Part II

Today while negotiating a rocky uneven curbcut (ha) puddles of rain hid what turned out to be a deep gouge in the street. Had I looked closer I would have avoided this unknown, veering right to remain on solid footing but my vision strayed. My front Rascal wheel made it up but as I continued, the left rear wheel collapsed into the gap and we, Rascal and me, began to slowly but surely tip left, me hitting the wet cobblestones with my head and side, the armrest breaking some of my collapse, Rascal coming to rest on top of me. I knew I was going down the moment the wheel lost contact with the pavement but was helpless, almost slow motion, like so many times before that I'd fallen but there was nothing I could do. My Sensational Sue was ahead 4 or 5 steps and heard my yelp but she too was powerless to do anything. Then, out of nowhere, a group of 4 or 6 or 10? Angels grabbed and righted the Rascal, me in it, my butt never leaving the seat. Several gathered fallen items, got me up the treacherous curbcut and back on the move. "Thank you. Thank you. Thank you, Angels." Then they were gone. (Who was that masked man?) These things happen to me all the time.

If I'm getting a little hesitant, a little sour, not looking forward to another extreme effort event, my SS is there to remind me "The Angels are out there, don't worry."

No matter where the journey, there always seem to be times I just cannot go any farther. Sometimes it's a sidewalk that had an upcut but no downcut. Other times the cobblestone path is just so uneven that forward progress is impossible. Because Europe is such an ancient landscape, many attractions just have no access for me. So many castles in Ireland remain unviewed by me. Versailles? Forget it. I could roll no swifter than 10 feet per minute and even then each few inches of progress was like falling off a cliff. But I'm okay. "I'll wait here and observe the walls. You go, tell me what you saw when you return."

Because my favorite person in the world is not only my wife, lover, and advocate, the times I see only an impenetrable end, my SS sees just another opportunity to "call on the Angels." At St. Mark's in Firenze on a rainy cool day, steps up and down blocked any entrance for me. "I'll just wait while you go in and see the sights," I said. "Nope." She found someone with a portable wooden ramp. I was in. Without her gentle shoves and urges I would see much less. Maybe someday I'll learn.

The limitations faced daily, are far out-weighed by the successes achieved by not giving in. Today we wanted to take Italian public transportation, specifically the autobus dodeici (12) up the hill to Piazza Michelangelo. No info we could gather would assure us any bus could or would take on the Rascal. We found the route to the nearest bus stop so we walked the narrow, crowded streets finally finding the pick-up point. But the Rascal seemed to be quickly losing power. The bus found us, lowered the ramp mid-coach and with a strong shove by SS I wheeled onboard. Little charge left in Rascal but the ride was free. This wasn't an isolated incident. We were able to borrow some electricity at a café at the Piazza, Sue and another strong Angel giving Rascal and me a final push to the café. There, for an hour, we had coffee, gelato, and watched the rain move to the east.

All through Italy we were welcomed into attractions, onto buses, and given free access: The Duomo, Uffizi, Pitti Palace, Boboli Garden, all the bus rides we took. Everything. We were welcomed by smiling guards, directing us to the front of waiting crowds, handing us free-admittance, and for the most part, allowing carry-on packs and satchels to enter without detail security checks: small favors greatly appreciated. It seems Italy has made it the law that persons with disabilities shall be allowed full free privilege to all state historical sights and museums. How nice.

In most cases, full exposure to art and history is often limited due to the structural inaccessibility; some places one must be able to walk to. Am I complaining? Do I feel left out? No way. Just how many Madonna and Child paintings does one need to see to understand the hold the Church had on its subjects? Same with statues and busts and frescoes. There's just so much magnificence it all blends into a unity.

The bottom line is the joys, the pains, the anger, the frustrations, and any other quality positive or negative can only maintain as much power as I allow.

Keep Your Eyes on the Road, Part III

Rejoining my opening truth about Rascaling, no matter how inviting and successful the day begins, calamity can instantly overtake the joy when one fails to pay attention.

In 2010 I joined my Sue and her travel team for a stay in a Villa in Tuscany. Poor Delta baggage handling had delivered my Rascal non-operational and lack of communication rendered no healing; in Italian it was non-fanzine: Rascal was kaput. The Italian ground crews just smiled and shrugged their shoulders as they lifted my scooter onto our group's rental van. I felt I was to be stranded in a Tuscany Villa, the hills overlooking Firenze. ("I'm complaining?") Four days later, though, after lots of semi-communicating with the very Italian villa maintenance man, who knew his friends in the Vespa shop could fix the problem, my Rascal rolled back almost as good as new. (Delta eventually made good on the loses) The next morning would be my first independent rolling-at-will. "I'll meet you guys at the van in the parking lot." I shouted at the group assembling for the short drive to Vinci. I speeded past a few quince trees and skirted the pool on a narrow path, a thick hedge of gnarly tea roses on my left, guarding the hillside slope, to a grove of Olive trees below. "I'm free," I cried. But there was a price to pay for losing concentration on the road ahead. The path had a little too much right-to-left slope and gently but firmly flipped me over, pinning The King between the Rascal and the thorny hedge. Stuck. I would have been freer had I bothered to search out a better route, or at least better managed the tilt but . . . live and learn.

After ten or so minutes of not getting to the van, a search party spotted me, all of us laughing at the stupidity of the situation. Several of the stronger were able to tilt me and Rascal back to near horizontal and with guides to the sides, I reversed to a more level playing field. Scraped and punctured and red-faced but no serious damage. KYEOTR

Keep Your Eyes on the Road, Part IV

On a recent visit to the beautiful Yosemite National Park, we walk 'n rolled to a cozy theater to hear a re-creation of some of the adventures of John Muir. The ramp up to the handicapped entrance was paved with a neutrally toned gravel surface, much the same as the surrounding patio and most of the adjacent area. In the daylight it was easy to see where the slope of the path began, its shadow obvious on the adjacent footing. But returning at show's end, I was paying no attention, just speeding down the path. The distinction between the path and surface it would soon reach was ignored and like flying off a curb, I went over the right edge, crashing to a stop, the 150-pound Rascal pinning me to the ground. I was almost immediately surrounding by exiting show-goers, who as usual managed to right the situation. Angels to the rescue. A head bump and some scrapes to me, scratches, dents and bends to the Rascal.

On several other occasions, instances like this have met with the same results. I've been lucky every time. The damage has been minimal and the Angels have come to my rescue.

We'll continue to travel as long as we can. With our Rascal-adapted Dodge Caravan, we've been able to take up to month-long trips driving multi-thousands of miles, my SS behind the wheel more than 90% of the time. When problems (car trouble, no reservations, bad weather) come up, we overcome, not letting circumstances control outcomes.

On a road trip to Lincoln, Nebraska last fall, a frozen water pump left us stranded in Colorado Springs with a cracked engine head, still 750 miles from our goal. Miraculously, we found TJ Auto, who not only repaired the van flawlessly, but also hunted down and had delivered to our hotel, another Caravan with full accessibility, electric ramp, no less—so we could continue our journey to Cousin Tyler's wedding. Five days later we returned to Colorado Springs, swapped vans and made our return to Southern California. This time, the Angels were Tim and Terry, hard working, honest, caring mechanics. We can't go wrong!

Of the half-dozen cruises we've enjoyed, the Rascal has been most welcomed. I see folks hobble, using only canes or walkers. Why haven't they given themselves permission to use tools designed to make their lives and the lives of those who love them easier? We get the most out of life when our movements can be free. Take advantage of everything the Universe has to offer. And always remember:

The Best Things in life aren't things.

If you think you can or you think you can't, you're probably right.

It's only with the heart that one can see rightly. What is essential is invisible to the eye.

You can change your thinking and change your life.

Find opportunities to be grateful.

The secret to happiness is gratitude.

Live a life centered on principle, not on circumstances.
All you need is love.

And, of course, Keep Your Eyes on the Road.

Acknowledgments

"Angels Everywhere." That's our traveling motto. This world, this wonderful world, is full of people who are thoughtful, kind, and willing to help those in need. We are grateful to all the Angels who have stepped forth to make our adventures so amazing, so incredibly educational and possible. We are sometimes overwhelmed with the kindness, the helpfulness, and the encouragement we receive from people all over this planet.

Cover designer Jeff Brown—you're the best.

A special thanks to our Angel travel agent Yolanda Hayden, who guides us to the best accessible accommodations. She has been a blessing in our lives for many years, many times, in many places.

Most of all, I am grateful to The King, both for his differently-abled experiences (KYEOTR), and his superb editing skills. Richard does things that evade my eye, often suggesting ways to simplify the flow of my narrative. Without The King, the travels and the tales wouldn't have had the same impact. And as I often say to him,

"You are endlessly fascinating. With all my heart Thee I Love."

I am often brought to tears by the Angels who have stepped forth to give us directions, to help Richard up and down steps, to get us out of sand traps and cobblestone holes and . . . well, you've read about the times my beloved has tipped over in his Rascal. We simply could not travel like we do without the freely-given assistance of all you Angels. Your love and brilliance brings to mind what W.A. Mozart said about genius.

"Neither a lofty degree of intelligence nor imagination nor both
together go to the making of genius.
Love, love, love, that is the soul of genius."

And I think that is what arises in the hearts of all of our Angels: love, love, love. Thank you. Thank you. Thank you.

About the Author

Sue grew up on a little farm in Dominguez Hills, and graduated from Compton High School in 1960. For 30 years she worked in public education, first as a teachers aide at La Vista in Fullerton, an attendance clerk at Yorba Middle School, then a district insurance clerk for Orange Unified, an English teacher at Anaheim High and finally as an advisor to student teachers at Cal State Fullerton.

She is the proud mother of three amazing children, seven inspiring grandchildren, and eight great-grandchildren. Every one of them a blessing.

After retiring, she and her husband, Richard, also known to friends as The King, decided to travel, see the world, and connect with people everywhere. Life for them has been one adventure after another.

California natives, they now reside in the beautiful community of Laguna Woods Village in Orange County where they live and thrive among the most active retirees anywhere.

Made in the USA
Monee, IL
03 May 2023